Quissett

ISBN
1-58898-478-8

Front Cover Photo: "The Knob" located at Quissett Harbor,
Falmouth, Massachusetts

Quissett

Gordon Mathieson

GMCI Books
2001

Quissett

I dedicate this book to my best friend, Ann. We happen to have been friends since we were eighteen years old. She happens to support those things that I dream about. She happens to be the illustrator of this novel's cover. She happens to have married me thirty-four years ago. Things happen for a reason.

INTRODUCTION
The Village of Quissett

There are many little villages scattered on that sandy spit of land called Cape Cod. People describe the villages as "quaint" and "charming". These small coastal communities have retained the historical and cultural character of those early days when naïve but adventurous pilgrims from England and Europe brought their families to this so-called "New World".

Without compromising any of its original landscape, Cape Cod has kept pace with the rest of the world in business, technology, education and, recreation. It still is one of America's most favorite tourist and family vacation spots during the summertime and autumn. People from all over the world are drawn to the Cape's beaches, sand dunes, harbors and, to those quaint and charming little villages.

Quissett is one of these villages located within the historic town of Falmouth. With its secluded location and long history of conservation, it is just as beautiful today as it was when the Quamquissett Indians first lived there. It appears to rest peacefully; yet keeps a vigilant eye on the sailing vessels passing through the tricky currents of Woods Hole connecting Buzzards Bay with Martha's Vineyard Sound. Pirates of the eighteenth century favored this hidden area to ambush treasure ships.

The world's leading marine biological research facility is nestled in this enclave. The buildings and laboratories surround Eel Pond with its famous and narrow pedestrian drawbridge.

The pre-historic glaciers were the primordial artists to visit Quissett. These oversized ice masses shaped and sculpted the Cape's landscape upon their retreat into the ocean. Their gradual recession left the abstract rocky moraines and intriguing coastal caves. They created natural works of art with countless nooks and crannies cut into coastline rock and sand. Today, these unique geological formations intrigue the soul and provide for wondrous discovery.

Quissett Harbor had been naturally chiseled out of the western coast. This is a small but picturesque bay offering safety and protection for smaller boats. It is shaped on the north by a thin isthmus, a mile long, that reaches out into Buzzards Bay. As this narrow stretch of land meets the water, it gradually elevates to create a hill with rocks, sand, wild sea roses and thick vines of bittersweet. From this pinnacle one can see across the water to the former whaling capital of the world, New Bedford, Massachusetts.

Early English settlers called any rise in the land or small hills, like this one, "knobs". But this particular geological gem of Quissett Harbor has been referred to simply as "The Knob" for nearly two hundred years.

Generations of folklore tell us that the Quissett Indian tribe thought of this unique natural formation as a mystical place. They visited this hill on the shore to communicate with the spiritual world. Anecdotes say that young Indians went there to rest and to meditate. Today, visitors who follow the mile-long wooded trail out to "The Knob" sense the same special peace and tranquillity.

Hundreds of years ago, the native American Indians held high regard for this land, later to be named Cape Cod. They revered this territory that abundantly gave of itself with sweet berries, fish, oysters, clams, lobsters, and wild game so that earthly nature and human life could coexist in harmony.

As more colonists came to the village of Quissett, they brought new ideas, tools, and equipment to improve hunting, fishing, and farming. The Indians traded their furs and animal hides for these useful inventions from across the ocean. These artifacts improved their means of sustenance and survival. They abandoned their teepees and moved into wooden-framed houses. They netted fish rather than tediously spearing them. They abandoned their animal skin-made garments and began wearing clothes woven from cotton or wool fabric. The native Americans needed and used these new ideas to advance the quality of life.

Smallpox was the one thing, however, brought over from the continents that they did not need. This microscopic, hitchhiking import from across the Atlantic ravaged the untested immune system of the native Americans.

With this disease spreading rapidly, it took only a few decades for the number of Cape Cod Indians to dwindle, quickly making them a minority race to the white-skinned immigrants. The Quissett tribe, the original village inhabitants, was totally wiped out by smallpox. The industrious immigrants from across the ocean soon became the only residents of this quaint village. Today, the Quissett tribe's name is the only memory of those native Indians.

The new village tenants continued to use the land for sustenance but not as their native friends had done so. The excess fish were sold and bartered for other goods and services. They brought over sheep, hogs, cattle and other livestock for their production. They later cultivated the local Cape's cranberries to be sold around the world. They built ships from the stately oak trees. As the generations passed, they built windmill driven pumps. These passive machines extracted the salt out of the sea's water to be sold worldwide by the bushel. The colonial Cape Codders' survival became dependent on a mercantile network of countries around the world.

Quissett had soon become one of the wealthiest villages on Cape Cod. The Hatches, the Mayhews, the Rowleys, and the Brooks families were all original land barons. They invested wisely in real estate on Martha's Vineyard, Nantucket, and on up towards the new town and shipping port of Boston. Their legacies and progeny still live in these scattered towns and villages today.

The beauty, the charm and the landscape of Quissett would forever stand still and go unnoticed over the centuries if it weren't for its people. It is the generations of inhabitants including the native Quamquissett Indians, the pilgrims, the colonists, the fishermen, the whalers, the farmers, and the marine biologists, who bring life to this quaint Cape Cod village.

The stories and events that unfold from each generation of Quissett villagers make this area most interesting. What follows is one of those stories.

CHAPTER ONE

Sam Parker

They could only stare quietly at his boots. Their eyes were fixed on the old pair of knee high, faded green, rubber wading boots. Although they were more than thirty feet away it was easy to recognize those familiar, scraped and patched, hideous galoshes.

Roger and Rita Anderson stood nearly paralyzed on the sandy beach as they stared at those boots. It was a cool, yet sunny, spring morning on Cape Cod. Roger still held his wife's hand as he had done so for over forty years.

They were friends with the distinguished and extraordinary Quissett man who wore those boots each morning as he walked along the same beach. The Andersons saw those waders almost every day at sunrise for the past five years. That was the usual time that they took their morning walk along Chapoquoit Beach, or as the local folks called it, "Chappy". It was a daily ritual that they enjoyed immensely. The invigorating walks in the sand and the talks with the interesting and handsome man who wore those boots, Sam Parker, made each day a new beginning in their lives.

Some days there would be no talking among them. Just a warm, casual, greeting and they would continue on their way. Most days, however, the three of them would sit on the large rocks of the jetty to share brief stories. As they chatted, the morning sun would quietly rise up behind the nearby sand dunes to warm their bodies and illuminate their faces.

On this early May morning, as he held his wife's hand, Roger reflected on their recent encounter just a few days ago.

"Hey, Roger, Rita. Look. I found these conch shells at the water's edge," Sam said, as he pulled two large shells, still slimy with algae, out of his white canvas sack. He slowly pivoted the shells in his hands so that his friends could admire the naturally artistic spiral edges of the hardened casing.

"They are absolutely beautiful!" remarked Rita.

"It's so good to see this marine life returning to Buzzards Bay. It means that our waters are getting cleaner. I haven't seen too many of these creatures over the past several years."

Sam then gave a brief, yet informative, discourse on the status of marine life in the Quissett area and how sea animals will only migrate to the most favorable of ocean waters. Sam loved to teach others some new or interesting fact from his area of expertise. As a marine biologist at the Woods Hole Oceanographic Institute for nearly 30 years, he enjoyed discovering new things each day. He loved even more to share these discoveries with colleagues, children, and others, including his befriended beachcombers, the Andersons.

As Roger stood on the sandy shore this day, still holding his wife's hand tightly, he further recollected their initial introduction to Sam over five years ago.

"My name is Sam Parker," he introduced himself while extending his hand to the retired couple.

"Rita and Roger Anderson," Roger replied. "We're taking in our morning exercise. We enjoy a nice walk on the sandy beach and breathing in the fresh salty air. This is one of the reasons we decided to retire on Cape Cod."

"Well folks, if you come here this time each morning you'll be sure to see me. I've been doing this same routine at Chappy for twenty-five years now." Sam flashed a pleasant and friendly smile filled with bright white even teeth that contrasted to his rugged tanned face.

"I gotta ask you something, Sam. Why do you have canvas sacks draped over each of your shoulders?" inquired Roger.

Sam chuckled. "Well, I guess you could call me a seashore collector of sorts," he answered.

"This white canvas bag is always over my left shoulder to collect shells, precious stones, or any found jewelry. This other black canvas bag is always over my right shoulder to collect junk, garbage, and trash. We all have to do our share to keep our beaches and our planet clean."

Sam reached into the black canvas sack and pulled out a rusted soda can, some green-tinted fishing line, and an empty plastic milk container to show his trash findings for the day.

"Unfortunately, my black bag fills up more often than my white one does!"

"No doubt," interjected Rita.

"I am also a creature of habit." Sam explained. "I parole the same two miles each day and end up walking out on that jetty. I'll stay out there for a while meditating and drinking in the beauty of the nature that surrounds us. That's *my* morning cup of coffee," he laughed.

Sam continued, ".....and you'll never see me without the same fishing cap, the same fisherman's vest, the same white and black canvas sacks, and of course my favorite wading boots."

Both Rita and Roger looked down at the hideous looking rubber boots. They had to be nearly forty years old. They restrained their giggles.

"My wife, Paula, thinks it funny when she launders these same clothes each week so they stay fresh. She refers to them as my 'uniform'. I'm the one who takes care of these rubber boots though. I'll never give them up. I got these old boot-shoe trees that keep these waders dry and standing tall," Sam proudly smiled.

The green rubber boots were not standing tall on this early spring morning. They were lying horizontal. The toes of the boots pointed toward the sky, bobbing up and down with each wave that fell upon the Chapoquoit shore. Rita and Roger knew that the man inside of those boots, who was grotesquely floating at the water's edge, was their special friend who walked the beach each morning.

"His name is Sam Parker," Rita wept as she called the Falmouth police from her car cell phone.

***

The police cars and ambulance arrived at Chapoquoit Beach within minutes. The uniformed police officer interviewed the Andersons. The Chief of Police, Jack Ogren, and Detective Jesse Souza quickly cordoned off the site of the drowned body with yellow police tape. It was still early in the day. That was an advantage.

"This is not how I wanted to start my day today," said Jack in a disgusted tone. "Especially Sam. Jesus Christ, I just can't believe it. Of all people."

He then stared down at Sam's slightly swollen and bloated body, so commonly characteristic of a drowning victim.

"He was a good friend, Jesse. A good friend and a good man."

It was Sam Parker all right. Everyone in Quissett village knew him for his early morning walks along Chapoquoit beach. They all knew of his efforts to keep it clean for the others; especially the local families with little children who so loved this beach in the summer months.

" I never saw anything like this," said Detective Souza.

"What? Is this your first drown victim, Jesse?" asked Jack incredulously.

"No. No, I've seen a few, but this is the first time I found a drowned victim with such a big smile on his face. And look. He has his eyes wide opened.

"Yeah, it's a little creepy ain't it?"

"I hate to say it Jack, but…. that look, that smile. I'd say the guy looks real happy."

Detective Jesse Souza was right. Jack stared down into Sam's face and saw this man's characteristically wide smile exposing a beautiful set of shining white teeth. He looked as if he were telling one of his typical stories about the inherent benefits of seaweed, or a lecture about the future promise of marine life helping mankind in medical research. He looked genuinely happy. How could someone surface from under the water like that?

Ogren thought back of the many times he had been in Sam's presence. Whenever Sam spoke, he engaged his audience with not only his words, but also with his broad smile and twinkling, luminous eyes. It was that same expression that veiled his face today, looking straight up to the sky.

Sam Parker had always felt strongly about people taking care of the sea and all that it provided to mankind. He would tell children to always clean up after themselves at the beach. His motto to them was that "the only thing that you leave behind at the beach is your footprints". He would lecture to adults and caution that if we all didn't take conservation efforts seriously, there would be nothing left for our grandchildren to enjoy. He engaged their attention with his style and encouraged them with his words to be good environmental citizens.

Jack had heard Dr. Parker's lectures many times over the past two decades. Sam consistently stressed in his lectures that all living organisms are perfect creations of God. He was emphatic that all organic things are linked in ways we don't understand. This included every living thing—the fish, the trees, the grass, the animals, and the seaweed —everything that was comprised of living cells.

He always, however, intimated that we would be enlightened about this natural connectivity some day. He would speak on a quasi-spiritual theme when he talked of nature. It was rather unusual for a Molecular Cell Biologist, to juxtapose elements of the Divine with factual scientific data. But Sam Parker was his own man. He was well respected by his academic peers; not only those in Woods Hole, but also those scientists around the world. They would never argue this issue with him. They considered his personal spiritual beliefs to be his individual right.

Jack then stopped reflecting how this dead man had been so well known and so well loved. His mind shifted quickly to Paula, who had been Sam's wife for nearly twenty-five years. Jack had always held a special place in his heart for Paula since he was seventeen years of age. They had been school classmates for several years as they grew up. During and after high school, he often regretted never dating her. Paula was such a prize among all of the girls at Quissett High School. She had it all; intelligence, beauty, sex appeal and personality. And most important, she had liked Jack Ogren very much. He had a deep and painful void in his heart that he never went after the girl who meant so much to him.

"OK, Jesse. Let's get Sam's body photographed. I need to get it over to the Medical Examiners office.

"Sure thing boss," replied Jesse as he adjusted his Polaroid camera.

"I just can't get over this one, Jess."

"It's a good thing that this didn't happen next month, with all the families and kids playing on the beach in the morning."

"That's true. Sam wouldn't have wanted to scare the little kids with his body floating up to meet their sand castles."

Jesse couldn't keep his eyes off of the drowned body as he inserted a new film pack into his camera.

"He certainly was his 'own man' wasn't he?" said Jesse, as he looked down on the outfit that that Sam had worn. The tan fishing vest was covered with his two large canvas sacks draped over each of his shoulders.

"That he was, Jesse. He was his 'own man' and he will be missed."

"Want me to contact his wife, Jack?"

"No! No!" Jack replied emphatically. "I will call on Paula."

Jack then reflected back again on his days at high school with Paula as he walked back to his car. She was Paula Larson then. Jack and Paula were always good friends growing up. At times Jack flirted with her, and she flirted back, but they never dated. They were both a bit shy and didn't have the courage to ask one another out on a date. They were perhaps afraid of losing their long time platonic friendship if things didn't work out.

As the years went on, Jack deeply regretted not having the

courage to ask Paula Larson out on a date. His well-hidden crush for her had never gone away after all of this time. Living in the same town made it difficult at times when he encountered Paula and Sam together. His heart still skipped a bit when he looked into Paula's eyes.

It didn't matter that Jack had later married a young, beautiful debutante from New York City. Even during his short seven year marriage to Gail, his unrequited crush on Paula Larson, had never lost its intensity.

When Paula Larson married Sam Parker on New Year's Eve in 1977, Jack was the traffic officer on duty for her wedding outside at St. Ann's church. In a way, he was happy to see that she was happy. She looked so beautiful in her wedding gown. He vividly remembered the little white tiara resting on her auburn hair. At the reception line outside of the church, Jack gave Paula a quick but heartfelt congratulatory kiss on the cheek. He shook Sam's hand with a brotherly smile and masked his jealousy well that New Year's Eve. It was the first of many handshakes between these two men. Later, as the years went on, they would work together on several town projects and committees. His outward affection for Paula would have to be suppressed.

Jack walked slowly over to the Andersons who were sitting on the huge boulders that served as a natural sea wall. He noticed that Rita was still teary-eyed. Her husband, Roger did not look much better. His face was an ashen white and he appeared to be shivering slightly.

"Look folks, I am sorry that you had to come across this situation this morning. I know it must be rough on you seeing your friend this way. I also want to thank you for immediately calling in this drowning to us. Because you acted so quickly, we can process things more efficiently without attracting a crowd of onlookers. Poor Sam deserves that." Jack looked back at the floating body.

Jesse was moving around the corpse at close range to take several photographs from different angles. He used two packs of film. Jesse was thorough.

"We may be in touch with you if we have any more questions."

"Thank you, Chief Ogren."

"Look, we are going to have to bag the body now and get it moved. Why don't you folks go on home and try to get your minds on something else."

After leaving the drowning scene, Jack didn't drive back to the police station, nor did he go directly to Paula Parker's house. Instead, he drove straight to Quissett Harbor. He got out of his car and walked around the parking lot. Then he slowly strolled onto the public dock. There was nobody else around at the harbor at this time of day during early May. He lit up a cigarette. He walked around looking at the boats that were tied up to their moorings. He kept pacing and looking around to see if anyone else might be around. He glanced at the silly names painted on the boats' sterns.

As he walked off of the dock, he briefly glanced out at the "Knob" just coming to life as the sun brightened that area of the bay. He thought about Paula and the fact that he had to tell her the news. As he flipped his lit cigarette into the bay, his mind flashed to how Sam would have been hurt to see this pollution created by the Chief of Police. But then Jack thought that Sam could not feel hurt about anything from now on. Sam was dead. Jack could not help Sam feel anything now. But he could help Paula. Perhaps he could help make her feel better. This is the way he always saw it. He could make her feel better and love him as she did once before.

Jack slowly looked around at the harbor parking lot making sure that he was still alone. He then left without anyone seeing him. He got into his unmarked police car and headed out towards Woods Hole to give Paula the tragic news.

When Jack arrived at her house, it appeared that Paula was not at home. This seemed odd, given the early time of day. Jack thought that Paula, who had retired early from her teaching career, might be sleeping late. He rang the doorbell and knocked loudly on the door but there was no response or noise from inside of the Parkers' house.

He walked around to the back of the modest house to see if she might be outside. He could see that her early vegetable and flower gardens were already neatly groomed and weeded. The daffodils were just past their peak and were showing signs of wilting. The bright orange, white and ruby azaleas however were blooming vibrantly as he walked by. The yard had a wooden outdoor swing set for two. It faced the bay to the southwest. He envisioned Sam and Paula casually swinging back and forth on it on warm evenings. He walked away from the house knowing that he would now have to contact her by phone as soon as possible. He walked back to his car and picked up his police radio handset.

"Jesse! Make sure that this drowning doesn't get out to the press yet. I still haven't located and notified his wife." Jack spoke loudly into the police radio as he drove along Quissett harbor.

"Will do," replied Jesse.

Detective Jesse Souza knew that Jack would be more involved with this drowning case than he should. It always happened this way when the case included friends or relatives. This disappointed Jesse. He wanted to handle it all by himself. He needed to prove to the chief how thorough he could be on any case. He was a good detective and he always wanted a chance to prove it.

***

When Jack returned to his office, he called the Parker residence and left a message on the answering machine for Paula to call Jack as soon as she returned home.

Jack couldn't sit still. He kept pacing back and forth from his desk to the water cooler. He was thinking how he wanted to wrap up this drowning case as quickly as possible. Then he could bring closure to this incident and get on with his life. He thought again about Paula. Perhaps, he might have a life with a new opportunity.

"Laura! Where are those interview notes with the Andersons?" Jack yelled out from his office.

"Here they are. I just got them. I haven't put them into the system yet," replied Jack's secretary.

"Thanks, Laura," Jack said in a low breath as he clenched the papers.

Jack stared at the notes written on the standard Falmouth Police Department case interview form. The form had been thoroughly filled out by an experienced police officer. The top section was neatly printed with the name of the police officer, Sergeant Jeff MacDonald. The location, Chapoquoit Beach. The date, May 10, 2000. The time, 7:25am. The next part of the form was filled out with the biographic and demographic data on the Andersons. The detailed interview followed.

The essence of these interview notes outlined the Andersons' past five year association with the victim, Sam Parker. They were not close social friends but did see him almost every morning on "Chappy" beach.

They described Sam's habit of wearing the same outlandish outfit each day— the same cap, the same vest, the white and black canvas sacks, and the beloved green, rubber, wading boots.

They also described Sam's daily routine. They discussed his habit of walking the sandy beach picking up his "treasures" and ultimately ending his routine on the rocky jetty for his morning meditation. They speculated with the police officer that this slippery walk could be risky if the bay was active with wind and crashing waves.

Jack saw in the interview notes that the Andersons hadn't seen Sam for the past two mornings. They thought that unusual. They also knew, however, and told the police officer, that he had been bothered with severe migraine headaches recently. They thought he might have taken a brief break from his usual morning routine.

Jack put the notes down on his desk and turned to look out of his window onto the traffic on Rte 28. He was in deep thought. In his mind he was seeing the face of Paula Larson, the widow.

The buzzing of his intercom startled him. Laura told him that Mrs. Paula Parker was on the phone.

"Hi Jack! What's up? I just got in and got your voice mail. I haven't heard from you in a dog's age," Paula said in her usual bubbly way.

"Well, Paula, ah.....unfortunately, this is an official call. Are you going to be home within the next half hour?"

"Sure thing. Come on by."

Jack, like most police professionals hated this part of the job. It is not so much getting the words out about the death of the victim, as the anxiety of wondering how the family members will react.

Paula would be the only family member there. Jack and Paula had no children. They had spent many years caring for Jack's disabled mother who had lived with them until she passed on a few years ago. Then it was just the two of them again. Now, suddenly, Paula would be alone without anyone else in her personal life.

Soon after Jack entered into her home, he asked that Paula sit down. She refused. She sensed that bad news was coming and she wanted to be standing. As Jack slowly told Paula of the discovery of Sam's drowned body earlier that morning, she turned immediately away from him. She did not want him to see her face. As Jack went on with some of the details, Paula kept a fixed gaze out upon the bay. She focused on that peculiar unique appendage of Woods Hole, known as Penzance Point. She never moved. She only kept her water-filled eyes fixed on the land, the sea, and salty air that Sam had loved so deeply.

As Jack spoke to her, she was facing the shocking reality that she would no longer share her life with the man she loved so much for nearly twenty-five years. Sam was not only her husband; he had always been her best friend. Paula wept loudly yet controllably. She was trying to be strong so that she didn't need Jack's arms for support. She held onto the back of Sam's favorite chair for support. She could somehow feel his strength, his energy, still within that chair.

"You don't know how sorry I feel for you. If there is anything that I can do Paula, please, please, do not hesitate."

"Sure Jack, I just need some time," she sniffled. "This is such a shock. I...I.... need some time alone."

"Paula, there is just one other thing. We are going to need to have an autopsy done."

"An autopsy? But why?" Paula protested, raising her voice in anger.

"Well, it's just a....."

Paula interrupted, "I don't think that an autopsy is necessary. Don't I have any say on this? For God's sake! I am still his wife!"

"I know, I know, Paula, but we have to do this. We must rule out any foul play and see if we can determine the exact cause of death. It's a state law. Unfortunately, family members have no decision on these types of cases."

"Oh, Christ! I hate the thought of autopsies. I hate the thought of....." She paused and took in some needed air with a long and audible gulp.

Jack thought that she was going to become sick. She looked extremely pale, and appeared dizzy. He walked over to her kitchen sink and got her a glass of cold water. Paula then exploded into loud sobbing.

"Paula. Paula! Here. I know. I know. I feel so badly for you. " He grabbed her forearms and held them tightly in his hands. He was trying to steady her so that she didn't fall. She took in deep breaths to regain her composure.

"Oh God. Drowned? I'll be all right. Damn it ! How long will this autopsy take Jack? I do want to have services for Sam." Paula was sniffling her words out through her now pink colored nose.

Jack gave her his clean handkerchief. She took it from him and again turned away. She couldn't face him.

"I've already contacted the Medical Examiner's office in Barnstable. She is expected to finish early this evening. I will let you know how it goes, and when you can schedule the wake."

Jack put his hand lightly on Paula's shoulder. He squeezed her flesh very gently. He felt the warmth of her skin. He wanted to desperately grab her and hold her in his arms. Jack imagined the pain that Paula was going through. It made him very uncomfortable. He did not like seeing her this way. But it was unavoidable.

"Are you going to be all right, Paula?" Jack asked. "Can your sister, Pat, or a friend come here and stay with you?"

"Thanks Jack," she wept and then took in a very deep breath.

"I don't think that you should be alone tonight."

"I think that I will call Pat and let her know. I was just thinking that maybe she can get a private charter boat to take her over from the Vineyard. There are no other late ferries scheduled this time of year."

"Look. Let me phone Steve Hatch. He's the chief over there at Vineyard Haven. He and I can arrange for a boat to bring Pat over to Woods Hole as soon as she is ready."

Jack started walking down the front entrance steps. He was relieved that this part of his job was over. He opened the front door to let himself out. He took a deep breath without her seeing him as he headed down the stairs towards his car. He exhaled slowly.

Then, without conscientiously thinking, he slipped back into his police role. He had to ask just one more question before leaving. He turned slowly and looked up at Paula standing in the doorway. She was leaning against the wall for support.

"Paula. By the way, when was the *last time* that you saw Sam?"

"Me? Oh. That was yesterday morning," she replied.

He paused. He hated asking this next question because of its prying and personal nature. But he just had to know. It was his job to ask the question and to record the answer into the case notes.

"Paula. Weren't you surprised that Sam didn't come home last evening?"

She stared at him. There was suddenly a brief but sharp sense of tension between them.

"He wasn't supposed to come home, Jack. He was scheduled to leave on a two-day research trip out of Woods Hole yesterday." She put the handkerchief to her nose. "I said 'Goodbye' to him", she wept "...and then took the morning ferry to the Vineyard to visit Pat and the kids as I do each week."

Paula gave Jack a cold and biting look. It was a look that he would never forget. It penetrated his whole being. It was the look that impacts your soul whenever your trust or friendship is being questioned. Now he didn't feel good. Jack couldn't look back at her.

He nodded and turned away from her. He quickly got inside of his police car and drove off.

As Jack drove along, he thought that this was the other part of his job that was difficult. Performing an investigation with people who are friends or relatives was never easy. Wise policemen and policewomen always delegated this task to others. Jack would consider this situation very carefully, but he knew what he had to do. He thought that he had to be in control of this one.

Paula Parker was the last person on earth whom Jack wanted to get upset. She was still his friend. He didn't want her to grow distant from him. He was going to make sure that never happened again. He wanted to protect this beautiful woman. He wanted to console her. He wanted to hold her in his arms. He still had intense feelings for her. He has to conceal these affectionate feelings for a while longer—but not much longer.

After Jack drove off, Paula closed the front door. She burst out crying and walked into her bedroom for a good, long cry. She lay on her bed for almost an hour just crying and staring up at the ceiling. Later, she washed her face and tried to get herself together before she called her sister. It was terrible to be alone just now. She had never been alone before. Then she thought to herself that she had better start getting used to it.

She walked over to the portable bar in her den. She poured herself about 3 fingers of brandy over ice. She then carried her snifter of liquor, swirling the ice, out through the sliding door to her deck. Paula slowly walked back and forth on the deck as she relived that horrible session two weeks ago at Boston General Hospital. On that day she learned from the Chief of Neurology that Sam's headaches were not typical migraines. The recent seizures were due to an advanced brain tumor in his anterior left lobe. It had been metastasizing rapidly. It was inoperable. The best that Paula could do was to keep her husband, her best friend, as comfortable as possible for the next several weeks.

The doctor wrote her a prescription for a very strong drug to give to Sam when the pain became too excruciating. He didn't have much longer to live in this world. The doctor was brutally candid.

Paula placed her brandy on her deck railing. She sat down on a chaise lounge and stared at the sun setting through her glass. She stared at the bright light rays radiating from the amber prism. She put her head back and began to recall her life with Sam.

Tears involuntarily rolled down her face as she reminisced all of those beautiful, love-filled years with her husband. Prior to the visit to Boston General, she never thought of life without Sam. Living without Sam seemed impossible. Now all of a sudden, it was reality. She had no idea what she was going to do. She had always been a strong person and always overcame the many disappointments in her life. Now, she didn't know if the resilient Paula Larson Parker had the strength to continue life without her friend, her lover, and her husband, Sam.

CHAPTER TWO

The Investigation

The phone in Chief Ogren's office rang each day with inquiry calls about the drowning. The calls came from the local and regional radio, TV, and newspaper reporters. These journalists were anxious to learn how the investigation into Sam Parker's death was coming. The public needed to know the final details of this case. It was still a shocking mystery as to how and why a marine biologist could have drowned in his own bay.

Since Dr. Sam Parker was so well known, the news of his drowned body on Chapoquoit beach was considered a "high profile" case. The news of this tragedy had spread not only around Cape Cod, but also in the greater Boston area and throughout the scientific community around the world. Jack had promised the reporters that he would hold a brief press conference as soon as there was a firm conclusion to the case. This drowning case was leaning heavily towards a possible suicide. Sam had been a well-respected man. If a report got out that he had taken his own life, it would go down hard with the locals. Suicide carries with it a stigma that implies weakness or emotional troubles. That was not Sam Parker. He was a giant in the minds and hearts of the local community. He had a gentle strength that his colleagues and friends admired.

Chief Jack Ogren was constantly thinking about the widow, Paula. He could not get her out of his mind. If a conclusion was reached that Sam did take his own life, he did not want the pain to endure with her any longer than it should. He would expedite this case in every way that he could.

Jack Ogren looked at the clock on his office wall. It had only been twenty-four hours since Sam Parker's body had floated up on the shores of Chapoquoit Beach. It had been a long and nerve wracking day for Jack. He felt very uncomfortable. He was anxious to hear from the Medical Examiner's office. After he had her report, he could take control of the investigation. Then he would feel better.

The call from the Barnstable County Medical Examiners office came at 10:30 that morning. Doctor Karen Schmidt wanted to speak with Falmouth's Chief of Police, Jack Ogren, immediately.

"Jack, I have completed my work on the Parker case," said Karen.

"Good, I'll be glad to get this one over."

"Well, there's a few things that you have to know, Chief."

"Like what?" asked Jack, seemingly perturbed.

"First of all, Sam Parker had a massive brain tumor that was spreading so fast that I don't think he would have lived much longer."

"You're kidding!"

"Oh yeah...Jack, you know us M.E.'s...we are always kidding and joking after we perform autopsies."

"You know, I remember reading in the interview sheet that some friends said he had complained about migraine headaches."

"Well, he had some headaches all right. This was a serious malignant tumor that must have been extremely painful for him during his final days."

"Final days?"

"Oh yeah...He couldn't have had but more than a few weeks."

"Hmmmm.....I didn't know.....Poor Sam."

"There is another thing that you must know."

"Yeah, what's that?"

"Sam had ingested a large quantity of a flavored morphine derivative just prior to his death."

"Like how much?"

"Enough to kill an adult within minutes."

There was a very long pause. Jack was silent. He couldn't think of what to say to Dr. Schmidt. He wanted her to speak. But she didn't. She too, was silent.

"Well! Do you think that perhaps Sam committed suicide? I mean he must have known he was dying with little time left."

"Hey Jack! That's *your* job to figure that out. I just report the findings. But I need to tell you something very important."

"Such as...?"

"He was dead before he drowned. That is... he had been dead before his lungs filled up with the sea water."

Another long pause. Jack 's mind was now racing. He wondered if Karen had any more revelations with her autopsy of Sam's body. He was getting a little nervous.

"Ah...shit!...I didn't want to hear that!"

"Sorry...I just call 'em as I see 'em. Jack, you'll have the detailed written report in your office by tomorrow afternoon."

"Yeah. Thanks, Karen. I appreciate it."

Jack hung up the phone and stared out at the cars just barely moving along Rte 28. The weekend traffic begins building exponentially each weekend in May on Cape Cod. This Friday was no exception. He was upset. He had hoped that the autopsy would have been done quickly without anything abnormal discovered. But it was. As of now, only two people knew this little twist—he and Dr. Karen Schmidt. He had to keep this little tidbit of information as tight as possible.

Jack was hesitant to get Detective Souza worked up over this new information, but he was obligated to bring him up to date. He had to come up with an action plan. Jack decided that would handle all of the interviews with Paula. Jesse would interview the neighbors and Sam's colleagues in Woods Hole for any leads.

Jack paced around his office. He was really steamed over the results of the autopsy. With these new findings, this case could be far from being closed. Jack thought to himself as he paced. He knew that if, or when, this new information from the M.E. got out, the press would quickly speculate that there were three possible ways that Sam could have drowned.

It could have been an accident that he somehow became disoriented from his medication fortified with the morphine and fell into the bay.

He may have committed suicide by drinking the lethal drug and purposely falling into the bay. This was even more plausible since his life was soon to end in a painful and undignified way.

And then there was the possibility of homicide. It was possible that he was administered the lethal drug unknowingly and then was pushed into the bay.

The drive out to Paula's house in Quissett didn't last long enough. Jack could have used more time to strategize, but he did want to let Paula know in person that she could now arrange funeral services for her husband. He knew that this was weighing heavy on her mind. She needed the proper memorial service for Sam. She needed to begin the grieving process so that it could eventually be brought to closure.

When Jack arrived he took her up on her offer to have a cup of coffee. He sat down at the kitchen table while Paula turned the percolator on. Paula was relieved to hear the news from Jack that the autopsy was completed quickly. She could now post the services in the newspaper.

"Thanks for arranging for Pat to get shuttled over here the other night, Jack."

"No problem. Is she still here?" He looked around and down her hallway as if to see if Paula was within earshot.

"Yes. But she just stepped out. She just went downtown for a while."

"Paula. I have to tell you something. There were a couple of things that the M.E. found that you should know about."

There was a pause, as she pushed the sugar bowl closer to Jack. Paula looked warily at him.

"What is it Jack?"

"Well, unfortunately this case is going to remain open until we can get some answers."

"Answers to what?" Paula responded, somewhat agitated.

"We can't officially determine if Sam's drowning was an accident, a suicide or a murder."

"Oh Jack – really! Suicide? Murder? What are you saying for God's sake?"

Jack then told Paula about the Medical Examiners findings including the lethal morphine drug and the fact that he was dead before he was in the water.

Paula listened. Her face showed an expression of disbelief.

"Paula, I wasn't going to reveal all of this to you now, but I thought that you should know. Besides it could become public knowledge soon, and others might inform you later."

"Oh my God. I just don't understand. It doesn't make any sense. Morphine?"

Paula got up from the table and walked towards the kitchen sink. She poured herself a glass of water. She was angry. For the next several minutes, Paula told Jack about Sam's brain tumor and its prognosis. She told him how Sam never felt defeated and would never give up on his research work or on his life. She mentioned the prescription drugs for Sam's pain, but there never was a script for morphine. The prescribed drugs had worked and reduced his pain. Sam was confident that he could make this brief exploration on the Woods Hole research vessel since it was for only two days.

She further told Jack how she didn't want to leave for her weekly visit with her sister over at the Vineyard. Sam insisted that he was all right and that she should still take the ferry over there. She described his spirit as being upbeat and positive. He felt that he was invincible to any disease. She emphasized that suicide was something that Sam would never consider.

"There was never any morphine prescribed, Jack. I am totally confused with that news."

"Well, it is pretty easy to get a hold of that stuff. "

"Yeah, but I can't envision Sam injecting himself. As a matter of fact, he was afraid of injections with needles."

"Oh, Paula, the morphine drug wasn't injected. It was administered orally. He probably drank it since it was masked with some flavoring. It was found in his stomach."

" I see." Paula began to cry.

"Look Paula, I am so sorry. This discussion can wait until after the services. Let me go and leave you with your sister, Pat, to make arrangements."

"I'm sorry, Jack. Its ...its just that suicide and murder are so foreign to the life that Sam had lived." Paula was shaking her head back and forth as the tears started rolling down her cheeks.

"Well, we are still not ruling out accidental death. He may have taken the morphine for pain, took too much and then collapsed into the sea from the jetty."

"Well Jack, that's a more plausible way for my poor Sam to die." Paula left the room as she burst out crying.

* * *

The tension was high at the police station the next day. Jesse knew that they were in for a lot of investigative work. The pressure from the newspaper people would be turned up high. Jesse knew that he would have to satisfy the hounding reporters or as he called them, "the media mavens". He was anxious to start bringing together some of the information that he already had begun to collect. He wanted to solve this case as soon as possible. If, there was going to be a case.

Jack was pacing around again in his office like a nervous cat.

"Jesse, I want to wrap up this case soon. Real soon." Jack said to his detective as he walked into Souza's office.

"Well Jack, everything is checking out so far. I interviewed some colleagues of Sam's at Woods Hole. His reputation was solid as steel. No marital or financial problems that anyone knew about. He got along with everyone. No suspects."

"Well, I would have bet on that. Anything else?" Jack was more than a little sarcastic towards the younger detective.

"I did speak with his closest colleague—another scientist by the name of Ted Burford."

"Yeah?"

"He told me how he received an e-mail at his Woods Hole office. Sam had sent it from his house early Wednesday morning. In fact, here's the hard-copy of the e-mail."

Jesse handed Jack the piece of paper. The e-mail read:

Hi Ted,

I am not feeling too well with these migraine headaches and have decided not to go on the two-day expedition.

My wife just left to visit her sister on the island, and I could use the day to rest up. I am just leaving for my walk now along Chappy for some fresh air. I will return and take a nap. The medication makes me sleepy. See you next week.   Sam

"When was the time stamp on the electronic mail message?"

"6:30AM."

"It all fits in Jesse. You see. I am now thinking that he did take some of "his own" extra medication in the form of morphine. He took his usual beach-combing walk and then strolled out to the jetty as he does each day. With the pain medications taking effect, he got dizzy, maybe disoriented, and then he slid into the sea from the slippery jetty."

"Intentionally or unintentionally?"

"Goddamnit! Does it really matter, Jesse?" Jack was getting angry.

"Yeah, OK. Jack it doesn't matter."

"Look," said Jack, getting very red in the face. "The man was terminally ill. Maybe he had a month of life left on this earth. He was smart enough to know that those final weeks would be ungodly. He would endure severe pain, suffering, and God only knows what kind of embarrassment. What the hell difference does it make? I probably would do the same thing."

"OK, Jack, but what about him dying....... before he drowned? That doesn't make sense, and it is documented in the ME's notes."

"It still could have happened. He could have expired on the rocks and his body just fell or slid into the water. The waves could have knocked him over. Who knows? What else could have happened? His wife loved him dearly. He loved her. There were no financial problems. There was no evidence of a robbery at the scene. There was no motive for murder. Your investigation found that he had no enemies."

"Hey wait a second, Jack. Let's take it a little slow now, OK? I didn't say that he didn't have *any* enemies."

Jack gave Jesse a piercing look. "What do you mean, Jesse?"

"Well, it turns out that Sam did have one person who had watched him closely. I interviewed some folks in town. This guy had one, long-standing beef with Sam."

"And who would that be?"

"A local by the name of Vincenzo Vendrasco."

"Yeah, so, what about him?"

"I learned that Sam had a boat mooring in a prime spot at Quissett Harbor. Sam's 16-foot skiff was tied up to that ball. I think it was a Boston Whaler. Well, this Vincenzo knew from the Quissett Harbor Master that Sam was thinking about giving up his mooring space. He hadn't used it much lately. Vincenzo had been on the waiting list for over 5 years to get a mooring at Quissett."

"Yeah. So?"

"As you know, Quissett is one of the best harbors on Cape Cod."

"Where are you going with this, Jesse?" asked Jack.

"Listen. Some time ago, Vendrasco tried to buy the mooring from Sam. But Sam wouldn't budge. Vendrasco became really pissed off at Sam. The rumors are that the two of them had a real shouting match. In the last year, Sam used his little whaler only a few times to go for a quick spin out to the bay with his wife. Vendrasco knew this and it bothered him beyond no end. Vendrasco is a very serious fisherman and really wanted that hook and ball in the water for his bigger boat."

"Come on Jesse. For Christ's sake, you're not telling me......."

"Jack, the Harbormaster told me that Vendrasco called him just this morning. He wanted to know when he could get Sam's mooring. Now that Sam is dead."

"Jesse. This is bullshit! For Christ's sake, do you *really think* that a guy would push another man into the sea and drown him to get his mooring?"

"Why not? You know they take out guns and shoot people over parking spaces in New York City!"

"Yeah...but come on...that's New York City...not Quissett."

"Hey, Jack...."

"Jesse! Get your head out of your ass. There is no case here!"

Now Jesse was getting angry with Jack. He stared at Jack, thinking to himself—you do your job, you dig up some information, you come up with a potential theory, and then you get ridiculed.

Jesse also thought that Jack was too damned close to this one case. It was evident that Jack wanted this case closed quickly. But there were still some loose ends. What the hell was the rush? This puzzled Jesse. It didn't make sense to him.

"I suppose, Jesse, that this guy, ah...Vendrasco, has an alibi?" Jack gave his Detective Souza an exaggerated condescending look.

"It's weak. With no real witnesses. The ME puts the death sometime between late Tuesday and early on Thursday. She didn't want to pin it down any finer than that."

"And where was our friend, Vincenzo, at this time period?"

"Out on the open sea. He was southwest of Nantucket, doing some tuna fishing."

"Tuna fishing, eh? Well then he wasn't out there by himself."

"No. Not at all...but he was only with his wife.... A real blonde beauty, I might add. About twenty years younger than him."

"So we have Vendrasco, Sam's only possible enemy, out tuna fishing with his wife during the time of death."

"Yep."

"Jesse. Did you ask if he caught any tuna? If so, we could check with the fishmongers then."

"I did that, Jack." He replied sarcastically and loudly. Jesse was now pissed off at his boss for the obvious condescending question.

"And?"

"He told me that they got nothing. Supposedly they got skunked during that fishing trip."

"Hmmm....did he have any priors?"

"I'm working on that. I am waiting to hear from the Boston PD. He spent most of his early years in the Boston area. I hear the fax machine now. Let me go see if it is something that we can use."

Jesse left Jack's office pleased to be out of there. This was the first time that his boss was so involved with one of his cases. He knew it wasn't just because it was a high profile case. He had heard too often about how Jack had pined for Sam's wife, Paula, for many years. Some of his friends had told him how Jack often talked about his high school crush on Paula at Jake's bar, a popular drinking spot. Evidently that crush had lasted for a lifetime. It wasn't right that only Jack would deal with Paula. Jesse was assigned to investigate and interview all others. But not Paula Parker. This wasn't S.O.P. and Jesse felt that Jack was out of line with this approach to the case.

As Jesse was looking at the fax coming in, Jack closed the door to his office. His mind was on Paula. He needed to talk with her. He dialed her number.

"Paula. It's me. Jack."

"Yes Jack. What is it?"

"Listen. I need to speak with you. Can I meet with you in private?"

"In private? What do you mean?"

"Is your sister, Pat, still there?"

"Actually she is. But she has a hair appointment at 6:30."

"Good. I'll be at your house about that time. Don't worry. This won't take long."

Jesse knocked on Jack's office door. Jack hand signaled for him to come in through the door window.

"Jack. Look at these faxes, " Jesse said as he entered the office. This Vendrasco character is one mean son of a bitch."

"Jesse. For God's sake, let me look." He grabbed the papers and began reading them.

The Boston Police Department reported that Vincenzo Vendrasco had a long list of priors. He was connected with the mob in that city and in Providence, Rhode Island. He did some prison time for drug running and some assaults. None of them for long sentences. He was also pinned down for some money laundering. He was, however, implicated in two different murder cases. They had to do with some small time drug dealers in the North Shore of Boston. In both cases the murder was done with a gaff hook like those used by fisherman for tuna and large game fish. The large hook was ripped through the victim's neck such that he couldn't move. He would be left to bleed to death. There were no convictions. Apparently, Vendrasco had some good connections in the DAs department.

"I told you Jack. This Vendrasco guy. He ain't no good."

"Yeah, but come on Jess. This guy was playing with the big boys up north. If his " m.o." was the gaff hook, he wouldn't change to something so delicate as a morphine derivative."

"But Jack. It's still drugs. The guy lived in the drug world, which includes illegal morphine. "

"I can't buy your theory right now. But I tell you what. You got about twenty fours hours to convince me."

Jack looked up at the clock. It was 6:15pm. He grabbed his coat and told Jesse that he was leaving for the day and rushed out of the office.

As he pulled his car up in front of the Parker house, he looked all around to see if there were any people who might see him getting out of his car.

"Paula. I need to let you in on something." He was still standing in the doorway. "Let's talk for a bit."

"What the hell is it Jack? You seem out of sorts... especially for you."

"Paula, Listen to me. There are a lot of people who want to drag this case on about Sam's death. I can't tell you who they are, but believe me; they are looking for some sensational twist to Sam's drowning. They can easily drag this out and waste time as a possible suicide or homicide. This could get very uncomfortable. Every little thing in Sam's life, and yours, will be exposed to the public. I need to warn you."

"Oh...Jack we already discussed this. I am not in the mood. Right now I don't think that I can handle......"

"I know, I know," Jack interrupted. "But listen. I can control the case and its conclusion pretty much right now. If it goes any further, too many people get involved. Since Sam worked on government research contracts, the FBI will step in. That's when I would lose the control and things might get out of hand. This is what I want you to understand and to agree with me."

"What? Agree with what?"

"I know that you don't want any suicide or homicide investigations. I am going to let the press know that the case was ruled an accidental drowning just like you and I discussed. In my official report I will not record that he was fortifying his prescribed medication with morphine that he may have taken from the lab in Woods Hole. On this occasion, during his morning walk out on the jetty, he became disoriented, died and fell or slid into the jetty. If I come out with this story now, I can be very convincing. Then there will be no further investigation. The reporters will write their stories. They will never know if there were any loose ends. Are you OK with this, Paula?"

"Well, of course, Jack, but why are you doing this?"

Jack looked at her and paused. He lightly grabbed her forearms with his hands. "I am doing this only for you Paula. You don't want some sensational news dragging on about Sam's death being a possible suicide or even a homicide do you?"

"No. No, of course not. Nothing will bring Sam back now."

"OK then. Let me arrange a press conference for tomorrow and announce that the case is closed."

"Thanks, Jack."

"OK. But there is just one other thing. *We never had this conversation. OK?* I am jeopardizing my career by doing this. Can we agree on this, Paula?"

"Sure. Sure Jack."

"Great!" He looked straight into her eyes. There was a silent pause.

"Yeah...Thanks."

"Remember, I am doing this only for you. You have had enough to deal with and a dragged out public investigation is not what you need right now."

Paula broke a slight smile on her face. "That's for sure Jack."

Jack noticed the little smile on her face and it warmed his heart. Then he did something that he was unprepared for. He instinctively grabbed both of her shoulders in a gentle and loving fashion and pulled Paula towards him. He then kissed her softly on her forehead.

"Good Night, Paula."

Surprised, Paula replied, "Good Night, Jack."

Paula watched through the front window as Jack Ogren pulled away. She was still somewhat confused with Jack's coming to her house and what he had to say to her. He seemed so rattled. He seemed to understand why *she* wanted to close the case as soon as possible. But, why was *he* so anxious to avoid a possible murder case or suicide case? Why did he really want to keep this quiet? What was he trying to avoid or hide? It made no sense to her. She would think about this for several days to come.

***

Jack called the Cape Cod Times, the Falmouth Enterprise, and the Boston Globe. He would hold a press conference call at 2pm for a news release on the Parker drowning.

"Jack, I still think we should wait a day or so, something may turn up." Jesse objected. "We still haven't found anyone who actually saw him walking that morning, but who knows, somebody may still come forward."

"It was an accident, Jesse. Let it go! For Christ's sake! Everyone in this town including the Andersons who saw him each morning knew about Sam's daily routine. He always ended up his walk with at trip out on the jetty. You know how goddamned slippery those rocks can be! Add some heavy drugs to the situation and he could have easily slipped into the bay."

"What about suicide, are you ruling that out too?"

"Yep. There is no suicide note for his dear wife, whom he loved. Of all people, I think that Sam would have left a note for Paula. In addition, you, Jesse, came across the e-mail indicating everything was normal except for his painful headaches. It corroborates that his wife had left for the Vineyard and that he was going for his morning constitutional at the beach. There is nothing to indicate that he was going to kill himself."

"What about Vendrasco?"

"I think that nothing will come of that. I am not going to bring him in based on his desire to get Sam's mooring at Quissett Harbor. Without any hard evidence, I'd be the laughing stock throughout the Commonwealth of Massachusetts."

The articles were succinct in all of the papers the following day. They described his morning walks at the beach for the past 25 years. There were excerpts from the Anderson interview about his routine meditation on the jetty each morning. The general conclusion was that Sam Parker was either knocked off of the jetty rocks with high waves, or he slipped on the wet rocks, and drowned. There was no mention of the morphine. There was no hint of foul play or suicide. There was no need for the public to know about Sam's terminal condition and his medication. The articles went on...'that the village of Quissett mourned the loss of one of its favorite and famous citizens..........'.

It was a well-crafted article. Jack was proud of his work as he read each newspaper clipping.

That afternoon, Paula Parker called the Falmouth Police Station.

"Jack, I just wanted to call and thank you for your quick work on Sam's accident. I realize how difficult it was for you. I know that you did the right thing."

"No problem, Paula. But please remember. I did it only for you."

There was a brief pause. Paula wasn't sure what to say.

"Yes Jack. I am grateful," she finally replied.

"And remember, if there is anything else that I can do for you, just pick up the phone. Don't ever hesitate."

"Thanks, Jack. I will."

"Is your sister still there with you?"

"Yes. She will stay with me until a few days after the funeral. But then, she has to get back to her clinic on the Vineyard. There aren't that many doctors to go around over there on the island and she is desperately needed."

"Take care, Paula." Jack hung up the phone and stared at nothing for a very long time out through his office window. His mind was wandering.

He thought long about the attractive and sexy girl of his high school years.... Paula Larson. Visions of her innocently teasing him with her sweet smile came back into his head. He recalled some of the times when they were together at teenage parties and dances. He pulled open his desk drawer. In a file folder at the back of the drawer were some old photographs. He took these out and looked at them for a long time. He could still remember the scent of her after all of these years. A smile came across his face. It was the first smile he had in several days.

He still had feelings for her as he did at seventeen years of age. His heart actually had beat a little faster when he was in her company these past few days. Soon he could do something about those feelings. He just did her a great favor. In a way, she now owed him.

Jack further thought that it was a shame that such a good person, such an attractive woman, had to now live alone. It was a waste of life when one had to live alone. Jack knew this all too well. He had been living alone for almost eight years now. It was eight years since his wife told him that she had found someone else and the divorce proceedings began. She wasn't living alone. She lived with her new attorney husband in a Westchester, New York mansion. She was very happy not living alone.

CHAPTER THREE

Paula Larson

Growing up on the shoreline of Cape Cod provides a wide variety of opportunities for every child. Every boy or girl can enjoy the true experience of nature and take advantage of all that the Cape environment offers. Most kids learn to sail, to fish, to swim, to dig for clams, and to catch blue crabs at an early age. The large wooded areas where native American Indian tribes once lived have challenging and beautiful hiking trails. Youngsters learn at an early age where the sweet, wild blueberries grow among those hidden trails in the woods.

The Cape environment also provides artistic beauty that make children and adults appreciate the natural scenery. The autumn cranberry season paints a variety of unique pictures never seen in any other part of this world. People will stop by these fruited bogs at harvest time. They will wonder at the bright, vibrant, crimson colored harvest as it raditates against a backdrop of warm, golden, New England foliage.

The wintertime is as active as the other three seasons. There are many cross-country skiing trails in the dense, pine-treed forests and state parks.

The local cranberry bogs are then flooded with fresh water each winter to freeze up and protect these tender plants. The iced over bogs become hard, smooth skating rinks. They are ideal for figure skating and hockey games on the coldest of winter days.

Like her friends, Paula Larson had learned to swim, to fish, and to sail in her native Quissett village at an early age. There was always something for her to do on the land, at the shore, or in the bay. She rarely got bored with nature's playground.

With the advent of her adolescence, however, Paula spent much of her time caring for younger children. During the summertime she baby-sat for neighbors as much as sixty hours a week. Paula discovered that this activity not only proved to be lucrative, but she truly enjoyed being with the younger kids. She was their friend, their teacher, and at times, their surrogate mother. Her baby-sitting services were in high demand by the Quissett parents all year round. But the demand increased even more by the visiting "summer people" in July and August. These couples needed a responsible teenager to look after their kids when they went out to dine, to golf, to sail or to attend the ubiquitous summer cocktail parties.

Paula got to know the children very well. They loved to be with her. She always played games with them, taught them how to swim and how to bait a fishhook. She took them on nature hikes, and patiently nursed their sicknesses and injuries. The little ones grew attached to Paula and never forgot her, as they grew older. They sent birthday and Christmas cards, Valentines and letters to her from their homes in Boston, New York, and New Jersey long after each summer ended. Paula began to look forward to the day when she would be a wife and mother with kids of her own.

The years at Quissett High School went by quickly for Paula. She was a good student, well liked by her classmates, and voted captain of her swim team. Her outgoing personality and willingness to do extra work or to help tutor the others did not go unnoticed by her teachers. She was elected Treasurer of her graduating class of 1970. She had dated a little bit and had one or two steady boyfriends, but these relationships never turned serious.

Paula was ecstatic that early spring day in 1970 when she received her letter from Bridgewater State College. Her application had been accepted to enter the elementary education program in the fall. While most of the graduating seniors didn't know which career they want to pursue, Paula knew exactly what she wanted to do with her professional life. She had visualized herself teaching elementary school since she was twelve years of age. She had never drifted away from that dream.

Paula rarely had any sibling competition with her sister, Patricia, who was four years her senior. Growing up in school, Pat always had an affinity towards the sciences. She was valedictorian of her Quissett high school class of 1966. After a successful "pre-med." curriculum at Tufts University in Boston, she was now going to attend the Harvard School of Medicine in the fall. She planned to concentrate in Internal Medicine.

Pat and Paula had always remained supportive sisters. More importantly, they were close friends. There was nothing that they would keep from one another. They shared their confidence with each other. They told each other their most intimate experiences. This secrecy was sacrosanct and never needed to be questioned. The two sisters helped each other with advice, guidance, protection, and money whenever it was needed.

Although Pat and Paula were close, the characters and personalities of these two sisters were as different as night and day. The older Pat was a driven, hard-nosed competitor, while Paula, was more sensitive, loving, and compassionate.

They did not look like one another physically. Pat was more of an ordinary looking woman of twenty-two, with a tall, slender stature. She had mousy-brown, hair which she always wore cut very short. She never wore makeup, or flashy clothes. She always minimized the look of her figure with baggy or masculine styled outfits. Paula loved to joke with Pat about her subdued femininity and playfully accused her of attracting lesbians. At times, she teased her older sister about this by calling her "Provincetown Patty."

Conversely, Paula had grown into a very attractive, sensuous, eighteen-year-old Quissett High School senior. She always kept her silky, auburn colored hair at a long length even during the swimming season. Her beautiful hair was always smooth and bounced around rhythmically when she walked. She had a soft, milky facial complexion that contrasted with her deep emerald-green eyes. Her sweet, wholesome smile was permanently fixed on her face. Because of the rigors of competitive swimming, her frame had very little body fat. She had softly defined muscles in her legs, arms and abdomen. Her breasts had blossomed more full in her senior year. This expansion made her narrow waist appear even smaller than it was. Although Paula knew that her physical body was sexy and appealing to both boys and girls, she never flaunted it. She always tried to emphasize her personality, her character, and her inner spirit to be her finest assets.

***

There are certain traditions and rites that accompany the passage of graduating from high school. Most are universal standards such as the senior yearbook, the senior prom, class day and class picnics. Other non-sanctioned rituals are specific to particular schools and are carried on year after year. These events are often shrouded in student secrecy, loyalty, and at times some intense peer pressure.

Quissett High seniors had one such secret ritual. For over a decade, a party known as the "Freedom Fest" was held on the Saturday night before the commencement ceremony. This annual party was held on Washburn Island, facing Vineyard Sound. The police had no easy access to this area and there were no homeowners in the vicinity to complain about loud noise and music. This night, in mid-June, was an icon for the seniors to come of age, and to celebrate their freedom from high school, teachers, homework, and oppressive parents. This was the night on which they claimed to reach the official status of "adult". The clandestine party was held each year so that the Quissett High seniors could engage in one last parent-free party of drinking, dancing, and swimming together in the moonlight.

The event was arranged by a small group of students to

coordinate all of the boats, beer kegs, food, and music. It was always a logistical challenge to coordinate the one hundred or so seniors and party supplies to be loaded onto boats to reach the island around twilight time.

Small campfires were lit nearby to provide some auxiliary light to the otherwise dim moonlit beach. The party went on for several hours, usually until the beer kegs went dry. The music, dancing and just "hanging out" with friends made the party a success!

The climax of the night was the so-called, "Class Skinny Dip". One anonymous senior was pre-selected by the Class President to yell out the words....... " Skinny Dip!!!" near the end of the evening. This was the long awaited signal for all of the students to disrobe as quickly as they could and run the short distance into the cold, dark, salty water. This rite of spring was always the high point of the seniors' "Fest". It climaxed weeks of anxious hallway chatter and hype among the graduating class.

Paula danced and spent most of the night with two of her closest girlfriends. This skinny dip thing was no big deal to them. In reality, there wasn't much light to expose their young, nude bodies. It was the "daring to do it" that made everyone participate.

At the signal, Paula laughed and giggled with her friends. They quickly and nervously took off their clothes and ran into the dark, cold water as fast as they could. Within a few minutes, all of the students were splashing, laughing, and acting silly as if they were little children at the beach for the first time. The frolicking went on for some time.

Paula was glad that she came. She always enjoyed "being part of the gang" even though she always kept her own personal standards and ambitions.

While Paula was splashing and frolicking in the chilly water with her friends, however, she was unaware that a pair of eyes was secretly riveted on her. From behind a stand of thick pine tree these eyes followed her every move and stared at her sensuous body. They had been focused on her for the entire evening.

This "skinny dip" event went off well as it did each year before.

The seniors all yelled, laughed, and cried tears of joy before quickly and modestly running on shore to dry off and get dressed. Some stayed in the water to continue swimming in the nude. Others resumed dancing, singing, smoking pot and drinking on the sandy beach.

Paula quickly dressed and began walking on the sand with her two girlfriends. She was still toweling off her long, auburn colored hair as they slowly strolled and talked.

Suddenly, a deep voice from the darkened hillside called out, "Paula! Paula!" interrupting their chatter.

All three girls turned to see who called, but they could only make out a tall, male silhouette standing among the pine trees. The light from his cigarette burned red against the black, darkened trees.

"Paula, can you come over here for a minute?" the voice asked.

Paula told her friends that she would return quickly and walked over toward the trees and the swaying dark silhouette.

"Who is that?" asked Paula as she moved slowly towards the figure.

There was no answer.

"Is that you Jack?" Paula asked

"It's me, David," the shadow seemed to say.

"Who?" inquired Paula walking closer.

"David, David Whitestone," replied the darkened silouhette.

As she approached, Paula said, "Oh, I thought that you were Jack. Jack Ogren"

"Sorry, Paula. Are you disappointed?"

"Huh? Oh, no, David. What are you doing up here in the dark? Do you want to join my friends and me for a walk along the beach?"

"No, No. I need to talk with you. Can you stay for a few minutes? Paula, I really, really need to talk with you tonight."

Paula was quite surprised by this encounter. She hardly knew David, as did any of the Quissett students. He was a recent transfer student from a New York City high school. He was very quiet and usually kept to himself. He was a tall, good-looking boy with shoulder length black hair, a thick mustache and coal-black eyes. Nobody seemed to know much about him, although he had been enrolled at Quissett High for over two months.

Paula did a quick mental scan of her class schedule and realized that David was in her American History class. She didn't take much notice of him simply because he always took a seat behind her in the classroom and she couldn't see him. There were times, however, when she sensed someone staring at her from behind. She thought more than once that it might have been David Whitestone.

Paula looked over to where she had left her two girlfriends. They had already started walking slowly towards the anchored boats for their return trip to the mainland. They were deep in conversation and giggling. They anticipated that Paula would catch up with them soon—if she wanted to do so.

"Well, what is it David? I really should get going," said Paula. " I have a busy day lined up for tomorrow and I want to get back home early."

"Please, Paula. I need your advice on something. Right now, I am really nervous about asking you."

Paula walked up to him and noticed his nervousness.

"Well it can't be *that* serious, David, what is it?"

" First, you've got to have a beer with me," said David in a noticeably trembling voice.

"Well, OK, David, but I really got to get going. What's your problem? Are you flunking American History or something?"

"No, no, not at all. Please sit down, I have some beer stashed in the water to keep cold. I'll get you one and then we'll talk."

David quickly walked away from Paula towards the water. He retrieved two cans of beer from the cold salt water where he had stored them earlier. With his back toward Paula, he flipped opened one can with his left hand, reached into his shirt pocket with his right hand, and pulled out what appeared to be a white, paper packet. He poured the contents inside the opened can and swished it around. He then walked toward Paula, gave her that can of beer, and then opened the second can for himself.

"Thanks for doing this Paula. I've been wanting to speak with you for some time," said David. "But first, let's toast to our graduation next week and our freedom. You know— no more teachers, no more books,— and all that bullshit."

They both chug-a-lugged their beer with long swigs, and then sat down on a large fallen oak tree trunk.

"So, David, what is so important that you got to talk to me about? Especially now. It is almost midnight!"

"Paula, I want to consider you a friend. Please promise me that what I tell you is held in strict confidence?" asked David.

"Sure," replied Paula. "Who the hell would I tell anyway?"

"You know, its a bitch coming here as a senior and trying to fit in during the last two months of the school year. I've really no friends or anybody that I can talk to."

"Sure, David, I can understand that, but what exactly is your freakin' problem?"

"This has to be confidential. Promise?"

"Promise!"

"How about a 'Promise Toast' then?"

They lightly clinked beer cans, raised them and swigged.

"Well it has to do with this girl who is in our class." David did not look at her.

"Yeah...So who is she?" asked Paula.

" Aha...I will tell you her name a little later."

" Do you like her?"

"Yes, yes. In fact, I am really infatuated with her. I think that I have been ever since I came here to this little town of Quissett."

"Village, David. It's Quissett village".

"Yeah, yeah. Whatever".

"Well tell her how you feel. Ask her out on a date, call her...what's the problem?" Paula asked sarcastically, as she was becoming somewhat annoyed with this conversation.

"Promise me that you won't tell anyone?" pleaded David.

"Of course, David."

"How about another 'promise toast'?" asked David raising his beer can and clinking with Paula's. They both chugged.

"Was this girl, without a name, here tonight, David? Did you see her at the party?" asked Paula struggling a bit to articulate her words.

"Well, yes, she was at the party tonight. But I could only stare at her. She is soooo hot!"

"Why didn't you go with her? Was she with another guy?" asked Paula sipping her beer.

"No, I don't think so."

"Well, how the hell can I help you David, if you don't tell me who this chick is?" Paula's tone was changing and becoming uncharacteristically angry.

"Tell you what. I will give you her name as soon as you finish your beer."

They both chugged again.

"Was she dancing before the class "Skinny Dip?" Did you see her dancing?" Paula slurred her words as she finished off her can of beer.

"Well, ah..., yes she was, it was so cool to watch her. She looked beautiful. I couldn't keep my eyes off of her," smiled David. His voice had now become calmer. He was more confident.

"Well, if you won't tell me her name, can you describe her to me? " asked Paula, losing her visual focus temporarily.

"Oh sure I can. Then you will *guess* who she is. She has beautiful green eyes, and a soft complexion, and a beautiful, sexy, figure."

"Well, whooooooo is sheeeeeeee? This game of yours is total bullshit!" said Paula struggling to keep her brain focused on the conversation. All of a sudden her head felt as though it was spinning or wobbling. She had lost control. She couldn't figure out why.

"She has beautiful, soft, auburn hair, "continued David.

Paula looked over at David. He was smiling coyly. She felt strange and suddenly uncomfortable and out of control.

" I don't think I know her," answered Paula, hardly keeping her eyes opened and now becoming very dizzy.

"Come on Paula. Let's you and I walk over there to that little dune. I think we need to rest," directed David as he helped her to her feet.

She struggled to walk over to the dune that David spoke about. Nothing seemed real to Paula. She thought that she was in a dream. She had no idea where she was. The party was long gone from her memory. She felt like she was floating rather than walking. She couldn't feel the ground beneath her feet. David was leading her. She couldn't comprehend why an old, green, Army blanket had been stretched out behind the dune, as though it was prepared for a couple to lie down on it. She felt like laughing. Everything was unimportant. She never felt carefree like this before. She tried to focus, to be serious, but it was impossible.

***

Paula never knew what happened. When she woke up an hour later, she stared straight up above her. The moon had climbed over to the western side of the sky with large, puffy, silver-gray clouds dancing by in front of it. She just lay still for a while, looking at the starry heavens above. She tried to mentally reconstruct what had happened. She did not know where she was. She could not understand why she was in this condition. She slowly moved her aching head from side to side. There was nobody around her. She was alone. She could hear only the sound of the waves breaking on the shore.

She stayed still for several minutes. The pieces of the puzzle slowly came together. She could feel some pain. She felt very damp. She was sore. As this frightening mystery unfolded, Paula knew exactly what had happened. She began to tremble. She thought she was going to get sick. Most of her clothes and underwear had been thrown on top of her. Some were bloodstained.

As her mind began to slowly clear, Paula remembered that she drank only one beer with the bastard. She now realized that she had been drugged and raped. She didn't know which drug he had used. She began to weep involuntarily. She thought she was paralyzed. She prayed to God. Her head ached and pounded with each heartbeat.

After a while, Paula managed to get dressed. She slowly got up and staggered around. She thought she might get some help from anyone who was still on the island. She had no idea what time it was. She just kept walking in circles for a while. She adjusted her clothes a little and tried to focus.

Paula struggled to walk a straight line. She then spotted what appeared to be a male figure standing about thirty yards away from her. She could see him only from his chest up. His lower body was hidden by a tall sweeping sand dune. He appeared to be swaying slowly from side to side. Her blurred eyes couldn't make out who it might be.

She quickened her wet, sandy, steps. She was whimpering to herself as she struggled to move along. Paula considered yelling out for help, but then thought better of that. As she got closer, she could make out the face of the boy who was behind the dune. It was Mark Rocco, a classmate of hers and Quissett High's star football hero. He was staring up at the sky slowly moving his head. Paula thought he was chanting or mumbling something. She thought that she was hallucinating. She thought that her own head still was not clear. She slowly walked up to the dune's crest without him seeing her. Then, looking down into the depth of the sandy dune, Paula saw another classmate. It was Sonny Brooks. The waning moonlight illuminated Sonny's kneeling body and face as her head bobbed up and down vigorously between Mark's legs.

Paula quickly turned and ran. She stopped. She vomited violently. Then she slowly labored to catch her breath. She now knew that she was on her own. There was no help to be found.

Paula cried as she ran straight into the cold, dark water. She washed herself as best she could with the chilled salty water. She then swam as fast as she could towards the mainland with a speed that she had typically reserved for scholastic swim meets. On land, she regained her bearings and soon her normal heart rate returned. She started walking more steadily towards the main road. Her head had cleared. Her clothing was soaked from head to toe. When she eventually reached Central Avenue she walked on the sandy shoulder of the road to escape the glare of on-coming headlights. She ambled along with her head looking straight towards the ground below her.

"Paula, Paula is that you? Are you all right?" The voice came from the slow moving Ford Mustang behind her.

Paula turned to look inside of the vehicle.

"Oh Tom, thank God, thank God!" she began to cry.

"Jump in, I'll take you home!" said Tom.

As Tom drove slowly in the direction of Paula's home in Quissett, he looked over to her sitting next to him. She was crying; shivering and looking very lost.

"Hey Paula, are you really OK? You look like you've been through hell," said Tom. "Here. I have some beach towels in the back seat. You can get yourself dried. I'll turn the heater on so that you can warm up."

He intentionally drove his Mustang down the darker side roads of town to avoid anyone seeing Paula in this condition.

"So. What the hell happened? I hate to say it but you look like shit."

" Oh, Tom...I...I ". She gulped uncontrollably to take in some much-needed air. " I don't think I can talk about it. Just take me home. Please!"

Although she was still weeping quietly, she was trying to recapture some of her composure with long deep breaths. Of all the people whom she might have encountered at this time of night, she was so relieved that it was Tom Donovan. No better person could have come to her rescue. He was a good friend. More importantly, he was also someone whom she could trust.

Tom Donovan was considered to be one of the sweetest, most sensitive students in Quissett's 1970 graduating class. At over six feet tall, sandy colored hair and a trim athletic build, Tom was easily selected as the best looking boy in the senior class. He was captain of the Boy's Swim Team, countering Paula who was captain of her swim team.

In the past, Paula would love to have dated him. She had actually asked Tom to go with her to a school dance during their junior year. As Tom now drove her along the back dirt roads, Paula had a brief flashback of that nervous encounter over a year ago.

"Gee, Paula. Thanks for asking me," replied Tom. I'd love more than anything to go to the dance with you— if I were available. But I guess that you haven't heard. Sonny Brooks and I have been going steady for about a week now."

"Oh really?" responded Paula. " No, I hadn't heard about you and Sonny. I guess the rumor mill has been a bit slow this week." Paula tried to hide her disappointment and total surprise with a false smile.

"Yeah, she asked me out a few weeks ago. It all happened so fast," Tom giggled, almost impishly.

"Well. Good luck, Tom," replied Paula.

Paula had never understood why those two could be going steady. Tom was always one of the hardest working, athletic, and caring students. He was the son whom every mother wanted. He was a good student, had been an altar boy at St. Ann's church and became an Eagle Scout at the age of 15.

Sonny Brooks, however, was the diametric opposite to Tom Donovan. She came from a long line of blue blood ancestors who originally settled the town of Quissett. The Brooks family was one of the wealthiest families on Cape Cod through real estate investments, business and good stock market strategy. Their wealth was considered to be "very old" money.

Sonny always got what she wanted. Sonny was beautiful. She was intelligent. She had pretty pouting lips and a thick mane of dirty blonde hair. She flaunted her sexy, slender body and knew how to emphasize certain parts of her figure whenever the mood struck her. She always had the best and latest trends in clothing. She traveled extensively with her family and claimed to be the youngest Quissett girl to swim topless in the Caribbean islands—during her sophomore year. This had been a story that she proudly shared with the entire class.

As Sonny grew up, she had turned rebellious towards her family and had gained a reputation of being promiscuous since the ninth grade. She had transferred to a private, prestigious school in Farmington, Connecticut during her freshman year, but soon returned home. The story followed that she got caught selling large quantities of marijuana to the other students and to one young, handsome, male faculty member.

"I didn't go to the 'Fest' tonight, Paula," said Tom from behind the steering wheel of his sporty car.

"I just could not bear to see Sonny there. Even though she broke up with me over a month ago, it is still hard for me to see her. At first, I was really pissed, but now I am working on getting over it. We were together everyday for almost a year and a half. I really, really, loved Sonny. I still don't know why she broke up with me. We could have been great together!"

Although Tom had a long list of positive attributes, he was also one of the most naive, young men around. It was a well-known fact that Mrs. Sarah Brooks did not want her daughter, Sonny, to see Tom Donovan any longer. She had been concerned that their romance had continued for almost eighteen months. Tom Donovan was not someone with whom Sonny Brooks should waste any more time.

That March, Sarah offered to buy her only daughter a brand new sports car of her choice if Sonny immediately dumped her boyfriend, Tom.

After a St. Patrick's night dance and a long session of heated love-making in the back seat of Tom's car, it was time to talk. Sonny looked at an exhausted and spent Tom Donovan and told him that it was all over for the two of them. She told him that she was falling for someone else. She thought that she shouldn't see him anymore. This would be their last night together.

Tom was totally confused and emotionally devastated. He initially thought it was a joke, but then as Sonny began putting on her clothes, he could sense that she was serious. He then figured it was an emotional thing and that they would be back together within a day or two. This, however, never happened as he had hoped.

The next day, Sonny picked up her bright, new, cherry-red, Corvette convertible. She was soon giving joyrides around town to all of her friends. Tom Donovan wasn't one of those friends.

***

"Are you feeling any better, Paula?" Tom asked, as he drove along the side roads.

"Yeah...I guess so. I'm getting there." She was still shaking.

"You know, Paula, I have to tell you that this is my last night in this freakin' place. I have to get away. I need to plan the rest of my life. I know that Sonny and I will never get back together. Screw her. I need to start a new life. The further away from her, the better."

"Good for you," mumbled Paula, not really paying much attention to what Tom was saying.

"I am not going to march at the goddamned commencement ceremony," he told her.

"Oh, Tom! The class will miss you! Don't be an asshole over her!"

"No, no...I don't even want to see her again!"

"There are others, Tom. There will be others."

"Yeah.. I know. But I also want to escape that bullshit war in Viet Nam, too. With the way my luck is going, I'll probably get drafted into the Army next week. I don't have money for college yet. I just know that I'll get snagged by the draft board and get sent over to Viet Nam. I'm telling you Paula, I'm not getting my ass killed over some stupid war that should have never been started in the first place!"

"Where will you go Tom?" asked a slightly more alert Paula.

"Canada. They can't get me up there. Thousands of draft dodgers are up there and I don't mind joining them. My grandmother lives up north on Prince Edward Island. I wrote to her that I am coming to help her on her potato farm. I told her that I need to think about what I want to do with my life. She is happy with that, and I could use the time away from here."

"Good for you, Tom."

"I don't feel like a coward, Paula. I think that this stupid war is "f"—ing ludicrous. I don't want to die for something that I don't believe in."

"Tom, Tommy. Stop! Stop here, I don't want to wake up my folks with the noise of your car. I can walk the rest of the way and then slip up the back stairs without waking them. Tom thanks a million...you will never know!"

"Take care Paula." He bent over and kissed her lightly on her forehead. They embraced briefly. "Hey. Good luck at college!"

"Yeah...You too. Take care, Tom. And good luck in Canada!"

* * *

Paula was in a deep, emotional shock for a few days. She couldn't bring herself to tell anyone about her rape. She only wanted for that entire, ugly night to go away. She had recurring nightmares. It was impossible for her to go to the police and report the rape. The "Freedom Fest" had underage drinking, illegal marijuana, the class skinny dip and everything else. She would not be looked upon as an innocent young girl in the eyes of the law. She couldn't go through all of that. She wouldn't put her parents through all of the embarrassment and stress. Neither the police, nor any jury would ever believe her story.

She then realized that David Whitestone knew this as well. She thought to herself over and over; That son of a bitch! He knew exactly what he was doing! It had all been planned by that creepy asshole. She kept wondering privately to herself. "Why me God? Why me? I didn't do anything wrong. I didn't deserve this to happen."

She became a recluse in her Quissett home during the next few days. She avoided the remaining senior class activities. Paula attended the graduation commencement exercises only to appease her parents and sister. At the ceremony, she didn't see David Whitestone, nor did she look for him. She said good-bye to her friends and retreated to her bedroom for a few weeks of peace and quiet.

The time in solitude was a healing time for Paula. She slowly began to regain her strength and recharge her spirit. After all, she was going to college in the fall. She began thinking logically to herself. Don't look backward. Look forward. She remembered an early sailing lesson many years ago—Look toward the bow of your ship, not the stern. Don't be negative. Be positive. She was going to become a schoolteacher. She would work with little children. That's what she wanted. Paula smiled. It was the first smile that she had for several days.

Paula realized that she had missed her friends, so she began meeting with them again. She missed talking with her sister in Boston, so she called her. She missed baby-sitting. So, she offered to do that again. She missed her morning strolls along the beach. So, she got up early and walked in the warm sand. And then she realized that she missed one other important thing in her life. She missed her menstrual period.

CHAPTER FOUR

Sonny Brooks

Sonny Brooks had set her alarm clock to wake up early in the morning after the Quissett High "Freedom Fest". Jared, her older brother, was returning home after completing his junior year at Dartmouth College. She was excited about this reunion. She looked forward to the two of them spending their summer vacation together. They had always enjoyed each other's company. Sonny had missed Jared while he was sequestered up in the isolated woods of Hanover, New Hampshire.

She was proud of her "brainy" brother. He had excelled in prep school. Each Ivy League college to which he applied during his senior year had accepted him. Sonny adored her older sibling. He was not only intelligent, but also fun-loving and patient. He always listened to and tried to understand his younger sister. He never judged her. She liked that.

Jared was much more than just an older brother to Sonny. He had always been her best friend since childhood. He supported her through thick and thin. They truly understood each other and supported each other regardless of the circumstances.

There wasn't much family love in their home. Like so many families, love had been replaced with expectations. The parents didn't love them for what they did in life or how hard they tried. They expected that of their children. Affection was just something that the generations of Brooks lineage never demonstrated. Jared and Sonny needed the brotherly and sisterly love that they had cultivated between themselves over the years.

Even though they got along so well, Jared and Sonny were two very opposite people. Jared did not condone his younger sister's current lifestyle. He worried that she was experiencing only the veneer of her life. He never lectured, but recently tried to set examples for her to look deeper within herself, and encouraged her to move beyond those liberal, teenage trappings that were occurring during these turbulent times.

Like his younger sister, Jared was also very good-looking. As a young man, he never had trouble dating the most attractive girls from Boston to Provincetown. Since adolescence, the only challenge that he had was to avoid getting girls pregnant. His handsome, mature, and easy ways attracted a wide community of women of varying character and backgrounds. This had included a few who were married. The younger girls would quickly "fall in love" with him. It was no secret that marrying into the Brooks family could become very comfortable. Jared faced this social challenge very well as he matured. He simply began living a life of sexual abstinence. He eventually stopped dating entirely during his junior year at Dartmouth.

Jared was very content with this new life style. He now was more interested in exploring and finding a deeper meaning to his own life. He recently had found more stimulation while researching what is commonly called the "paranormal experiences". He read all that he could about the metaphysical world and events that could not be explained in scientific terms. He would spend hours reading and researching about events that were never fully understood, never rationalized, nor explained in proven logic.

He recently dabbled in meditation. He interviewed clairvoyants, psychics, and hypnotists to learn more of what the so-called "fourth dimension" is all about. This research had excited him. Jared, however, had kept his personal interests in this new activity on a low, quiet level. His family had been unaware of this new and exciting world with which Jared was so fascinated. He had no intention of discussing this with his parents since he knew that they would be disinterested.

"Jared!" Sonny yelled waving her arms from her third floor bedroom window. It was eight-thirty on this warm sunny, spring morning. Sonny still had on her "baby doll" pajamas.

"Sonny!" Her brother answered back from his mud-splattered pick-up truck.

Peering through the screened windows, Sarah and Richard Brooks smiled at the sight of their son, ambling up the front staircase and onto the wrap-around style railed porch.

Jared was the most handsome progeny of the Brooks lineage. At over six feet tall, he always had a fit physique. He now had his long chestnut-brown hair pulled back in a smooth, ponytail. His early tanned face accented his bright white teeth and hazel colored eyes. His opened blue denim shirt contrasted with his light colored, tan, khaki cut-off shorts. His favorite leather moccasins, which had been worn for too many years, barely covered the soles of his feet. He carried a gym bag full of clothes in his left hand and an opened soda can in his right.

The Brooks couple saw their son as the pride and joy of their otherwise insipid and merely platonic marriage. Jared was the positive balance to their long standing, unhappy, relationship. He was the light that brightened their other darkened moments of their existence. Sarah and Richard bickered constantly. All of these disagreements centered on their daughter, Sonny, and her misguided, abusive behavior.

Richard and Sarah Brooks conveniently blamed each other for neglecting their only little girl during her childhood years. They intimated that she had been the cause of their own distant and cold relationship. They rationalized that her rebellious teenage attitude was predicated on something that went wrong during Sonny's earlier years. They privately felt that each had focused too much of their attention on Jared, their first born. They would, however, never openly admit to this to one another.

The couple had argued intensely through Sonny's adolescent drinking and experimenting with drugs. They kept it quiet and out of the newspapers when she stole a car at age fourteen "for the fun of it". Sarah reacted quickly to Sonny's early and active sexual life. She asked Dr. Thompson to prescribe birth control pills soon after Sonny's fifteenth birthday. She had been a constant emotional burden and source of stress for Sarah and Richard Brooks. They looked forward to the days when she would become an adult. Then she would be living on her own, away from them, and away from the Quissett homestead.

Jared greeted his parents politely. They hadn't seen each other since Christmas. He gave his mother an obligatory hug and shook his father's hand with a smile. The many generations of Brooks' families could never be labeled as warm and affectionate. They were always reserved. They were always in control.

Sonny, however, ran downstairs smiling and screaming towards her brother. She immediately jumped up upon him, locking her arms around his neck and clenching her legs around his waist. She hugged him tight, laughing loudly to celebrate Jared's return home.

"Jared! Jared! I missed you so much! You're finally back here where you belong!" She pounded Jared 's back with tears of joy in her eyes.

"Sonny, It's so good to see you. You're as beautiful as ever," he smiled. Missed you lots!"

Jared, with his sister's legs still scissored around him, swung her around in large circles, smiling and laughing. Later they both ran up the curving cherry wood staircase to get him unpacked and settled for his homecoming.

The luncheon meal was served at the standard Brooks 12:30 time. Every meal of every day was always scheduled at its same standard time.

Jared knew that Francois was also happy to see that he had returned home. The Brooks family's chef, and sometimes chauffeur for over twelve years, had prepared Jared's favorites — a light, creamy lobster bisque, with an entrée of Paella, complete with fresh shrimp, chicken, linguica, mussels, and saffron flavored rice. It was time to celebrate. The prodigal son of the Brooks bloodline was home.

Jared was the center of attention at the dining table. The dialogue during the meal was light, reserved and cordial. Dessert was a dish of sweet, locally picked strawberries topped with whipped cream. The small talk of Jared's latest college semester courses brought them to coffee. He spoke only of the weather, some of his friends and the core academic courses that he had taken during the last five months.

He was hiding a lot from his parents and sister. He had some startling news to tell them, but now was not the appropriate time.

Richard and Sarah Brooks sipped their chilled Riesling wine with renewed anticipation on this early afternoon in June. It was good that Jared, their only son, was back at the Quissett home. They had missed him. He was also very good for Sonny. For the next three months Jared would look after Sonny and keep her in check. She always behaved well when her older brother was at home. Richard Brooks was not the least bit ashamed that his twenty-year-old son was a much better father figure for Sonny than he was. He now felt relieved knowing that he did not have to get involved with his daughter's summertime activities.

As Jared pretended to listen to his parents discuss what was happening with them, the family business and the latest Quissett news, he engaged in an old habit that he had since childhood. Whenever Jared was absorbed in his own thoughts, he slowly tugged his left eyebrow with his thumb and index finger of his left hand. This routine irritated his parents. They had many times asked him to correct this childish behavior during his younger years, but he continued the habit. They thought it obnoxious and a flaw in his otherwise perfect character. Sonny found it to be cute.

"Hey Jared. Be careful. You're going to pull out all of your eyebrow if you don't stop thinking so hard," laughed Sonny.

Jared returned with a wide grin at his sister. He had missed her candor and wit.

"You know what I really want for my homecoming? I'd like to

go to Nantucket for the weekend. It would be great to be in the old cottage again. And ...and I could let off some pent-up steam after those final exams," proposed Jared.

"But you just got home, Jared. And we have so much to talk about, " replied his mother.

Jared smiled. "Well, I was thinking that a brief escape for a while with Sonny would be good. We could get caught up with one another in our recent studies and our latest love lives. We all have next week and the rest of the summer to become re-united on family matters."

Richard Brooks quickly answered. "Yes, Yes, of course, Jared. You young people need your own time. Go ahead. You and Sonny should go over to the island to get the cottage ready. That way, we can all use it this summer."

Sonny smiled, knowing exactly what Jared was doing. "Great idea, Jared! Let's get ready. We have to pack some things and get clean linens for the beds."

If their daughter, Sonny, went over to the island with Jared, then Sarah and Richard could breathe more easily. When their daughter was out of sight, she was out of mind. The inside joke for Sonny and Jared was that Richard and Sarah hadn't been to the Nantucket cottage for over eight years. It was a sure bet that their footsteps would not grace the family cottage again this summer.

At six o'clock that evening, Jared slowly taxied his single engine Piper Cherokee out to the Falmouth airport runway. The aircraft had been a gift for Jared's 18th birthday. He had been piloting small aircraft since he was fourteen years old and he flew at every opportunity. He was the respected president of Dartmouth's "Flying Eagles" aviation club.

The landing approach to Tom Never's airfield on Nantucket was always a spectacular sight but it was especially beautiful during the early dusk hours of this late spring day. The sun's fading light presented fuzzy shadows on the green pine tree-crested hills and light-tan colored sandy shores. The gray weather-beaten homes dotted the landscape at almost equal intervals. As the plane banked for its final approach, Jared marveled at the rippled dunes dancing with varying hues of color. These colors changed continuously and quickly so that no artist could ever capture and duplicate the scene on canvas. Sonny was just finishing her can of Heineken beer as they touched down on runway 4R.

They had lots to talk about. Sonny had been accepted to attend Wellesley College in the fall. Despite her aberrant social behavior, Sonny had always been a good student and always found academics to be an easy challenge for her. She was personally more excited about attending school away from home and far from the oppressive heels of her parents. She was looking forward to leaving her parents and to experience the freedom and the youthful excitement of the big city.

Wellesley, and the city of Boston, offered not only an escape from home but it was also a place much closer to her brother, Jared. She knew that she could drive up to the woods of Hanover, New Hampshire, and within an hour, she would be with him whenever she needed his advice or assurance.

The Brooks' Nantucket cottage, which consisted of seven large rooms, was perched on a beautiful bluff at Squibnockett Beach. The northeastern side of the building had a wrap around porch with a spectacular view of Nantucket Sound. The second story bedrooms were bright and airy. They provided a great view of the sailing and fishing vessels gliding by on the blue-green colored sea.

Jared prepared a glowing fire in the dark green, cast iron, wood burning stove. This was a ritual for them on each spring visit since the fire warmed the rooms quickly and eliminated the damp, mildew odor that attacked the inner cottage walls. While he did this, Sonny made up the beds with fresh, clean sheets.

Later, Jared poured a glass of Merlot for him and Sonny, and they both sat near the roaring fire. The chill of the cottage was soon forgotten.

"Sis, I have been planning and thinking about this trip here with you for the last few weeks. I have so much to tell you and I needed to talk with you before I spoke with anyone else."

"Sounds deep, Jared," Sonny replied.

She now felt very special again. She was happy that her older brother still regarded her as his number one confidante. It had always been that way. Knowing this, a warm and tender smile illuminated Sonny's face. She sat cross-legged on top of the sofa.

"I am serious Sonny, I have gone through some changes in my life that you just won't believe."

"I am all ears, 'Bro'. Just start telling me your news," as she sliced wedges of cheddar cheese and placed them around a plate of crackers. They both slouched back on two of the over stuffed sofas just a few feet from the warmth of the wood burning stove.

"Sonny, I have met the neatest group of people up north who have introduced me to something I never thought about before. They have introduced me to another dimension of life."

"Say what? Another dimension?" she replied swallowing her wine.

"It all started during a discussion about the famous psychologist, Carl Jung, in my Advanced Psychology class. Ya know.... He really was a very interesting person. Even though he was considered a scientist, he unwaveringly believed that there was a spiritual plane that existed. He also believed that people continued living on this spiritual plane after they died on earth. He saw it as a fourth dimension. It was what we were taught about the place called heaven. Only it is really a different plane. One that we cannot see, but it does exist. He referred to it as — the 'collective unconscious'. It is different in many ways from the heaven and hell that we were taught as kids."

"Oooooookaaaaaaay," replied Sonny with a skeptical look on her face.

"After one particular class lecture, a small group of us students and a teaching assistant got together and spun off our own discussion group. We were pretty excited about these topics and wanted to share information and experiences. We began meeting informally almost every night," Jared told his sister with heightened excitement.

"We talked about spiritual experiences, psychic phenomena, karma, and reincarnation. We also shared our most intimate and personal introspective selves with one another. It was unbelievable. You know what I learned? I learned that each of us is the same as one another. We all have the same positive elements in our souls. That is..... we.....we are really connected in our inner spirit-selves. It is this connection that we must work to improve upon. As we connect with people we become collectively more powerful. Powerful beyond anything we could imagine. We connect, not physically, but "spiritually". "

Jared held up and quickly curled the two fingers of each hand to indicate the phrase was to be in quotes.

"Sonny. Sharing our souls and our inner most thoughts and feelings is the most intimate thing that I have ever done with anybody! It really is!"

Sonny looked at him with a quizzical look on her face. She didn't know where he was going with this story but she had hoped that he would get there soon.

"It is much more exhilarating and fulfilling to share intimately in this way with others than merely sharing our physical bodies with another person." Jared intentionally looked squarely at his younger sister.

Sonny got his subtle message of that last sentence. She stared at him. She immediately felt that she was both pissed at him and embarrassed at the same time.

"I hope that this isn't one of those funky religious cult groups. Is it? You haven't joined some of those weirdo groups that drink donkey piss and pray over cabbages, have you?" asked his sister.

"No, not at all. In fact, Sonny, we aren't even an organization at all. We just exchange ideas and feelings about why we are here on earth. We try to help each other to understand the meaning of life. We hold informal discussions, meditations and dabble in out-of-body experiences and past life reincarnations."

"Oh, shit no, Jared, you're not going super weird on me are you? I mean out of body experiences. You aren't doing some stuff are you?"

"No. We are spiritualists. We are communicating with other

spirits with our spiritual capabilities."

"Oh no. Now I get it. Are you going to be one of those 'Born Again' freaks who thumps the bible at every chance you get?"

"No, no, it's not even close to that". Although Sonny, I have to admit that I feel stronger now about my Christian doctrine. What was recorded in the Bible was not fiction. And what Jesus and other spiritual leaders spoke about while they were on earth was accurate. The problems come in with the institutional interpretations. We have to overcome that. I have personally expanded my spiritual knowledge from these discussions and experiences."

"Experiences?" queried Sonny.

"I'll get to that later, but I will cut to the chase on what this has all meant to me. You know, Sonny, the one thing that has bothered me these past couple of years is the answer to the question— What is life all about? Why are we here? What are we supposed to do with our lives?"

"And now you have all of those answers?" asked Sonny putting a cracker in her mouth.

"No, but I have learned a good deal and I understand more about the purpose of life than I ever did before. I am serious about this, Sis. For the first time in my life I feel that there is a definite and predestined purpose for each of us living here on earth. As I learn more about it, I am purposely changing my attitude toward life every day. I feel better. I feel more, more...at peace."

Sonny poured more wine for each of them and lay back on the sofa. She had never seen Jared like this before. He was so intense, so passionately fired up. It was obvious the he was so immersed in this "new life" for him that she needed to focus on his every word, so she could understand what had happened to him.

She also knew that Jared would not let himself be lured into some cult, or get induced by some exotic, mind-altering drugs. That just wasn't Jared. Even though he always appeared carefree, outwardly, he always remained in control of himself. He wouldn't be sharing this with Sonny, in this way, at this cottage, if he didn't believe it to be so important. She would listen carefully to him since it was the most special person in her life speaking— her brother, her confidante, Jared.

As the night went on, Jared explained how he had been introduced to a new way of thinking about life. He now truly believed that there was a spirit or soul within each of us. He now had firm credence that each of us had come to earth to accomplish or learn some specific deed or deeds. Jared spoke of spirit guides. He explained what is known as bi-locational capabilities, better known as out-of-body experiences. He also introduced to her stories about how he had researched documented near-death-experiences. He also told his sister how he now completely believed in divine miracles. He had studied the life of the contemporary Padre Pio and others who had experienced the crucifixion wounds known as the stigmata syndrome of Jesus Christ. He told Sonny about the incorruptibility of the physical bodies of saints who had died. He talked about how there were different molecular vibrations and densities on the earthly plane from those on the spiritual plane. He told her about meditation and telepathic communication experiments including faith healings in which he had participated.

At times, while she was listening to his animated diatribe, Sonny thought that Jared had gone a little mad. She found herself getting somewhat nervous and uncomfortable with this new side to her brother.

She wasn't getting any of it. Her personal philosophy was, if she had one was, "If it felt good, do it". She now realized though, that Jared fully believed in this weird, new world of his. Even though she wasn't buying any of it, Sonny would never make light of anything that her adored brother felt was important. She did not interrupt him. She pretended to be listening intently and understanding him while she was quietly hoping that he would stop. She wanted to talk about the Red Sox, President Nixon, or some of the British rock bands that were becoming so popular in the United States.

At midnight, Jared told Sonny that he would temporarily stop his diatribe on spiritualism. He wanted his sister to take some time and reflect on what he had shared with her these past few hours. It was late and they should get ready for bed. He told her that he didn't want to hear her reactions just yet. Besides, he had more to tell her. He also wanted to save the most important information for later. It was important that Sonny listen to these experiences first so that she could understand what he was going to tell her later. This talk was almost as if it was a prerequisite lecture that she must listen to so that she could understand what he had to tell her the next day. This was how he had previously rehearsed this weekend in his head. He decided to change the subject, as they started to clean up the remains of their snacks.

"So, are you getting along any better with the folks?" asked Jared.

He intentionally shifted the tone of their dialogue from the lofty and sublime to the mundane. He knew that he had laid a lot of new stuff on his sister in the last few hours. Sonny answered her brother while picking up the wine bottles, remaining cheese and crackers.

"Are you kidding? The *real* Cold War is going on in Quissett between Sonny Brooks and her parents. Forget that
US-Soviet Union bullshit," she said in a tone of sarcasm.

"I take it then, that you're not talking much?"

"We spoke last week" said Sonny.

"Are they giving you any more freedom or latitude now that you are out of high school?"

"Jared, they are like my goddamned shadow. They worry about every move I make. I swear that they even have a private detective following me everywhere I go."

"Well, that's unfortunate. I do hope that you are just being paranoid about that private detective shit."

"It wouldn't matter. You *know* that I always figure out a way to get what I want —especially what I got last week"

"Oh yeah? Pray tell Sis! What did you get last week? I am almost afraid to ask."

"Sit down and I will show you," she smiled happily from the change in the mood.

Jared slumped down in one of the living room chairs.

Now it was her time to perform. She had listened to her brother long enough. She now wanted the limelight. It was her turn. She smiled at her brother in her famous impish way.

Sonny began singing in a very lusty, low tone. She hummed the music from that popular, earthy, bawdy tune, "The Stripper". It was background music that was commonly used for striptease acts across America.

"Dant dant da, da dant dant dah...." she sang.

She began to slowly wiggle her hips and make emphatic strip-tease dancing movements toward Jared who was stretching out his long legs on the ottoman.

Sonny, still humming the tune, theatrically winked at Jared and then turned around with her back towards him. She deliberately and slowly unbuttoned her oxford shirt as she hummed the tune a little more loudly. Still wiggling her hips, she took off her shirt and threw it in a large, swirling, stripper's motion to the floor. Her deep purple colored bra contrasted with the fairness of her pale skin. While still singing, she did one complete twirl, and then stopped short. With her back again to her brother, she slowly unbuckled the belt to her shorts. She shook her hips and wiggled out of the denim shorts. She let them drop to the floor. Her purple colored silk panties matched her bra. She then took high, deliberate steps out of her fallen shorts. Still singing the famous tune, "dant dant dah, dah dant dant, dah," a little louder now, she looked over her shoulder at Jared's smile.

She slowly backed up towards him kicking away the ottoman and letting his feet drop to the floor. Then, when she was very close to him, she began to languidly roll down the left side of her elastic topped panties. As she pulled her silk underwear down to the mid-point of her left buttock. Sonny then emphatically thrust her buttock out at him and.....and there it was. At first Jared couldn't make it out exactly. Then, peering more closely, he could see the small butterfly tattoo, freely flying in bright green, neon-blue and vibrant orange colors.

"Like it?" she asked.

Laughing, he said, "Sonny, you are something else!"

"It's not a big deal. The tattoo artist in Plymouth who did it told me that I was just ahead of my time."

She pulled her panties top back up to her waist. She started to pick up her dropped denim shorts from the floor.

"I am *sure* that you are well ahead of your time! Good night, little sister."

Jared got up from his chair and shook his head from side to side. He then picked up her oxford shirt and threw it at her....

"Good night, big brother," replied Sonny with an impish smile. It's great to have you back home!"

***

Jared and Sonny spent the next day lying on a blanket at the nearby Squibnockett beach. It was a very hot sunny day. They would work on developing their tans. Jared was anxious to finish his discussion with his sister from the previous night.

It turned out to be a bittersweet day for Sonny. She loved being with her brother. But while she listened to Jared ramble on for a long time about his recent transformation, she felt distant. She was quickly realizing that she and her brother were separating from that comfort blanket that they shared since childhood. They now seemed to have very little in common. Jared was stretching into directions that Sonny neither liked nor understood.

"So you see, Sonny, we are all connected. We all share everything in common. We are here on this physical plane to help and to serve others. That's what makes life more enjoyable for all of us. Jesus, Buddha, Abraham, Ghandi, and so many others have said it. Love one another. *That's all that we have to do in life!* Love one another. Everyday we should do things that will unite us. And we should not do things that will separate us. Imagine if everyone did that around the world for just five minutes simultaneously! It could change everything."

Sonny drained her cold beer washing down the last bite of her tuna sandwich.

"I am just not getting it 'Bro.' But don't blame me. I was always slower than you."

"I am not trying to convert you Sonny. We all have to live our own lives. We must however, respect each other's challenges in life. We need to love everyone. Even those people who upset us or try to harm us. We must be sensitive to everyone, especially those who we do not understand or who have done things that we have not experienced."

"What do you mean?"

"We should never judge others, because they are different from us. You know. We are constantly judging one another based on our own standards. Most times when people judge others they don't even know that they are doing it! We shouldn't discriminate against people because they look or live differently than ourselves."

"Jared, you know me. I am not that type of person. I am very open minded." responded Sonny, with a little defensiveness.

"I know Sis, but we must open our hearts. Not just our minds. Please help me to remember it all through my life and I will help to remind you."

"Deal!" said Sonny, now totally disinterested and bored with the entire sermon.

"Sonny, there is something else that I need to tell you."

"Oh shit, Jared, don't tell me that there is more!" Sonny dropped her head into her hands in an exasperated gesture.

"I hadn't planned this weekend out here on Nantucket just to tell you how my life has changed philosophically. I want you to know that I am not just blowing smoke. I am actually doing something to follow my convictions. I am committed to helping others. Last night and today I was merely building a foundation so you will understand what my plans are"

"Plans?" asked his sister with a quizzical look

"Sonny, I am leaving Dartmouth. I've learned all that I can in a classroom. Most courses were totally boring for me. I am not helping anyone sitting in lecture halls. I need to experience those things in life that I feel so strongly about. I need to do my part. I have passively lived what I consider to be a self-centered life. Now I want to do what I really should be doing."

"Jared you are doing what you should be doing! Don't give up Dartmouth. Where will you go?"

"That has already been arranged. I need to do my part. I want to go where so many of the other young people my age are going," he said emphatically.

"Oh, no! Don't tell me its up in some commune in Woodstock!"

"No, no. Listen. Last week, I drove into Boston and enlisted in the Marines Corps. I want to go to Viet Nam. I want to fly aircraft over there and do my share with my brothers and sisters and help bring this ugly, fucking war to an end!"

The shock of this news went through every cell of Sonny's being. She couldn't draw a breath of air. It was like every biological function of her body had shut down. Only her mind had activity. She knew that Jared was serious. Even as a small boy, he never lied or exaggerated about anything. She was sure that her brother had already enlisted in the Marines. There would be no reversing that commitment since the war was intensely heating up in this spring of 1970. The United States needed all of the best men and women it could get into uniform. The Armed Forces would love to add Jared Brooks, Ivy League aviator, to their ranks.

Sonny quickly realized that there would be no weekend trips for her to run up to Dartmouth from Wellesley. There would be no brother–sister talks into the wee hours of the morning as they had always enjoyed all of their lives. She couldn't pick up the phone and have Jared listen to her bitching about the parents' and their spying on her.

She wanted to cry. She wanted to bawl like she hadn't done in years. But she wouldn't. She still loved Jared. She loved him more than he would ever know. If she cried, it would make him feel badly about his decisions and this new pathway of life that he found. She swallowed hard. She suppressed her tears and she swallowed again.

"How about a beer?" she asked Jared, with a cracking and

weakened voice.

"Sure. Are you OK, Sonny?"

"Of course, Jared. Don't you see we are just changing. We are following different paths in our lives. We couldn't stay joined at the proverbial sibling-hip for the rest of our lives."

Her voice was weakening. There was internal trembling in her body.

"I am sure that you will be a great Marine pilot. If I know you, you will come back from Southeast Asia as a decorated war hero."

She smiled with her lips trembling a bit. She looked up into his eyes.

"Sonny...", Jared tried to interrupt.

" I can envision the whole damn village of Quissett honoring you in a special hometown ceremony."

Her voice was quivering. She was trying to be strong.

"That's not what I want, Sis. That's not why I am doing this. But if that special day should ever happen, I will only accept that award if you are with me and I can see you smiling."

Jared put his arms around his younger sister.

Then she cried. She fell sobbing into her big brother's arms. She let go. She cried uncontrollably. He held her while she cried and shook violently. He knew that she had been trying to absorb this shocking news. He held her for a long time. The explosive release of the pent-up tears made her feel better. And it was all right. Everything would be all right.

CHAPTER FIVE

Tom Donovan

Prince Edward Island is a unique and beautiful piece of the globe's mosaic puzzle. Its rolling green grassy hills etched with farmhouses and gray boulder walls look much like the countryside of England, Scotland and Ireland. The briny, blue waters of North America surround the serene, pastoral beauty of this northern Canadian island. It is one of the world's most enjoyable and pleasant places in which to live and to work.

During 1970, Prince Edward Island had still been a well-kept secret. The travel agents in the United States had not yet discovered this island's potential for commercial tourism. They still hadn't realized how the colorful landscape with its picturesque vistas of sailing harbors, recreational fishing, and lobster bakes could lure the Americans and others to this island gem for summer and fall vacations.

The original, native people and earliest settlers of this island were descendants of the British Isle's first wave of immigrants. The English accents, as well as the Scottish and Irish brogues are heard on every road, in every field, and in every pub. These island people are noted for their very friendly personalities and hard working ethic. They enjoy each day of their lives on earth like it might be their last. They are cognizant of the challenges and tragedies that their courageous ancestors endured. The winters on this island, located close to the North Pole can be very difficult. These Canadians have learned from those hard experiences, adjusted to them, and now live harmoniously with their land, their seas, and their neighbors.

Prince Edward Island was not a foreign place to Tom Donovan. As a youngster, he had spent many weeks vacationing with his grandparents on their expansive thirty-acre potato farm. He had always enjoyed going up north for a visit. He felt the warm, genuine love of his grandparents and enjoyed listening to their colorful stories spoken with a thick Irish brogue. His grandpa had let him drive the farming tractor in the potato fields from the time he was nine years old. Prince Edward Island was always a pleasant change from Tom's routine and youthful days living in Quissett.

The farm was quite different now. His grandpa, Thomas, had passed on a few years back and now his Nana O'Brien was getting on in years. He felt a special closeness with his grandmother soon after he returned to her home. She had a way of doing that with most people. Tom was happy that he was spending time with her now and helping her out during her later years. He would also provide her with some much needed company and lively conversation to keep her mind alert. The potato farm would also serve as his own therapeutic retreat from the Cape and his emotional loss of his former lover, Sonny Brooks.

"Tommy, I am so glad that you are up here with me," Nana said as she served him breakfast. "It had been so quiet and lonely here before you came."

She brought over a basket of steaming, hot, homemade biscuits to accompany his breakfast of scrambled eggs, ham and boiled potatoes.

"Me too, Nana. I really want to help you with the farm. I also need to do some physical work and get back into shape."

"Ah, we'll have you strong as a horse in no time."

"And by the way, I don't mind telling you that I am using your house to hide from my local Army draft board."

"That's OK my boy. War is always the work of the devil. I believe that those silly-ass politicians and President Nixon down in

Washington, D.C. don't know what the hell they are doing in Viet Nam. You know Tommy, they are scared themselves. But they keep listening to the devil and not to God. They could get out of Viet Nam today and save a lot of lives on both sides. They got themselves into a corner and now they don't know how to get out. I fear for the lads who will be killed over there."

"You'll have no argument from me on that, Nana." Tom said as he moved his scrambled eggs around with his biscuit.

"I want you to enjoy yourself up here too, Tommy. You know..... all work and no play......eh? You've got to get out and have some fun, you know. We have some lively pubs in Charlottetown. I hear that the local colleens are at the pubs every Saturday night for music and dancing. We have some pretty, lassies up here Tommy. And you're a young, healthy man...eh?"

She giggled a little and winked at her grandson.

"Well, I actually have had enough of romance for a while......Nana. You know it always doesn't work out the way you want it to."

"Hmmm...well, yes, I understand."

Nana now understood why his usual, permanent smile had been missing since he arrived. She first thought that he wasn't feeling well physically. He looked so much thinner and pale since she saw him at his last visit.

Tommy was embarrassed talking on this topic with his elderly grandmother. He quickly changed the subject to the farm, the maintenance of the equipment, and the part-time high school students she employed. Tom liked to work with these kids who were so useful for some of the routine lighter farm work. Teenagers were essential to help out with the potato harvesting in early autumn. The high schools typically closed in late September for the annual harvest period. Their younger bodies could endure the rigors of bending and lifting the heavy sacks of vegetables easier than the older workers could.

The days in Canada were very long and difficult since farm life required being up at sunrise and working almost non-stop through the early evening. The physical labor was good for Tom. He was trying desperately to get his mind off of Sonny—their love, their romance and their voracious appetites for sex. They had both enjoyed each other so much. There had definitely been a special chemistry between them. They were spontaneous and fun-loving teens. They were both quite smart. Sonny could pass any school exam given to her and she would have no difficulty with the academic challenges of college. A year ago he had been so grateful that they had found each other at a young age. He always thought that they were truly made for each other. He had often fantasized about living with Sonny for the rest of his life. Tom always thought of Sonny and him as true "soul mates."

The weeks went by quickly for Tom that summer. The cooler temperatures of the fall and the harvesting season were coming upon them. The nights were the most difficult time for Tom. When all of the hard work of the day was done, images of Sonny floated back into Tommy's mind. Nana could hear some light sobbing at night coming from his bedroom. She knew that the young man was going through a difficult emotional period. She wanted to help.

On one Saturday morning in October, Tom came bouncing down the stairs to the inviting aroma of hot coffee and a full breakfast of pancakes and sausages.

"Tommy. I've been thinking. Why don't you go into town this evening for some fun and relaxation? You've been working hard, lad, and really need a bit of a break...eh?"

Tom looked up at her holding the coffeepot.

"You know, I think I just might go out tonight... Nana... just for a change to my usual routine. Who knows? Maybe I will learn more about life up here. Maybe I will find truth and light." Tommy laughed somewhat sarcastically to himself.

"The only place you'll find that is with God, Tommy. Truth and light is only with God. Besides, I don't think that you need truth and light. I am hoping that you'll find a young lassie, dance a bit, laugh a bit, and she will make you feel.....Let's say.... Truly light....eh?"

They both laughed. Tommy thought about his adorable

grandmother as he helped her clear off the kitchen table. She had twinkling and mischievous blue eyes. She was always alert, always sharp, and never lost her sense of humor. She had been married at the age of fifteen and became a mother soon after. She lost a few children during birth and a couple through diseases. Fortunately, she had healthy births of his mother and her three brothers and two sisters. His mother, aunts and uncles always spoke fondly of their parents and their memorable childhood on the Canadian potato farm.

***

"Hello there. I've never seen you at Paddy's Shamrock before. My name is Seamus Flannagan".

Tom turned in his barstool, looked at the young man sitting next to him, and extended his hand.

"Hi.... I am Tom Donovan. Yeah, you're right, I am new to these parts. Helping out for a while on my grandmother's farm."

"Welcome then. It's good to see another guy here about my age. As you can see this place attracts a wide range of people".

"I can see that." Tom looked around at the crowd in the pub. "There must be people here ranging in age from seventeen to seventy."

"That's an interesting American accent that you have. Is it Boston?"

"Actually a bit south of Boston...Cape Cod."

"Ah, yes. I have heard of Cape Cod."

The music at Paddy's Shamrock was very different from that played in the states. It was totally eclectic. The small band played some contemporary Rock n' Roll, many Irish and Scottish ballads and several bagpipe standards. Noticeably missing were the dissident, anti-war tunes that were high on the pop charts back in Massachusetts. These islanders were all happily insulated and disconnected from the heinous bloodshed raging in Southeast Asia. They enjoyed life. They enjoyed each other.

Seamus was a very likable young man. A bit shorter than Tom, with deep, thoughtful, green eyes. He wore his long, brown hair neatly trimmed at his shoulders. He looked Tom straight in the eye when he spoke. They were both nineteen years old. They both knew that they were at an exciting and pivotal time of their lives. That night, these two strangers carried on interesting conversations about the war, the Peace Corps and how they both wanted to make an impact on helping humanity. They were very open with one another. Their discussions continued while they consumed several pints of draught beer. They also had a lot of fun and laughs that evening. They danced with a few of the local girls and closed the Shamrock down at one o'clock in the morning.

It didn't take long for Tom and Seamus to become good friends. Tom felt comfortable talking with him. Seamus understood the avoidance of military draft without any personal or philosophical reservation. As the weeks went on, Tom told his new friend about the only love of his young life, Sonny Brooks. Seamus reacted with a friendly sensitivity to Tom's personal and emotional plight. He knew that Tom was still in love with his high school sweetheart. He knew that he was still in emotional pain.

While driving to a professional soccer match, Seamus informed Tom that he too was a renegade from the New Brunswick area and now living in Charlottetown. But he was there for different reasons. Seamus told the story how he had made a critical mistake one evening and followed a group of teenagers whom he did not know to a house party. At the party there was some marijuana. Seamus had never used "pot" before and wanted to try it. He was on his second reefer, when the police busted in. The night was one that he would regret for the rest of his life.

The news of the arrest and its publicity shocked the Flannagan family, his girlfriend and her family. His longtime girlfriend, Elizabeth, under parental pressure, was immediately forced to break up with Seamus. Seamus was literally disowned by his conservative, puritanical family and he was figuratively banished from his small, provincial hometown. He was shocked how family and friends judged him so harshly for his making simply a bad decision. The public embarrassment was too much for his family to handle. This incident coupled with his long hair and liberal attitude was something that his family could not tolerate. They encouraged him to leave home and not return until he matured and gained a sense of responsibility.

Since arriving in PEI, Seamus had enrolled in a local Jesuit college and was giving some thought to continuing on to the seminary to become a catholic priest. He could never marry his former girlfriend, Elizabeth, whom he had deeply loved. He was now healing his emotional wounds at school much like Tom was doing at the potato farm. He wanted to find a life in which he could be happy, secure, and accepted. And perhaps forget.

He had talked with many seminarians at the college and thought about their future clerical work helping others. This appealed to Seamus in ways he had never thought about prior to his coming to Prince Edward Island.

Tom Donovan listened intently to Seamus Flannagan. He respected what he had been through and the fact that he moved on with his life rather than feel self-pity. Tom decided to join Seamus at some of his classes at the university.

That winter Tom found peace and purpose getting back into the academic challenges at the university. He buried himself in his studies with an overload of philosophy and theology courses. Tom felt that he was beginning to find light and truth. He thought that he was finally "finding himself". He was becoming happy with his life once again. It had purpose. It had direction. His thoughts of Quissett and Sonny Brooks eventually faded from his mind.

CHAPTER SIX

Paula and Patricia

Paula had returned into her depressed state of mind. She retreated into a solitary recluse since she had discovered the shock of her unwanted pregnancy. She stayed in her bedroom each day. She came out of her room only occasionally for some meals.

It was obvious to her parents that something was bothering their daughter emotionally. She had lost her usual effervescence. She could not look them in the eye as she always did when she spoke. Paula tried to disguise her sober and depressed mood as just "anxiety about attending college in the fall." Her parents didn't believe this. They speculated that she may have experienced a teenage romantic disappointment and they purposely stayed out of it.

Paula was experiencing her own personal hell. She was vomiting each morning. She had pounding headaches during the day and she was unable to get a good night's sleep. She often would doze off and then awaken with a jolt, screaming, as if she experienced some grotesque nightmares. At times, she succumbed to self-pity. Something she had never felt before. She felt trapped in a corner and couldn't see any way out.

She knew that she had to take control of her life again. But she would need help. This was something that she couldn't do alone. The only person with whom Paula could talk about the rape and pregnancy was her closest friend, her sister, Patricia. Her sister was her strength. She was her rock. Pat would quickly understand and help her get through this. She hesitated informing her over the phone. This was something that she had to tell her older sister face to face.

Paula drove to Pat's apartment on the west side of Brighton, located just outside the city limits of Boston. After she arrived, there was no small talk. Pat could see in her sister's pale and lackluster face that she was seriously troubled.

Paula tearfully told her sister the entire ugly story that occurred on Freedom Fest night. After she had finished telling Pat of her being drugged and raped in a semi-conscious state, she broke down in an explosion of uncontrollable shaking and crying. Pat quickly sat down next to her and hugged her tightly. There were no words spoken between them for a very long time. There were rivers of tears streaming down each of their faces. Her older sister fully understood why Paula could not have gone to the police to report the rape. Nobody would believe her.

Later, as Pat made a pot of tea, she asked Paula what she wanted to do about her pregnancy.

"Pat, this isn't a baby created from love. It was conceived out of sickness, a total mistake, a crime of violence and rape."

"Of course, sweetie."

"This baby was created from the seed of a bad, twisted, sick, fucked-up person. I don't want to carry such a life inside of me. I can't give birth to such a demonic person. I want it out of my body now!" She began crying again.

"I know, I know. I think I can help Paula, but we have to act quickly. There have been some unwanted pregnancies within the medical school. They have been aborted by a well-respected midwife in Cambridge."

"Pat, I am so scared! I can't believe that this is happening to me. I didn't do anything wrong! Why me." Paula asked. "Why me?" She then broke into tears again.

"I'm sorry, sweetie. I can't answer that for you, Paula. I wish I could. But listen, don't you worry about anything. I will take care of arranging this and will always be there for you. Don't worry. I will call you at home as soon as it is scheduled. Don't worry about anything. Obviously, don't tell anybody anything. Performing illegal abortions carries long prison sentences in the state of Massachusetts."

Paula nodded stirring her tea. "Thanks, Pat."

"By the way, what was this asshole's name?"

Paula's face turned an ashen white.

"David Whi...Whi....Whitestone." she blurted out.

Paula quickly jumped up from the sofa and ran for the bathroom. She made it just in time to kneel in front of the toilet as the vomit erupted out of her. She stayed there for a while shaking and crying.

***

The next evening, Pat made a telephone call to her home in Quissett. After chatting a bit with her mother, she asked to speak with Paula.

"It's all set Paula. This Friday morning at 10am. Tell Mom and Dad that you have to shop for some clothes for school in Boston and that you will spend the weekend with me at my place."

That Friday morning, neither of them spoke as Pat drove her 1964 Volkswagen bug to Cambridge. They both were oblivious to the traffic snarls, the jaywalkers, and the cacophony of sounds coming from the various car and truck horns. They were both nervous and anxious driving to the abortionist's office.

The building wasn't dank and dark as described in some of the horrific stories she had heard regarding illegal abortions. Paula had always envisioned a dreary and not so sterile building where an old mid-wife or quack doctor performed these procedures during the dark of night. This office suite was located in a typical five-story brick office building. The huge glass case sign outside of the entrance listed multiple business offices for accountants, lawyers, and real estate agencies.

Pat looked at notes that she had previously scribbled on a piece of paper as they rounded one corridor after another. She finally spotted the address of the office for which they were looking. Paula said nothing. She thought that she was going to be sick. The sign painted in black letters on the glass door was for some fictitious Insurance Agency. As Pat slowly opened the door they were reminded to close it quickly by the older, gray-haired receptionist.

The receptionist called the mid-wife as Pat and Paula sat on two waiting chairs. She came out to greet them a few minutes later. She smiled and softly introduced herself only as 'Nancy'. She had a face with a smile that appeared to be very understanding and gentle. She was one of those people who had an air of confidence and yet maintained their compassion. Paula wondered how many abortions she had performed as they introduced themselves. Nancy motioned for her to go into the next room and to disrobe.

The room was well lit and clean. Her sister, Pat, would have it no other way. She kissed her younger sister, wished her well, and told Paula that she would remain just outside in the waiting area.

Alone in the procedure room, Paula looked around as she took off her jersey and skirt. She hung them up on the clothes hangers and hooks anchored to the back of the door. She could see the operation tools laid out on the sterile white cloth next to the examining table. As Paula took off her bra and panties she stared at the stirrups that seem to be looming large in the tiny room. She was turning cold and shivered while she hurriedly put on the hospital "Johnny coat" as she was instructed. For the first time she was deathly afraid of what was going to happen to her. She was nervous and had a quick fantasy that she might die on that table while trying to eradicate someone else's sin inside of her. She prayed that she would be strong. She hoped that she wouldn't get sick. Before she could think any more, Nancy entered the room.

During the procedure, Paula said to herself every prayer that she had learned as a child and asked God to look over her. She looked only up at the ceiling and paid no attention to the sounds coming from Nancy's manipulative hands down below.

The procedure was over sooner than Paula expected. After a brief recovery period, in an adjoining room, Nancy informed her that all went well. Paula was to go home and to rest for a few days. As Pat came in to help her, she held a little unsteadily onto her sister's arm. Pat stopped briefly to pay the $450 in cash to the receptionist as she had been previously instructed. They quickly exited from the building and never looked back.

Back at her sister's apartment, Paula slept most of the day and into the evening. She had been very tired from the many sleepless nights anticipating this day. Pat stayed with her and every hour would walk over to feel Paula's forehead with the palm of her hand to insure that she hadn't spiked an infection-induced fever.

The next morning, Paula woke up feeling much better. She was well rested. She felt different. She felt renewed. She felt lighter. A burden had been lifted from her soul. There was no fever. Apparently there would be no infection from Friday's procedure. She felt fine. Her prayers had been answered.

Pat, too, was now more relaxed about Paula's condition. The look of relief had consumed her face. She smiled as she looked down at her younger, brave, innocent sister. She told Paula that she should still take it easy and rest while she went out shopping for some groceries.

After taking a long, warm, shower, Paula realized again that a heavy, emotional burden had been lifted from her. She started feeling more like her old self. The shower made her feel clean and she could sense a new beginning was unfolding for her. She had to regain her old self-confidence. She was fortunate that she had a lot to look forward to in her life. She did not want to lose focus on all that she had planned for so many years.

After her shower, she got into her jeans and short-sleeved sweatshirt and sat in the living room chair. As she picked up a magazine, flipping through the pages, Paula's thoughts drifted to her sister Pat and how she had helped her through this horrible ordeal. Her older sister was always so strong and so courageously independent. She was the most forceful, decisive member of the entire family. She was never intimidated by anyone. Never showing any weaknesses or vulnerabilities, it was no surprise that she would be accepted into a prestigious medical school. She was always in control. Pat was a "take charge" person all of her life. She had to be tough. For any woman of the 70's who wanted to break through traditional lines and become a doctor, there was no other way.

Paula then reflected on how Pat had always been very private when it came to her personal feelings and never showed an emotional side. This always perplexed Paula. How could anyone be so strong, so ironclad, and so independent? She respected her sister's strength and courage but often wondered if she had a softer side that nobody knew about.

As she sat there, turning the pages, Paula needed something sweet to taste for her dry mouth. She remembered that her sister always carried some kind of hard candy in her coat pockets. She walked over to the closet and found the coat that Pat had worn to Cambridge the previous day.

She reached into the right pocket of the coat and felt only a large soft ball of tissues —very damp tissues. She pulled out the crumbled ball and lightly squeezed it with her hand. Paula looked down as her fingers felt the energy of her sister's tears. Paula was amazed that she could actually feel Patricia's love through the dampness of her sister's tears. Paula was surprised. She now felt sad and a little guilty that she had put her older sister through this ordeal. But she also felt immense comfort knowing that her older sister's love was unconditional.

She then remembered the hard candy that she still wanted. She put her hand inside the other coat pocket. Her hand felt something this time that she never expected. It was not the hard candy that she expected to find.

She pulled out a string of golden rosary beads and softly laid them across both of her hands. As she stared at the bright string of elliptical objects, she felt a strange peace come over her. She rolled one individual bead between the tips of her fingers. Then something extraordinary happened to Paula. As she lightly squeezed the bead she could again feel Pat's energy. She not only could feel her energy but she also had a clear and real vision that took place on the previous day.

Pat was sitting outside of that dreadful room praying for her younger sister. The vision was not imaginary. It was real. It was as though she had been watching a movie. As her fingers felt the bead between her thumb and finger, she could feel Pat's love. She felt her spirit. She could see her sister weeping and using the tissues to dry her tears. Her older sister's anguish and emotional pain vibrated through that rosary bead. As she lightly squeezed the bead, she actually heard Pat's voice pray. She also learned through the bead's energy that Pat harbored no anger but rather a positive closeness to God. It was this positive spiritual attitude that gave Pat all of her strength. Paula now learned her sister's secret. She got her strength from love. Love of God, love of her sister, and love of everyone. She had no anger towards anyone. She had no hate stored in her soul.

She again looked down at the gold beads carefully. Paula knew that she had seen them before, but at first glance, couldn't quite remember when. As she looked down and focused on the beads, she then recollected a vision of many years ago. She smiled. Now she remembered where these beads had come from.

Paula was only eleven years old when her Grandpa Larson had died. Paula was allowed to briefly see him at rest in the casket during the wake. She could never forget the image of Grandpa with his silver hair and his closed eyes, lying peacefully in his dark, blue, vested suit. His gold rosary beads were draped in his hands, folded across his abdomen.

Paula then had a distant recollection of her grandfather. One day when she was a little girl of five years old, she had seen her grandfather resting in his rocking chair with his gold rosary beads in his hands.

"Grandpa, what is that toy you have in your hands?"

He grinned at her. "Oh my little Paula, this is not a toy. These are my beads. When I hold these in my hands they give me strength". He smiled warmly at his little granddaughter.

At his wake, Grandma Larson had wanted his favorite rosary beads to be buried with him. She had the undertaker place them across his body. Unbeknownst to Grandma, Pat had different ideas.

Paula's face broke into a wide, beautiful smile. She could imagine Pat, the teenage granddaughter, boldly running back into the funeral parlor. She could see her snatching the gold beads before the casket was finally closed. A tear of happiness involuntarily rolled down her cheek. She started giggling a little to herself. She carefully placed the rosary beads back into the coat pocket and walked back to her chair. She now knew a lot more about her beloved older sister, Patricia.

CHAPTER SEVEN

Paula and Sam

Sunday mornings were always special for Paula and Sam Parker.
It was their time. It was slow and it was sleepy. There were no jobs, no mundane chores to be done, and no errands to run. The usual busy pedestrian traffic for Woods Hole becomes practically non-existent on Sunday mornings. Each weekend, the marine biological research laboratories were darkened and still. Outside, there were no scientists, residents or tourists wandering around the village.

Sam always got up early on Sunday mornings. He put on his beach combing clothes and would start out for his routine two-mile walk at Chapaquoit Beach. On his way back to the house, he would stop by the local convenience store to pick up his Sunday newspapers.

Paula usually remained in bed on Sunday mornings, sometimes not hearing Sam get dressed and leave the house. She enjoyed the extra hour or so of sleep that she allowed herself on the weekend.

On this morning she awakened as Sam was finishing his morning shower. He walked out onto the deck with his stack of newspapers and a fresh cup of coffee. This particular June day was bright and beautiful as the sun rose slowly in the eastern sky and quietly reflected off of the Quissett village rooftops.

Cape Cod does not usually experience a typical spring season. The months of March, April, and May are still very chilly, similar to the winter season. Most people still wear heavy wool sweaters or jackets while outside since the afternoon temperatures drop quickly. Wood-burning stoves still warm many of the Cape homes during the spring season.

Summer, however, arrives in early June with the warm coastal air coaxing brilliant flowers to burst from their chilled buds. The maple, oak and elm shade trees simultaneously display their deep green colored leaves as if on queue. It is a time that Cape Codders spend every minute that they can outdoors. They have endured a long season of cabin fever and now work and play outside in the warm air as much as they can. They frequently cook outside and often eat their meals on decks or patios.

Paula was towel-drying her hair as she walked around the living room. Her shower had taken the sleepiness away and she now looked forward to spending an entire day with her husband. She could see Sam as she peered through the screened slider leading to the deck. A soft and happy smile graced her lips. She had just put on her dark green Chinese silk robe. It felt good against her nude and lightly scented and powder dusted body. The outdoor sunlight would complete the drying of her long, wavy, auburn hair. It would then have that soft shine to it that Sam had loved so much.

Paula was so much at peace with her life. She had the teaching career that she wanted. She could conceive of doing nothing else but teaching elementary school students. She was assigned to teach the sixth graders this past year. She thoroughly enjoyed it. The little minds of the twelve-year olds were still inquisitive, yet responsive and malleable.

She was still very much in love with the man whom she married. This was not so with many of her friends who had married at the same time. Paula and Sam had never been happier in their lives and cherished every day they had together. They were as much in love today as they were on the day that they married several years ago.

Paula briefly recalled that May evening when Pat and she walked over to the local Woods Hole pub, the "Purple Duck". They just wanted to have a beer and to talk. They had a lot to catch up on. It had been too long since their last sister-to-sister chatting session. Pat was beginning her residency at Boston's Beth Israel Hospital and was seriously dating a construction engineer. Paula had just landed her first teaching job. And it was in her hometown of Quissett. There would be a lot of talking going on that night.

That evening, however, was the first time that she had met Sam. Paula's life would change forever after that night.

Sam, a few years older than Paula, had just finished his Ph.D. program in Marine Molecular Biology at the Woods Hole Oceanographic Institute. He had been making plans to return to his hometown area on the California coast. There were more opportunities out west for young marine biologists. After his eyes met Paula's, he politely introduced himself. Later while sitting at the bar, the three of them talked and had several laughs until closing time.

Soon after that evening, Sam and Paula began dating. Sam never again thought about moving back to the west. He fell in love with her as fast as she did with him. It was the best time of their lives. They became inseparable. They both knew that they were meant for each other.

Paula, who had just received her bachelor's degree in elementary education, had been looking forward to her first teaching assignment in the Quissett school system that September. She had already begun planning her first week's lesson plan. She had no idea that very soon after that night at the "Purple Duck", that she would also be planning her wedding. They planned it for the following New Year's Eve. For Paula and Sam, their marriage couldn't begin soon enough.

Sam was the perfect man for Paula. He was gentle, sensitive, and ruggedly handsome. He had a distinct twinkle in his eyes that spoke of excitement, interest, and sincerity. His intelligence and life experiences were so broad that Sam could talk comfortably on almost any subject. Paula sometimes found herself in awe of her lover's breadth of knowledge. But it was his kindness that attracted her to him. Despite his advanced intellect, he was never condescending towards others; he was never gratuitous towards others.

Sam was always in awe of Paula's beauty. The perfection and love from inside of her soul captured him as much as her exterior physical beauty. At twenty-two, she finally felt what love was all about.

Since his childhood, Sam always had a voracious appetite for reading. He was often found with his nose in a book, magazine or a technical periodical. He read everything. At times he was like a walking encyclopedia. He was, however never pompous nor boring. People liked Sam. They enjoyed listening to him because his warm personality and humility always shone through the technical jargon. He enjoyed patiently explaining things to others, especially to the delight of young children.

After they married, Paula would often invite Sam to her sixth grade classroom to speak to her students about marine life. He was excellent with the youngsters. He often took them on field trips to the salt marshes, the shore, and to some of the Cape's biologically enriched tidal pools. Sam loved children just as Paula had loved being with kids all of her life.

Paula felt that their life now was exceptional. They were still very much in love, enjoyed their professions and had a fine circle of friends nearby and around the world. Life was just great for the two of them.

But they wanted there to be three of them. They wanted to share this great life with children of their own. It was something that they never spoke about directly since they felt that their healthy sexual relationship would eventually create a new life and bless them with a child.

"Need some more orange juice, honey?" Paula asked through the screen slider.

"Sure," replied Sam. "It's getting warm out here already. Going to be a fine day."

Sam pulled out the Cape Cod Times from the stack and put it near Paula's seat at the picnic table. Paula first gave Sam a light kiss, and asked about his morning walk on "Chappy" beach.

"Oh... it was good.... No trash or treasures this morning...my canvas sacks are empty today." He chuckled and continued reading the *Sunday Boston Globe.*

"Well, that's good. Everything is status quo." She smiled back at him.

Paula never joined Sam on his morning walks along the shore. She knew that this was his own special time to be alone, to think and to meditate. She knew that he needed this private space each morning and never asked to go with him.

"Say, Paula, did you ever know a girl by the name of Sonny Brooks who came from Quissett?" said Sam still looking down at the newspaper.

"Sonny? Yes, in fact she was in my class at high school. Why?"

"Well, the former Ms. Sonny Brooks is now Mrs. James Westcott. There is a big wedding article here in the Globe. I just happened to catch a glimpse of the word, 'Quissett' in the headlines and started reading it."

"Sonny and I were not close friends in high school, just acquaintances."

"Yeah, well, let me tell you. She just married one of the wealthiest men on the eastern seaboard. The Westcott family is very big into the chemicals and plastics resin manufacturing. They really have a monopoly in that business. Here, you might want to read this."

He handed the social page section to his wife.

Reaching for the paper, Paula told Sam, "Well, the Brooks family was never anywhere near the so-called 'poverty line'. You know that huge mansion on Bayberry Road with the blue shutters that you like so much? That's where Sonny lived."

"Wow."

"In fact, her ancestors owned almost of all of Quissett property in the very early days. The Brooks were some of the original settlers of this area. I am not sure, but they may have come over on the Mayflower."

"Is that so?"

"Yeah. I would bet that her great-grand daddy had sheep and

cattle roaming on this hill right underneath our deck."

"You know Paula, I have never seen anyone coming or going into that big house of theirs. Does anyone live there now?"

"You know, it is kind of a sad story." Paula poured herself a cup of coffee.

"How so?"

"Sonny and her brother, Jared, lived in that house with their parents while they were growing up. I didn't really know Jared, since he was a few years older than I was. He was cute though and I remember a lot of the girls swooning over him."

"Not you, of course!" teased Sam.

Paula replied by affectionately sticking her tongue out at her husband.

"Anyway, Jared enlisted in the service before finishing college. I remember hearing that this was a huge shock to his family. He abruptly dropped out of a prestigious university and volunteered to serve in the Viet Nam conflict."

"Where did he go to school?"

"I'm not sure, but I believe it was one of the Ivies. After enlisting, he was assigned as a marine helicopter pilot in the South Viet Nam. According to the newspaper articles, he was a decorated hero. He had saved a lot of GI's lives. I guess he was awarded with several medals for bravery.

"So, what happened?"

"My folks still have the newspaper clipping at the house. It was so tragic. I remember some parts of it. Jared had just completed a flying mission at Da Nang, near the North Viet Nam border and was heading towards his barracks. After he landed, he and his crew were riding in one of those open, convertible, Army jeeps near a place called Monkey Mountain. According to the report, a sniper shot him in the head. The driver rushed him to Da Nang hospital but he had already died. It was such a sad time for the people of Quissett. He was the first local casualty of the war. He had been a very well-liked young man."

"That is a tragedy. What happened to the Brooks family? Did they move?"

"No, The parents split up a few years later and I believe that Mr. Brooks had died just recently. Sarah, the mother, stayed at one of her townhouses in Boston and never returned to the Cape. The whole family just fell apart."

"Damn! That really is a sad story. There wasn't any 'good' that came from that war. Well at least now it looks like his sister is happily married. "

"You know, the one who took Jared's death the worst was his sister, Sonny. According to my friends and family, she changed her entire life-style. She became more quiet, turned into a loner and for a long time she never went out except to go to church."

"Hmm."

"Believe me, Sam! This was quite a dramatic change from the former Miss Sonny Brooks of Quissett High!"

"And the house? What happened to the house?"

"Sonny more or less boarded up the house. Occasionally, I have seen Hans, their utility man, come and check the place out for damage or vandalism. Other than that, there hasn't been any life there for years."

"That's too bad. Such a waste. The whole family broken up over the loss."

Paula put down her cup of coffee, and grabbed the Cape Cod Times. She routinely would read the Times quickly for local news and then start on the Sunday Globe.

"Oh my God!"

Sam looked over at the astonished look on Paula's face

"What is it?"

"I can't believe it," said Paula. Her mouth opened wide.

Sam glanced over to see the title line of the front-page article. It read, "**Local Falmouth Man Ordained as Catholic Priest**".

"It's Tommy! Tommy Donovan!"

"And who, may I ask is this Tommy Donovan?"

"He was another Quissett High School class mate. In fact, this is unbelievable! He used to date Sonny Brooks in high school. How ironic! What a coincidence! Good for him! Good for him! He deserves the best. Everyone liked Tommy. He was always such a good guy! I can't believe it! Tommy's now a priest! Good for him! Good for him!"

Sam smiled as Paula quickly read the article. She learned how he had lived in Canada since graduating from Quissett High School. He had attended college and later St. Joan's seminary in Ontario. Tom was interviewed and quoted in the article. It reported that he wanted to "return to Falmouth and truly serve others as a shepherd in the fields where he grew up." He would become a curate at the same church parish in Quissett where he had been an altar boy.

Sam watched Paula. Her face suddenly changed expression from an excited smile to a more distant, pensive look. She was no longer reading the text in the newspaper. She was into some deep thought. Her eyes had a distant look. It appeared that she was recollecting something serious, perhaps painful. This was quickly followed by a deep frown. He was going to ask why the sudden change but he knew that his wife was focusing on a private, personal thought. He wouldn't go there. He knew better. Sam always respected everyone's privacy. This included his loving wife.

Paula was reflecting back to the last time when she saw Tom Donovan. It was that horrid, dreadful night when he gave her a lift to her house. She was scared and dripping wet. He had picked her up in his car to safely take her home. She had mentally repressed that evening for many years, but now it all came back to her with all of its ugly details. She recalled him saying something that night about moving to Canada to avoid the draft. That was the last time that she had seen Tommy.

She quickly snapped out of her trance. A smile returned. Her thoughts shifted back to Tommy and his good nature, his naiveté, and his heartfelt benevolence of that night. He was one of the sweetest boys from Quissett whom she had known.

"Good for him, good for him." Paula said one more time.

Sam and Paula enjoyed the warm and peaceful Sunday morning. Sam had cut up some fresh strawberries and they leisurely popped the sweet fruit into their mouths while their eyes consumed the printed words of the newspapers. It was their time.

Later, Sam looked over at his wife. The sun's rays were reflecting off of her head. The blond highlights of her auburn hair looked like fine threads of gold woven into the deeper reds and browns. His mouth widened into a handsome smile showing his bright white teeth. He was happy. He knew that his bride, his wife Paula, was happy too.

Paula had laid her head back against the deck rail so that she could face the sunlight and have some peaceful thoughts. She thought that it was a good time to relax. It was a good time to be with your husband, your friend, and your lover. She also smiled to herself and thought that it was a great time to be ovulating.

She then turned her head towards Sam and saw his wide and warm smile.

"What are you thinking about, Sam?'

"You, Paula. You are just so beautiful."

She smiled back at him and slowly stood up to walk over to him. She stood behind his chair and then bent over him and kissed him softly on his forehead. She lightly caressed his face with the tips of her fingers. He looked at her as she walked around to face him.

"Come here, sweetheart. You know how I love to caress your hair after you have just washed it."

"I know that you do Sam," she replied, still smiling. "And I want you to caress my nice clean hair now."

Sam closed his eyes and raised his hand in an attempt to touch her head. She stopped him by catching his wrist with her hand and bringing it down to his lap. His eyes opened, surprised at her quick interception.

"Not there, Sam," she said softly.

Slowly she opened her green silk robe exposing her nude, beautiful, slender body. She seductively thrust her pelvis towards Sam's hand still held in hers. "Here honey. Right here."

CHAPTER EIGHT

Sonny and James Westcott

A virtual cascade of emotions poured through every living cell of Sonny Westcott during that Christmas week of 1977. She felt bewilderment, disappointment, pity for her husband, and self-pity for her. But underneath it all, Sonny was angry— very, very angry.

Every since she had been living with Jim Westcott, which began one year before her marriage to him, Sonny hoped to become pregnant. Soon after she moved in with him, she told Jim that she purposely discontinued using birth control pills. She confided in him that she always wanted to become a mother. She also did not feel comfortable taking the synthetic pills much longer. Jim did not know that she had been using them off and on since the age of fifteen.

The thought of parenting did not bother Jim at all. They were engaged. They were to be married next spring. Jim wanted to have a child almost as much as she did. He always enjoyed being with his young nieces and nephews. He loved the energy and excitement of children running around a home. Besides, children would never burden their intimacy of marriage. There would be ample support from nannies, housekeepers or whoever Sonny and he wanted to look after a child when they had other things to do. They both knew that the two of them could produce offspring who would be financially and intellectually advantaged with their wealth and "blue blood" lineage. If Sonny became pregnant before the scheduled wedding, the nuptial date would conveniently be moved up earlier on the calendar.

Sonny, however, hadn't become pregnant after being married for six months. They had failed to conceive after more than eighteen months of lovemaking on a routine and very frequent basis. This situation bothered her tremendously. She read several manuals about conception and followed her cycles and temperatures faithfully to schedule their sessions in bed. After several months into their marriage, she had privately worried that she may have eliminated or diminished her chances of getting pregnant from her early teenage promiscuity and recreational drug usage. She talked to her gynecologist about this concern. The doctor seemed confident that no harm was done during her activities of the late '60's.

Conceiving a child was not only Sonny's top priority; it had become her *only* priority. She became obsessed with this mission. Jim was noticing that it had altered her personality. She was becoming less social with others, including him at times.

Sonny had scheduled a visit with her gynecologist to have tests performed for any infertility problems. Within a few days, she received a phone call from the doctor. She had passed all of the fertility exams and lab tests with flying colors. She should have no problem becoming pregnant. The doctor strongly suggested that her husband should be tested before other alternatives are recommended.

Early in November, Sonny again reminded Jim how she had in intense desire to have children with him. She told him that she wanted to become pregnant soon. She did not want to wait until she was into her thirty's or later to begin a family. She told her husband about her fertility testing and the positive outcome. It was time for him to be tested. She explained that she wanted to have this done before they both left for their three-month business tour of the Far East scheduled soon after Christmas.

"Please Jim. It would mean a lot to me to eliminate any physical or medical cloud from preventing us having a child."

"Sure, Sonny. I think it appropriate that I be tested," he replied in a seemingly cavalier attitude.

Although he was lax in setting up the appointment and even made jokes about it with Sonny, he finally was tested in early December.

After some re-testing, Jim was informed of the final results. They were not good. Jim could not believe the news. For several days he was in denial and went for further testing at another clinic. The results were the same.

His doctors theorized that Jim might have become sterile during his boyhood years when he struggled with a long and complicated case of pneumonia. Jim was in complete shock when he had heard the news. He was devastated. Intellectually, he knew that his sterility didn't make him any less of a man, but he could not escape the emotional pain. He fell into a deep depression with the reality that he and Sonny could not produce a child of their own.

It was just a week before Christmas when Jim told Sonny that he was sterile. Her husband of these past six months would never be able to make her pregnant. At first there were a lot of tears, with both Jim and Sonny weeping together. But then they both wept to themselves in solitude.

Then there was the distance. Jim sensed that Sonny was quickly retreating further away from him. He also sensed that she was blaming him for their disappointing news. He was worried. On Christmas Eve, Jim proposed the idea of adopting a child.

"We can adopt, Sonny. We can get the best baby possible."

"I don't want to talk about that now."

"But look, in two days, you and I will leave for our trip to the Far East. We'll have almost three months traveling together to discuss it and we can decide how to plan."

"I have a lot of thinking to do, Jim. This is a big thing. It isn't just some business deal."

"Listen. With my contacts we can select the best and most beautiful and intelligent child there is available for adoption. We will soon forget that we didn't conceive the child. We will bring it up from its early infancy and accept it as our own. That's what happens in these cases."

"Jim. Read my lips. I am not interested in adopting someone else's kid."

The icy words resonated through Jim's heart. He felt that he was at a loss for words. He now knew that he had a tremendous challenge on his hands. His own depression was now overtaken with a fear that his marriage was slipping away. He felt helpless.

"Look Sonny, we are both speaking from raw nerves and emotion. This is not a good time. Let's try to enjoy the holiday with the family for now."

Sonny was not in any Christmas festive mood. She didn't want to discuss any options now. She was distraught. She was angry. This was not what she expected when she married Jim. Even though her husband was handsome, athletic, and interesting with all of his life experiences, she often felt that she wasn't really much in love with him. She had dated others who gave her much more excitement and passion. There had been others who gave her more physical satisfaction. Jim was the wealthy, good-looking man who was supposed to give her children— so that the Brooks bloodline from Cape Cod, Massachusetts could continue on for generations. Since her brother Jared, was killed in Viet Nam, Sonny knew that she was the very last chance to continue the proud and respected Brooks' progeny. It was her responsibility. It was up to her. She would do it for her deceased brother. She had been determined not to fail.

***

Christmas day at the paternal Westcott home on the picturesque Marblehead shore, located north of Boston, was always a special event. The entire day and dinner had been planned, catered and arranged by holiday consultants. There was a twenty-foot tall Christmas tree in the family Great Room. Professional decorators had artistically arranged the bright lights, shiny balls, and tinsel. The entire house had holly and fresh evergreen branches on staircases, fireplace mantels and doorways. Background Christmas music could be heard in each room equipped with in-wall speakers. The entire home looked beautiful with a Christmas fragrance in each room. The house had once been featured in a popular home-decorating magazine for its tasteful holiday appearance. This year was no different.

There would be over fifty family members and close friends attending the Christmas dinner. While the children where opening gifts and playing with toys, the adults would chat informally over cocktails and hors douvres. All of the fireplaces were lit providing inviting warmth from the frigid temperatures and light, snow flurries that were outside.

The men were dressed in suits and festive colored ties. The women wore semi-formal dresses with bright holiday colors. Some had corsages. Many women showed off their newest sparkling jewelry as gifts from their husbands or fiancées.

The new dress that Jim had bought for Sonny to wear this day still hung in her bedroom closet. Jim had seen the dress at the Neiman Marcus store in Boston soon after Thanksgiving. He couldn't wait to buy it for her. When he gave it to her that November weekend, he had asked that she wear the bright, red, silk dress with a moderately cut bodice to his family celebration on Christmas day. He told her that it would go well with the diamond necklace he had given her on her last birthday. But on this Christmas day, the holiday dress remained on the hanger and the diamond necklace was still locked in her jewelry safe.

Sonny entered the room looking very different from the rest of the gathering. She had decided to wear dark colors to mirror her mood. She had a straight black wool dress on with plain black pumps. Her hair was pulled back in a straight ponytail. She wore a small maroon barrette on her head. There was only the slightest hint of make-up with a dull, subdued, red-colored lipstick. She looked quite pale. She stood out from the others in a most unimpressive way. There was only the hint of a forced obligatory smile on her face as she met with the other guests. It was obvious to everyone that Sonny didn't want to be there. The whispers were spreading quickly from room to room.

"It's quite a beautiful view isn't it? " said John Westcott, who was Jim's older brother.

He had come up from behind Sonny as she gazed at the ocean's waves crashing against the rocks. The seascape view from that corner of the house was spectacular.

Without turning towards him, she replied. "Yes it is. It's still the Atlantic Ocean, but it is so different from the Cape Cod shores." She continued staring out through the panes of glass in the French doors.

"So.... you're not used to the North Shore's rocky coastline, eh?"

"No. I still really like the sandy beaches and dunes on the Cape. I guess I am feeling a little homesick. I really miss Quissett." She turned and walked by him with a slight devilish smile on her face.

As dinner was being served, Jim's mother leaned over to Sonny.

"Well my dear, I do envy you! Going off to the Far East has always been one of my favorite trips. If you'd like, I can tell you later where some of the best shops are in Hong Kong, Singapore, and Taipei. I never come back from the Orient empty-handed."

"Oh, Mother!" Jim interjected. "Sonny can explore for herself. Besides with her academic background from Wellesley, I am sure that she will be interested in visiting some of the cultural and historical sites. She can find boutiques and shops anytime."

"Is that really true, Sonny?" smiled Jim's mother with a twinkle in her eyes.

Sonny slowly put her fork down and picked up her napkin to lightly brush against her lips. She lowered her head down for a moment. Then she slowly lifted it up and looked squarely at her mother-in-law.

"Actually, Jessica, I am *not going* on this three month trip with Jim as we had planned. I just got some news that has changed all of that."

Both Jim and Jessica could not hide their surprised facial expressions.

"Oh, really dear, what is that?" replied Jessica.

"I have to return to my home in Quissett and take care of some legal and family real estate matters that have been neglected."

Now it was Jim's turn to become angry. It was bad enough that she publicly displayed her mood with her black, mourning costume. Now, Sonny had further embarrassed him in front of his mother and the other guests who were within earshot. Jim was seething inside. He was very uncomfortable that his family now learned that Jim knew nothing about Sonny's plans.

The wait staff served a sumptuous dinner with pheasant, turkey, and prime rib along with all of the fixings. But Jim had now lost his appetite. Sonny hardly ate one bite and did not speak much during the meal. She later excused herself from the dining table. She whispered to Jim that she wanted to leave early so that she could do some packing for her trip back to her Cape Cod home.

The half-hour drive back to their Boston town house in Back Bay was quiet. Jim was still angry at Sonny's behavior, but he was more concerned about the future of their marriage. He deeply loved his beautiful wife and did not want to lose her. He decided to stay calm. He showed his patience and compassion and not anger. It was his best trait. He always had control of his temper. Sonny was seeing this for the first time. It would not be the last time she would be impressed with his self-control and with his ability to discard anger. It would not be the last time that she truly saw how much he loved her.

It was a very cold and quiet Christmas evening both outside and inside of the Sonny and Jim Westcott home.

The next evening at five o'clock, Jim was gazing out the window of his first class seat as the Northwest Airlines jetliner took off from Logan International Airport, headed for Taipei, Taiwan.

At precisely the same time, Sonny's car was crossing the Cape Cod Canal over the Bourne Bridge. There was again some light, snow flurries. The "Welcome to Cape Cod " shrubbery was brightly lit up at the Bourne traffic rotary. This familiar sight put a smile on Sonny's face. It was the first smile she had managed in several weeks. She began to feel good. She was going home.

***

At first, Sonny felt a little awkward, even a bit scared being in the old family home all by herself. It had been several years since she had been inside the big house. After her parents had split up and she had discovered more to do in the Boston area, she never returned to Quissett. The house now had a hollow, empty feel to it. The temperature inside the home was icy cold. It was obvious that nobody had lived there for a long time. It was missing the usual pleasant fragrance of fresh flowers that had always been a part of the Brooks decor. The house was missing the aromatic cooking odors coming from the kitchen stove with their cook, Francois, leaning over the steaming pots and pans. The home had been abandoned. It had no life. It had no character.

As she walked around inspecting the first floor rooms she saw the neglect, almost like an orphaned child. Sonny then began to reflect on her discussion with Jim about adoption. She now felt that perhaps she was too harsh. She really wasn't opposed to adopting children. It was just that she was so fixed on continuing the Brooks bloodline that adoption never crossed her mind. She was glad that she would be away from him and Boston for a while. It was her retreat away from problems, and over time, she knew that she would come up with a solution.

She telephoned Hans to come over to warm the place up and to make sure that the water pipes were not damaged since there had been such a long period of vacancy.

She began rolling back the heavy sheets that had been draped over the pieces of furniture several years ago. There was a lot of work to do and Sonny was anxious to get started. She decided to take inventory. She visited each room, one by one, to see what she wanted to change.

After Hans arrived, he quickly checked out all of the plumbing and soon the warm air drifted up through the old-fashioned metal-grated heat registers in each of the rooms.

Sonny slowly walked upstairs to the third floor where she had her own private bedroom-suite as a teenager. This floor housed her large bedroom, a private bathroom, and a bookshelf-walled study.

She always had her privacy and physical separation from her parents. It was better for them. It was better for her.

She opened the door and looked into her old bedroom. She could see some of the old paintings and posters on the walls. Everything seemed distant and foreign to her now. She walked over to her old vanity table. She looked at the souvenirs and memorabilia from rock concerts, and parties that she had attended. Her room reminded her of an old late 60's and early 70's shrine. There were some faded photographs that had curled up on the top of the vanity table. She picked up the long smoking pipe that she once used for recreational drugs. It was lying there next to some loose change and an old book of matches. She opened the door to her closet and lightly felt the old clothes that she once wore. There were some flimsy tank tops, T-shirts with obscene expressions printed on them and skirts; very, very, short skirts. They were all rebellious and totally obscene. She felt uncomfortable seeing these clothes. It brought her back to a time in her life that was not a happy one. This room was not Sonny; it was a room for another girl at another time. She slammed the door as if she wanted the bedroom, and all that it held, to instantly disappear. The next morning she would ask that Hans throw everything out and have the bedroom completely redone.

She walked down the one flight of stairs where her parent's had their bedroom. She didn't walk into that room. That room meant nothing to her in her younger years. It meant less to her today. There were two guest bedrooms with private bathrooms adjacent to their master bedroom.

Jared's old bedroom was further down the hall. Sonny opened the door slowly and looked inside. As she looked around, it seemed as if her brother had never left. Everything was always in its place. His books, his drawings, everything seemed to neatly balance inside of his room. Even the design on his bedspread was symmetrical with deep blues, and vibrant cranberry colors. She looked inside of his bureau drawers. He had all of his underwear evenly folded next to his rolled up socks. The room had never changed since the last day he was here.

She opened his closet door. She could not resist touching his clothes that were neatly hung up in an orderly fashion. She tugged lightly at the off-white Irish knit sweater that she always loved for him to wear. As her fingers caressed the thick woolen sleeve, she closed her eyes. She could feel him. She sensed his energy. She heard Jared's voice and his laughter all over again. She reflected on the two of them playing touch football in the backyard. She mentally saw him walking along the beach wearing that sweater with his pant legs rolled up, barefoot, kicking the shallow water. This was something that they did often. Walks along the beach. Sonny smiled yet again. This time, however, she smiled for a different reason. There was love in her heart.

The heated air from the furnace was now beginning to waft through the registers of the bedroom. Sonny gently fell onto Jared's bed and closed her eyes. She pulled a woolen, knitted afghan up over her chilled body. She took in a deep breath and relaxed deeply. As she rolled over onto her side, she thought to herself that it was good to be inside of her brother's room. Sonny became very relaxed lying on her brother's bed. With the heat warming the room, she became very drowsy and relaxed.

Then something suddenly happened that surprised her. She thought that the bed was shaking but it was not. Then she realized that she was vibrating. But her physical body wasn't vibrating. It was something deep inside of her that she couldn't identify. It was her soul that was vibrating. Then she felt a presence that she had never felt before. She closed her eyes and fell deeper into relaxation while the internal vibrations continued. This time she could sense two arms hugging her gently, keeping her protected and safe from harm. She knew that those arms were Jared's. She knew that he was in that room with her. There was an overwhelming feeling of joy and tranquillity. Sonny remained laying in that position until she drifted off into a peaceful, gentle, sleep.

She woke up about an hour later. At first, she did not realize where she was for a while. She knew that she had a peaceful dream about her brother Jared speaking to her, but now, somehow she couldn't reconstruct the details of the dream. She couldn't remember what he had said to her. The brief nap did her good. She felt better. She felt refreshed. The past few weeks of emotional depression had left her. Then, after getting her bearings, she said out loud, in a soft, yet deliberate tone,

"Well, Jared, it looks like I am moving in with you. I 'm sure that you won't mind me taking over your old bedroom here. Maybe some of your goodness and spirituality will rub off on me. Ya know something, 'Bro', I miss you so much."

***

A few days later, Sonny was looking out of the picture window while she spoke on the telephone.

"Look Jim, this is something that I have to do *and* it's something that I want to do," said Sonny, gripping the phone more firmly.

"Well, Sonny, exactly how long are you going to stay there on the Cape? My family is quite concerned. As am I, of course."

Jim's voice on the telephone was so clear that it seemed like he was nearby rather than half way around the world. Sonny could hear the tension in his voice. She knew that he was worried about losing her and their marriage.

" I don't know. I am getting my family's house back in order. Hans is helping me to find remodeling contractors, and today I interviewed a delightful Miss MacDonald. She can help me with the household chores on a permanent basis. I really am excited about doing this, Jim."

"Well, we have to talk as soon as I return. I sincerely hope that you're doing some thinking yourself."

There was a pause that lasted much too long. Jim was getting nervous on the other end of the line. Finally, Sonny replied.

"Oh, I am Jim. Of course I am doing some thinking." She nervously switched the telephone handset to her other hand.

"OK, Sonny. Well, please, please remember that I love you and miss you. I am off to Tai Nan tomorrow, and then we are scheduled to go to Manila. I will call you from the Philippines to see how you're doing. These manufacturers' meetings are going better than we expected. We are on schedule and I should be home by March 15th as planned."

"Well, that's good Jim. I will talk with you later."

Sonny hung up the phone and gazed out through the front window for several minutes. She really didn't know what she was doing now. She also didn't know what she wanted to do with the rest of her life. She didn't *feel* anything. About her marriage. About her future. About her husband. For the first time in her life she wasn't sure who she was. This didn't bother her. She felt that she was at the right place at the right time. Something was telling her to "go with flow". Was that the message she got laying in Jared's bed the other day? She wasn't sure.

The only thing in her life now that was stimulating for her was working on the Quissett home. For some strange reason, she felt that this was the work that she was supposed to be doing at this time.

Was her brother Jared, closer than she thought; telling her that this was what she should be doing? Or was she living through some denial phase, knowing that her marriage was in shambles and she needed to do this work as a catharsis to get through this?

CHAPTER NINE

Reunion

Her first week back in the family Quissett home went by quickly for Sonny. She felt relieved to get her mind off of her childless marriage. There was very little thought given to her barren predicament or her hollow marriage to Jim. Her focus now was only on restoring the family home to a comfortable condition. The re-modeling work served as an effective therapy in smoothing out Sonny's rocky emotional state. She became totally immersed in these projects. As each day went by she became re-acclimated to her girlhood home. Likewise, each day made her more emotionally distant from her husband, Jim. She felt better. She felt healthier. She began to sleep better. The solution to her problems would be coming soon. She just knew it.

She soon began to feel a great deal of personal satisfaction as she brought the old Brooks' homestead back to life. But this time it was going to be a new life in the old house. It would not be anything like it had been while she was a bratty, irascible teenager. She would make this house into a home for which she would be proud. Sonny sensed that she would stay in this house forever.

On an early and cold January morning, she came down to the kitchen in her flannel pajamas and bathrobe. She put the kettle on for some tea and began reading through some catalogs for new curtains and drapes. Suddenly, she felt a little anguish. She did not want this remodeling project to come to an end, forcing her to return to Boston and to her husband. On the other hand, she realized that this redecorating could not go on forever. She thought that she needed more time than just a few months to work through her marriage dilemma. She needed more time, but his project would end soon. As she was making her cup of tea an idea came to her that solved this problem. Then she smiled, thinking that she would not have to end her "retreat" with this project. She would continue by moving out to the Nantucket cottage and begin remodeling projects out there. This would extend the hiatus from her marriage. By then, she thought, even her husband, Jim, should see the writing on the wall. She was now sure of one thing. She had come home to live and had no desire to return to Boston.

The following Sunday, Sonny decided that she would go to church in her old parish. She may bump into some of her old friends from the days gone by. She showered and dressed to get ready to attend a later Mass. She would relax from the painting, the hammering, and the wallpapering this day. After Mass, she would enjoy returning home to light a fire in the fireplace and to spend the afternoon reading newspapers and magazines. As she was applying her make-up, she thought that she might make some phone calls to old friends and let them know that she was back in town. She smiled as she thought about contacting her old high school classmates. It would be good to rekindle some old acquaintances. When they learned that Sonny Brooks was back in town, they would be shocked and surprised.

***

The only person, however, on that Sunday, who was shocked and surprised was Sonny. With the beginning of Mass at St. Ann's Church, she joined the congregation in routine fashion by standing up to face the procession of altar boys, deacons, lectors, and the priest slowly walking down the center aisle.

She thought that she was hallucinating when she saw Tommy

Donovan. His face was the same; his hair was the same. His curled up smile was still there. He looked the same as he did when he was a teenager at Quissett High School. He looked the same as when they were going steady. He looked that same as he did when she made love with him in various locations; including the back seat of his car. But there was something very odd about the way he looked.

He was walking down the center aisle wearing gold and green colored priests' vestments and preparing to say the 11:30am mass at St. Ann's church.

She was unaware that her mouth was wide opened as she stood in awe and disbelief. She had to grab hold of the back of the pew in front of her to steady her balance. After he walked up to the altar, she unsuccessfully tried to concentrate on the steps of the Mass. As she looked down at her missal, she realized that her hands were trembling involuntarily.

It was as if she were living in a weird dream. It didn't seem real to her! Fortunately, she had sat in a pew that was far back in the church. Tommy could not make her out from where he stood upon the distant alter. The sound of his voice delivering the homily was very disconcerting to her. She could not stop her heart from pounding vigorously inside of her chest. She felt some beads of perspiration at the top of her forehead. She remembered that deep voice of his and she mentally recalled the many times they spent together in their junior and senior years at high school. She tried to put them out of her mind but it was impossible.

Sonny did not remember driving home from church that Sunday. Every synapse in her head was electrified with unbridled energy after seeing the Reverend Father Tom Donovan. After returning home, she again put on some tea, and could not stop pacing through the house. She was oblivious to the tools, the ladders and the paint cans and drop cloths that she walked around as she paced.

Sonny hadn't given a lot of thought to Tom since their high school days. Soon after graduation she had heard rumors that he had become a Viet Nam war "draft-dodger" and ran away to Canada. She did, however, reminisce about Tommy from time to time. Many nights in her bed, she remembered him and those highly charged, sexually active years in high school. He was the most energetic and physically satisfying man with whom she had ever been. She thought back to their teenage romance. She knew that Tom had been madly in love with her, but her mother had insisted that she never marry below her social station. She often had wondered what would have happened if they had stayed together.

Little did she or anyone know that Tom Donovan would eventually become a Catholic priest. She wondered if he had dated much, or at all, after their break up. Or, was she the last girl with whom Tommy Donovan had embraced and kissed? Her mind still wandered out of control.

She continued pacing for a while and then sat down to have her hot cup of tea and some cookies. She couldn't get Tom out of her mind. Father Tom Donovan. The Reverend Tom Donovan. She didn't buy any Sunday newspapers as she had planned that day. She didn't call any of her high school friends that afternoon to tell them that she was back in town. Instead, she picked up the phone with some nervousness and called St. Ann's rectory.

"Tom, I couldn't believe my eyes this morning. I had no idea that you had become a priest! How...How....How wonderful!"

"Oh, Sonny, I thought you might have read about my ordination in the Cape newspapers."

"I haven't lived on the Cape for several years now. Actually, I just returned here a few weeks ago."

"Oh.. Are you married now, Sonny?"

There was a long pause.

"Well, um... Tom, yes, yes I am married.... For about seven months now."

"Well congratulations! It looks like we both found our calling."

Another pause.

"Sonny, why don't you stop by the rectory for a cup of coffee and we can get caught up on our lives? I'd also like to know how your folks and your brother Jared are doing."

"Oh.....Tom. Jared's...ah...Jared". This wasn't the right place and time.

Tom interrupted. "Sonny. You know, I am happy to know that you were in church today. I know how you struggled with Catholicism and with religion in general, when we were younger."

"Yeah, well, it took some doing, but I'm on board now. Tom, there is so much for the two of us to get caught up on. I'd like to stop by the rectory for that cup of coffee with you. Do you have any free time next week?"

***

Sonny had never before been inside of St. Ann's rectory. She found it a bit intimidating walking up the front steps. As soon as she stepped into the foyer, however, Sonny felt a sense of peace and serenity inside of this home. There was an aroma permeating the rectory that seemed to calm the senses. She thought that it might be the scent of burning wax coming from the lit candles on the fireplace and on top of the piano in the reading room.

The rooms were conservatively decorated with their hand-carved oak bookcases. There were elegant brass candleholders with white candles in each room. The deep, dark, maroon carpeting was immaculate. There were religious paintings neatly hung on the wall with additional photos of former popes and bishops.

The secretary, Christine Stanton, had asked Sonny to wait in the sitting room and she would call Father Donovan to come out to greet her. Sonny was again feeling a little anxious. She wasn't sure how she should greet her former lover.

"Sonny. It is so good to see you! "

A smiling Tom Donovan walked toward her, warmly grabbed her hand, and then kissed her softly on the cheek.

"Hello Tom,....ah .... Father Donovan," replied Sonny.

"Christine. This is Sonny Brooks or ....," Tom looked over at

Sonny for help.

"It's Westcott now. Sonny Westcott."

Christine stood up and smiled warmly at Sonny.

"Sonny and I were high school classmates together, Christine. We have a lot to catch up on. Can you please bring some coffee for us into my office? Sonny and I will be meeting in there."

"Of course, Father." Christine dutifully replied.

"And please hold all calls until we are finished," he told her in a more subdued tone.

Sonny couldn't believe nor comprehend this entire situation taking place. She thought that this setting was surreal. It seemed to her that she was performing inside of a movie set for Hollywood. She gazed at the boy with whom she once was madly in love with and with whom she made passionate love. He is now wearing a black cassock, a white cleric collar and sitting behind this mahogany desk at the church rectory. At first, she felt a little nervous speaking with him. She didn't know her script. Again, she could feel her heart pounding.

Tom sensed her anxiety and made her feel at ease by asking her some questions. He felt very sad after Sonny explained that her brother, Jared, had been killed in the Viet Nam war. He learned that her father had lost his struggle with cancer. He was also saddened when Sonny told him that her mother was currently in a rest home. She hadn't recognized any family or friends, since her diagnosis of Alzheimer's disease.

The time in Father Donovan's office went by too quickly for the two of them. They talked about many of their experiences of the past several years. After an hour, Christine buzzed his office. She informed him that there was another parishioner waiting to see him about scheduling a funeral Mass.

Sonny, upon leaving, turned to Tom in front of Miss Stanton's desk.

"Father Donovan, I would *love* to have you come by for dinner some time. Do you think that you could make it?"

"Why, of course, I really want to meet your husband."

"Well.....ah....how about next Thursday evening? Say seven-thirty?"

On that following Thursday, Sonny had asked Miss MacDonald, or "Mac", as she preferred to be called, to stay a little later that evening to prepare a dinner for her guest, Father Donovan.

Sonny spent an unusually longer time; showering, dressing, and putting on her makeup that evening before the arrival of Father Tom. She smiled in the mirror as he put on her earrings. For the first time in a very long time, she felt a twinge of excitement go through her body. She wanted to "show off" for Tom this evening.

Tom was impressed with the work that Sonny had undertaken to remodel the Brooks' homestead. He had still remembered how it looked when they were back in high school. She explained to Tom that she was nearly finished remodeling the interior of the house. She apologized for the disarray in some of the rooms. The dinner was cordial and somewhat reserved with small talk. After serving the coffee and dessert, Mac went home to leave her boss alone with the priest.

Sonny still did not feel very comfortable talking with her former lover under these circumstances. Tom, likewise, was somewhat less than comfortable with this reunion. It seemed that he did not know exactly how to act with his former sweetheart, now that he had chosen the vocation and taken the vows of a celibate catholic priest. The air was filled, during pauses, with a bizarre awkwardness.

"Oh, Tom, you don't have to help with clearing the table. I'll do that."

"My pleasure. Besides, I want to sit with you in the drawing room. You said earlier, when I asked about your husband, Jim is it?...that you would talk about it after dinner. I hope that everything is all right."

"Sure. We can make some room for us in there. Just move a ladder or two. But let me get us an after-dinner brandy, Tom. This is going take all of my courage and then some," replied Sonny.

Tom could not disguise his inquisitive expression as he looked back at her.

She handed Tom his snifter of brandy and they both sat down on the oversized drawing room couch. Sonny did not hold back much. As she spoke, she felt as if a burden was being lifted from her that she had been carrying for some time.

She began her story at the time when her brother, Jared, was killed in Viet Nam. His death had taken a serious toll on her. She explained how she went into a deep and long depression. His death had significantly changed her life in many ways. Later, she settled down. She knew that she wanted marriage and a family of her own. She told of her living with Jim before their marriage and that she thought that she "loved him". But now, several months into their marriage she was having her doubts that she did the right thing. She confessed that she didn't know if she was ever "in love" with Jim. She explained to Tom, that she always wanted to be closer to her husband, to understand his passions for his business but found that difficult at times. She had wished that there were something that would bring Jim and her closer. Tom listened intently as she told Tom that there was something missing in their marriage. She looked at him as though she wanted his approval. Although it was still early in their marriage, she felt that they were already at serious crossroads.

Sonny never mentioned the childless state of their marriage. That topic was much too private and much too personal. She told Tom that now she felt that maybe her marriage wasn't meant to be. She may have rushed into it too quickly. She told him that, now in retrospect, that she may have married Jim too soon during her post-depression period.

"Tom, I am only telling you this so that there is no mystery as to why my husband is traveling all over the Far East and I am on a 'Quissett retreat' of sorts. I need time away to think and to make my mind up as to what I should do."

There was a brief pause in the conversation. Tom knew that he must respond to all that she had just told him. It was expected that a priest should have consoling and encouraging words at these times. He looked at her squarely in the eyes.

"Sonny, I will help you only, when and if, you seek my counsel.

This is a very private matter between you and Jim. I will pray that you do the right thing. I want you to be happy. And I want the same for your husband, Jim. I don't have the answers. I will never interfere, but I will help you in any way that I can. But remember I will get involved, only if you hold your hand out to me. Remember that."

Sonny looked long into Tom's eyes. She remembered his strength and comfort from many years ago.

"I will remember that Tom. I will hold out my hand for your help when I need you. Thank you"

***

The next few weeks kept Sonny busy redecorating the house. With Mac's help, everything was beginning to feel comfortable, warm, and more "homey". The carpenters, plumbers, and painters were following her instructions well. The home began to have a new life and character to it. She felt that she was doing something good not just for saving the home but for the Brooks family.

Sonny played music each day. She was beginning to enjoy her life again. She discovered an independence and happiness that she had never experienced before. She felt that she was learning who she really was and perhaps why she was here on earth. She remembered the words of her brother that day so many years ago on the Nantucket beach. We all have a purpose for being here. We must help and serve one another.

Sonny's life was changing again. Everything seemed lighter and clearer to her. Also, she and her housekeeper, Mac got along well with one another. They had developed a relationship that was closer than that of the typical employer to employee. It was as though Mac was becoming her substitute mother. She certainly had the qualities that her own mother never possessed. Mac had a sense of humor. She was a good listener and was not shy about offering her own opinions. She liked to laugh. She was not afraid to show love. Single, and in her late forties, it was evident that she would not have a family or a daughter of her own. Mac was intuitive and non-judgmental. Sonny felt that there was a reason for Mac to come into her life at this time. She and Sonny had bonded quickly.

Jim had called Sonny almost every day from various cities in the Far East. Their telephone conversations were short, sometimes just a few minutes long. Jim could feel the emotional distance growing between he and his wife. He was becoming more depressed and anxious. He had hoped that the time away from each other would be healing for both of them. He didn't want to live without Sonny. He couldn't wait for this business trip to end in March so that he could return home and be with her again. Sonny did her best to be polite, but affection and warmth never came through during their telephone talks.

Sonny was very proud of her redecorating efforts. She slowly walked around each room, enjoying the fruits of her labor. She couldn't have done it without Mac's help and a considerable amount of money hiring the Cape's most reputable tradesmen. She had remodeled the entire kitchen so that it reflected a modern appearance. The new appliances blended in well with her design. There were polished granite counters installed. New oak cabinets and cranberry colored wainscoting surrounded the eating area. Delicate brass chandeliers were hung, and new ceramic tiled floors were installed. Light pastel paint and cheery wallpaper helped improve the color and brightness in all of the rooms. The home was now a place in which to enjoy and to live comfortably.

Now, Sonny wanted to show off the merits of her good work to someone who would appreciate it beyond her and Mac. The transformation of the Brooks' home should be shared with someone other than just herself. She wanted to celebrate her completed project with someone. She needed to invite a guest to visit her. After giving it some thought, she knew exactly who the person would be who would understand her pride. Sonny telephoned St. Ann's rectory.

"Yes," Christine said. "I just checked and Father Donovan could come over for dinner during the evening of February 8th."

***

The snow was coming down heavily that evening around 6pm. The temperature was dropping quickly as an enormous low-pressure area was heading up the eastern coast of the United States.

"Tom, why don't you park your car in the garage, we're supposed to get a little more snow tonight, and you won't have to brush off your car later."

Tom pulled the car into garage, shut the doors and ran towards the house using the backdoor entrance.

"I haven't heard any weather reports, Sonny. I've been at meetings most of the day. Are we supposed to get much?" asked Tom, stomping the remaining loose snow off from his shoes in the back door hallway entrance.

"I'm not sure," replied Sonny.

She lied. She purposely did not tell him about the latest forecast. She wanted nothing to spoil the evening that she had planned for the two of them.

Earlier, the Boston meteorologist on Channel 7 was referring to this snowstorm as "The Blizzard of '78". He cautioned viewers that Cape Cod would face the brunt of this "monster" storm. The National Weather Service reports were indicating that this storm could turn out to be the worst snow blizzard of the century.

Sonny helped him take off his coat and hung it up. She admired the way he looked in his casual clothes. He was dressed neatly in a woolen, sport shirt with a subdued plaid pattern and navy-blue colored slacks.

Sonny had given Mac the rest of the day off after she had earlier shopped for groceries, wine, liquor, and pastries. This was going to be one event that Sonny planned, prepared and served completely by herself. Sonny was capable of some very good gourmet cooking. When she was younger she spent a lot of time in the kitchen with the family chef, Francois. At times, while her brother Jared was away at college, Francois was the only one in her house who she could really talk with. While they talked he gave her some good cooking lessons.

She was noticeably excited when she gave Tom a tour of the redecorated house, room by room. She was a little embarrassed after pausing for a minute. She couldn't believe how much pride she felt in her work as she described each component of the remodeling effort.

Tom could sense it too. She seemed happier now and it showed. It was probably the first undertaking that Sonny had done by herself in her entire life. It was no wonder that she felt so happy. She thought that the best part was showing off her work to her old friend and new friend, The Reverend Tom Donovan.

Sonny had Tom relax in the love seat near the fireplace. She served cocktails and appetizers of avocado and crabmeat-filled mushroom caps, sprinkled with Beluga caviar. She enjoyed entertaining people who really appreciated it. Tom was one of those people.

This visit on the snowy evening was very different from their previous encounter. Both Sonny and Tom were much more relaxed. The initial sharp edge of reuniting with each other had now become smooth. Sonny felt better now that Tom knew of her marital stress and he didn't think any less of her.

After a delicious gourmet dinner and a bottle of wine, Sonny cleared the table while Tom refueled the fireplace with dried maple logs so that a beautiful hot roaring fire illuminated the dimly lit room. It was a relaxing time for Tom. He had never enjoyed such an evening of Epicurean delights and comfortable amenities. As he relaxed, he thought to himself that it was good once in a while to sample and to appreciate the finer things in life. While Sonny was in the kitchen, Tom's mind began to wander and to reminisce about his times with her so many years ago. He knew that he had better leave this house and get back to the rectory.

"I poured us a couple of brandies to enjoy by the fire," said Sonny carrying two snifters into the room.

Tom turned towards her as she slowly walked into the room. The trip back to the rectory could wait a little longer.

They talked again for a while about where their lives had taken them from their high school days. Sonny was interested in Tom's Canadian experiences at Prince Edward Island. Tom wanted to hear all about her campus experiences at Wellesley and her year abroad in

France. The conversation was light; yet interesting, for both of them.

During a pause in their conversation, Tom stared at his hostess for a very long minute.

"What is it, Tom?"

"You know Sonny, you haven't changed a bit since high school," he smiled at her.

"Au contraire, *mon ami*. I have changed quite a bit! I am not as shallow as I used to be. I am much better educated. And now I go to church regularly!" replied Sonny in a very animated fashion.

They chuckled and both sipped their brandies.

"I meant the way that you look, Sonny. You are just as beautiful and as fresh as our senior year at Quissett High."

"Thanks, Tom." Sonny stared back at her teenage heartthrob.

Her eyes seemed to be getting a little larger. There was a momentary pause.

"And, my friend, you haven't lost your good looks either. You're still in great physical shape. Do you still swim as often as you did back in the 'good old days'?"

Tom didn't know what to say. Her last remark caught him off guard. He had not thought much about how he looked in the past several years.

He was at a loss for words.

The ringing of the telephone interrupted their first awkward and silent moment. Sonny said that she thought she should answer it, since it was probably Jim and he would only keep calling.

"Excuse me Tom, I'll be right back. Help yourself to more brandy."

As Sonny left the room, Tom heard the wind howling outside. He had forgotten about the snowstorm. He stood up and walked toward the large picture window facing the road. He looked outside but couldn't see or recognize anything. The snow was falling so rapidly that it created what is known as "white-out conditions". There was no visibility. There had to be at least twelve inches on the ground already.

As Tom walked over to the closet to get his coat and gloves,

Sonny walked slowly back into the room. Tom turned and stopped what he was doing. He was surprised to see the tears rolling down her face. His heart sank. In all of the years that he had known and had loved Sonny, he never knew her to feel pain. He had never before seen her cry. For the first time in his life, he saw her vulnerability. She picked up her snifter of brandy and walked toward the fireplace. She sipped from it and then put it on the mantel. Tom walked over to her.

"I, ..I...I'm sorry." Sonny sobbed, shaking her head back and forth and turned towards Tom.

"Don't say anything, Sonny," as he took her into his arms and hugged her gently but firmly.

They stood together like this for a while and then Tom began to pull Sonny's body closer and tighter with his own. He could feel her teardrops fall on his plaid shirt. After a very long and warm embrace, Sonny looked up at Tom, and whispered softly into Tom's ear.

"It feels so good to be in your arms again, Tom. You have no idea how good this feels to me."

Tom's heart was racing faster. His chest hadn't pounded like this in a very long time. He didn't know what to do. He didn't know what to say. His mind was spinning much too fast. He felt weak in his legs and knees. Something was happening to him that had not happened to him in years. He mumbled something about how happy he was to be with her. He was happy that he could console her. He wasn't even sure what he was saying to her. He just spoke softly and closed his eyes. Nothing was making sense to him as his body began to slightly quiver.

Sonny looked up again at Tom's face. She could feel his tense, hard body. She looked deep into his eyes for a long quiet minute. Then she reached up and gently stroked his face. She brought her lips up to his. The kiss was gentle at first, exploring and revisiting the sweet taste of each other. The second kiss was more passionate, more meaningful, more like the heated hunger of old times.

Sonny remembered what Tom had said to her that day at the rectory. If she needed him she should reach out her hand to him.

As they embraced in their kiss, she slid her hand from his face and slowly caressed his inner thigh. She could feel Toms' reaction and she slowly and lightly gave him her hand.

That evening, Sonny never felt Jared's spirit in her brother's former bedroom. She wasn't connecting with the light vibrations of the spiritual dimension. Everything was earthly, dense and physical. She didn't feel Jared's presence at all, even though they were lying in his old bed. She could feel only Tom. She felt him many times that night of the blizzard. She felt every inch of him return to her after so many years of being away.

***

It took several days for the Town of Falmouth road crews to clear the roads from the 32 inches of snow that fell from the "Blizzard of '78". Quissett was one of the last villages to have its roads plowed. Tom had stayed with Sonny at the Brooks' home for three uninterrupted days. They had become friends and lovers much like they were at 18 years of age. But it was different now that they had some maturity, food, liquor, a warm fire, and a bedroom that they could share.

Tom had never been happier in his life. He had disconnected all thought and energy about his life as a priest. He didn't even think about it since his mind and his heart were filled only with his love for Sonny Brooks. There was no room for anything else at all.

He was realizing a fantasy that he had harbored since he was a junior in high school. During that time, he had often envisioned himself married to Sonny, living a life of romance, love and children. Tom loved children and wanted to have lots of kids with the love of his life, Sonny. Sonny Brooks Donovan. Tom always loved the sound of that name.

Sonny was equally happy. Tom had recharged an energy in her that had died long ago. She felt fulfilled. She was happy. She enjoyed having Tom live with her. He was easy to look at, a joy to make love with, and was honest in everything he said and did.

When things returned to normal after the storm, Tom had to return to his solitary room at the rectory. It was a time for the two of them to think independently and evaluate who they were, as individuals, and as a couple. The task was daunting given the circumstances. At times, Sonny thought that she knew exactly what she wanted and then vacillated to tears in a mild state of confusion. They both agreed that it would take some time. Tom continued to see Sonny after the snowstorm. He was more certain of his convictions and what he wanted to do with his life. The rest of his life should be lived with Sonny.

***

A week later, Sonny received an unexpected phone call from the Westcott home in Marblehead. It was her father-in-law, Jack Westcott, on the other end of the line. She could hear the shaking anxiety and concern in his voice.

"Sonny! Hello, this is Jack ....Jack Westcott."

"Yes, Jack what is it?" asked a surprised Sonny.

"Sonny, I have some bad news. Jim's mother, Jessica, has had a massive heart attack. She is resting comfortably now at the hospital. I think that she is going to be all right, but I must admit, I am really nervous. She is still in the intensive care unit. I've been with her around the clock."

"God, Jack, I am so sorry. Is there anything that I can do?"

"Well, to be honest, that is why I am calling. I had asked her this morning if she was up to seeing the children, even for a brief time."

"Yes?"

"She said that the only person besides me who she wanted to see, was you, for now. I hate to impose upon you, Sonny. I understand that you have some family obligations but do you think that you could take a run up to the Boston General Hospital and pay her a visit?"

"Ah....of course Jack, of course. Let me get some things together down here and I will come up."

"Thanks, Sonny. Jessica will be happy when I tell her that you're coming to see her."

Later that evening Tom stopped by to see Sonny. He was not shy anymore about pulling up into her driveway, opening the garage door and driving inside. After a brief kiss, Tom looked at Sonny and he quickly knew something was different.

"What's up, Sonny?"

She explained the phone call from Marblehead. She told Tom how surprised she was with the call since she hardly knew her father-in-law. She was more astonished to learn that her mother-in-law, Jessica, wanted to see her now while she was in the hospital.

"Why me? Why see *me* before seeing her own children? For God's sake the woman is dying and she wants to see me before seeing any of her own family. It doesn't make sense!"

"Sonny, is she aware of the troubles that you and Jim are going through?" Tom asked somewhat shyly.

Sonny shrugged her shoulders. "I don't know. I don't think that I will be gone long, Tom, but I am not sure. I am not even sure what Jessica wants to talk to me about."

"Can you call me from there, Sonny? I am going to miss you so much."

"Sure, sweetheart." She gave him a gentle kiss on his lips. "But first, let's have a proper goodbye."

It was upstairs in Jared's old bedroom, which had been their love nest for these past few weeks, where Tom opened up his entire heart to Sonny. As they lay there in a relaxed exhaustion, after two heated acts of lovemaking, Tom asked for Sonny's attention.

"Sonny, I love you. I love you as much as life itself. I now realize that I had never stopped loving you. There has never been anyone else in my life. I want to marry you just as I wanted to do several years ago. I now know that I made a mistake in becoming a priest. This vocation was only an escape from the pain that I felt from not being able to have you as my wife. I have used the vocation rather than have tried to follow it."

"Tom, please...I don't want us to rush....."

"I am not rushing, Sonny, in fact, this is long overdue."

"But Tom, we have so much to think about."

"And I will do that thinking while you are up in Boston."

She nodded her approval. She turned to him once again. He pulled her into his arms.

"Sonny, I have never been so happy in all of my life. I really believe that God has answered all of my unspoken prayers."

CHAPTER TEN
Truth and Consequences

Sonny walked apprehensively through the main entrance of the Boston General Hospital. She approached the receptionist station to learn where to find her ailing mother-in-law. As she skirted around moving gurneys, nurses and doctors dressed in sea-foam green scrubs, she thought about Jessica Westcott. She had never been comfortable with Jim's mother. They had very little in common and Sonny always felt that Jessica was disappointed with her son's choice for his bride. With retrospect, Sonny thought, she was probably right. The two women saw each other only on holidays or obligatory special occasions. She thought back to the recent Christmas dinner at her Marblehead home. That was not an especially good time for any of them. Sonny could not imagine why Jessica wanted to have Sonny by her bedside, especially now that she could be close to death.

"Hello Jessica," said Sonny as she entered the hospital room.

Jessica Westcott had two drip bags hanging from a pole which fed into her body. She slowly turned a very pale face towards Sonny as she entered the room. She managed to wave an arm up slowly as Sonny began taking off her gloves, scarf and overcoat. After some gentle, polite chatting, Jessica got right to the point of why she wanted to see Sonny alone. She asked that her daughter-in-law sit on the chair close to the bed.

"Sonny, I know that you and James are going through some

rough waters right now. I know that your marriage isn't as smooth as when your relationship first began." Her voice was weak but her words were direct.

"Most marriages have problems and regrettably people leave one another too quickly when it would be better for them to be patient and work things out."

"Oh Jessica....." Sonny started to interrupt.

"No, Sonny. Now please listen to me!" Jessica weakly held up her hand. "I just want you to know that I will support James *and you* in whatever you two do. But please listen to me....I also want you to know that as an old woman, I have learned a thing or two."

"Come on Jessica, you're still a young woman." Sonny politely patronized her.

"I may not be an old woman, but I am an 'old soul.' My spirit has been around for a long time, if you know what that means. I know that we are here on earth for a purpose. Most times we aren't sure what that purpose is."

"Where are you going with this Jessica?" Sonny frowned. She was a little uneasy.

"I think that you should reconsider your relationship with my son James. He may not be what your ideal is, but he is a very loving person and you can learn about love from him. Oh, I know that he gets hung up on his business, but you will find that he is still a very loving, selfless and serving person. Listen to me. James is a very special man. There is something very different about him from most of us here on earth. More than you know now. If you stay with him, you will find out what I am talking about. He is not like my other children. He is not like most children."

"Jessica, this is awkward. Jim and I haven't even ...."

"This old soul knows what is going on Sonny. And I know that he will always be good *to* you and—be good *for* you. He will provide you with something that you may never find in others. He has a special gift of healing powers that most people don't know about, except me."

"What are you talking about?"

"If you stay with him you will know. He helps people with their problems. He makes pain go away. His heart is always open. He is very slow to anger if ever at all."

"Well, Jim is due back soon, and I am anxious to talk to him," responded Sonny.

"He will forgive you your sins Sonny and he will never judge you. He has unconditional love for you as he does for others. You won't find many people in this life who remember that simple golden rule."

Sonny briefly thought of her brother, Jared, telling her that same message so many years ago at the cottage on Nantucket Island. She left the hospital thinking about Jessica. That visit and conversation was the most bizarre discussion she had ever had with that woman, or anyone else for that matter. She thought about what Jessica had said to her and then she thought about her husband in a different way.

A week later, in mid-March, Sonny greeted Jim's return to their Boston home more warmly and sincerely than she had planned. Jim looked good to her. He was well tanned from the heat and sun of the Far East tour. He had lost some weight that made him look more lean and athletic. For a moment she actually felt as though she genuinely missed Jim. Their reunion was much better than she expected. It was not as awkward as she had anguished about.

Jim was so happy to learn that his wife had made hospital visits to see his ailing mother. It meant a lot to him and to his father. Sonny gave of herself the best she could on Jim's arrival. She tried not to let her mind drift. She tried to be upbeat. She tried not to worry. She tried to focus on her husband and on his needs. She knew that she would feel more relaxed tomorrow— after she learned the results of her pregnancy test.

***

It was a cold and rainy evening when Jim's mother had passed. Even though it was expected, it was still difficult for Jim to accept.

Jim had to console his father but he also had personal troubles of his own that he needed to address. Things weren't right in his own personal life.

Since his return home, his wife had been extremely nervous. She never sat still. Her mind wandered. She was not focused. Her responses to him were only superficial. She was not happy. She had something to say and now Jim had to hear what that was. He could not or would not go on living like this.

As they returned home from Jessica's funeral, Jim had decided that they needed to talk. They had to talk about their future — the future of their marriage. Sonny had been only acting like a wife these past couple of weeks. And her acting wasn't that good. She was not being open with Jim. He now was determined to find out exactly what the problem was so that they could begin a healing process.

They decided to talk in their kitchen's breakfast nook that overlooked Boston's famous Beacon Street. Jim was very direct in asking Sonny why she had been acting so strange in the last few weeks.

"Jim, I have something terribly important to tell you. It can't wait any longer."

Sonny put her head down looking straight at the floor then slowly lifted her tear filled eyes up towards her husband.

"Jim, I'm pregnant."

There was no other way to candy coat this news and Sonny wanted to get this night over as quickly as she could. She had tears rolling down her cheeks.

"I know that you will want a divorce and I will grant it as soon as you want. I had an affair while you were gone and now I am carrying another man's child."

Jim looked at her, in a controlled, but sad, way. It appeared that he was not as shocked as Sonny expected. There was a long silence. She looked across the kitchen table at her husband. He showed no emotion at all. Sonny expected an explosive reaction any time now after she disclosed the news to him. Instead, Jim surprised her when he reached over the table and held her hands in his. He then sincerely asked his wife just one question.

"Sonny, are you feeling OK? I mean physically, are you doing OK?"

Sonny was completely taken off guard with Jim's reaction. She expected rage; perhaps some violent yelling and screaming as any husband would upon learning of his wife's infidelity and resulting pregnancy.

She didn't know why, but she stood up and ran into his arms sobbing. He held her warmly. She could feel his love for her. She could sense no anger or hatred. She sobbed for several minutes. She somehow felt that all of her anxiety that she had held within her was now absorbed by Jim and discarded. They didn't talk much that late evening. They were both tired and needed sleep. Jim knew that it was best to wait until the next morning

The next morning brought bright sunlight through their bedroom window as they both lay under the bedcovers. They looked out through the windows but said nothing. The first signs of new life were growing with the flowers and trees budding. Young baby squirrels were chasing each other and running about in the street below. The grass had begun to turn its vibrant, green color. The sweet smell of spring was coming through the narrowly opened windows. Spring was a harbinger of new things to come and of new life to be brought into this world. New life is a time for celebration. New life is precious. It is the time for people to come together and to join hands with happy expectation. Spring is a time to start over again. It is a time for renewal.

"Are you in love with him?" Jim asked, breaking the silence as they remained in bed looking up at the bedroom ceiling.

"I don't think so. No. I think now that it was all a total mistake. I was just overreacting to the news at Christmas time and feeling deeply sorry for myself."

"Does he know that you are pregnant?" again questioned Jim.

"No, not at all, I haven't spoken to him in a while."

Sonny felt that she should tell Jim the entire story from the teenage romance through the surprising priesthood, and culminating with the "Blizzard of '78". It was during those three days, taking refuge from the snowstorm, that the conception took place.

As she told the story, she inwardly questioned herself about any deep feelings she might have for Tom Donovan. She again wasn't sure that she loved him. Perhaps it was always and only a physical attraction. She felt terribly confused. There was a deep-seated guilt that she had misled Tom once again and she wasn't sure how she would confront him with the news.

There was a long and poignant silence.

"Sonny, I want you to think about something." Jim broke the silence again.

"Jim, I will do whatever you want. You have been the innocent one through all of this. Everything is my fault."

"Sonny, I would like nothing more than to parent and love this child who is growing inside of you now. As you and I are so grimly aware, I am unable to give you our own child. God has given me that challenge and pain to overcome in my life."

"Jim..."

"Sonny, I believe that this child is a gift for you and me. A gift from God. We can love it for the rest of our lives. We can give it the best life possible. But there are two conditions on which I must ask your absolute agreement for the rest of our lives".

Sonny was weeping. "And they are?"

"First we must agree to never let Tom Donovan know that he has fathered a child with you."

There was another period of silence. Sonny was thinking quickly.

"That is not a problem," said Sonny. "And the second condition?"

"We must agree to never, never, let our child know that I am not the biological father. He or she should never know about being conceived out of wedlock."

Sonny gave a lot of thought to the situation. She also now recalled her conversation with Jessica Westcott. Jim's mother was right. She could now see a character and a gift within Jim that was formerly unknown to her. He was forgiving and he had a healing presence. His love overcame any anger. He did not judge her actions. She felt that her life was changing yet again. Jim Westcott truly loved her. He loved her unconditionally.

They got out of bed and began a new life together and with the new life growing inside of Sonny. She was getting what she wanted. She was having it her way. She would still be married to one of the most influential men in the world's business community and she would continue the Brooks bloodline with the birth of this new child. She considered herself saved and blessed all at once.

After breakfast, as they were washing the dishes at the sink, Sonny asked Jim to listen to her once again.

"I have some requests of my own that we must agree upon," said Sonny.

She walked over to him, reached up, and draped her arms lovingly around Jim's shoulders.

"And what are they?" smiled her husband.

"I want us to live in Quissett full time. It will give you more time to spend with *our child* and give you more distance from your business."

"All right. OK. Not easy, but I am willing to do it. What else?" asked Jim.

"If it's a boy, I want to name him —Jared . After my dear brother."

"OK. But if it's a girl, I want her to be named.... Jessica, after my mother."

Sonny and Jim were happy once again. They had created a bond that Sonny thought impossible. She was happy. She was a wife once again. She would soon become a mother. She would continue the Brooks lineage. She would be living in Quissett. She would do it for her deceased brother, Jared. She really hoped that her unborn child would be a boy.

There were lots of things for her to do. She had to design another room at the Quissett home to be the baby's nursery. She had to buy baby furniture. She had to pick out baby clothes. She had to find an obstetrician down on the Cape. And she had to do one more thing. She had to tell Tom Donovan that it was over between them. Again.

***

She had to do it over the phone. She just couldn't bear to see him face to face. It was cruel and heartless, but Sonny would do it. She rationalized to herself that it was the best thing for Tom. He now could return to his vocation as a priest and help so many others who needed his guidance and good heart. Late on that Sunday evening, Sonny telephoned Father Tom Donovan at St. Ann's rectory.

"Tom, I'm sorry to tell you this over the phone. This is very, very difficult for me."

She had explained to Tom that Jim and she had reconciled. They were working hard on restoring their marriage. She needed Tom to understand this and to support their reconciliation.

She wept, "Tom, do you remember me telling you that I wished that there was something that would bring Jim and me closer together?"

"But what about us, Sonny, I can't believe this! I love you! Don't you understand? I love you more than life itself!"

"Tom. Please try to understand. Please listen to me. There is something else that I have to tell you. I am three and a half months pregnant," she lied.

There was a long pause.

"What?" responded Tom incredulously.

"Listen Tom. Jim and I had conceived on the night that he left for the Far East. I am expecting a baby. I didn't know this when you and I were together in Quissett. I couldn't have known"

The lie rolled off of her tongue much easier than she had thought it would. She was breathing more steady now. Her work was done.

Father Tom Donovan cried out loud. His world of love and

renewed life had just come crashing down all around him. Everything that he wanted in life was taken away in just a few minutes. He went through this at the age of eighteen and now had to relive it all over again. This time the hurt was deep. This wound could not heal. He never felt so alone in his life before. Nobody would understand him. His heart stopped its normal beating. His mind was swimming out of control.

He reluctantly wished her well and hung up the phone, sobbing and getting nauseous. He looked down at the words he had earlier typed on St. Ann's letterhead. It was addressed to the Archbishop of the Fall River Diocese. This was the letter that would free him from the chains of his vocation and enable him to marry the woman whom he loved so much.

***

The next morning, Christine Stanton, the secretary for St. Ann's rectory, arrived at work a little early. This was her typical routine on Mondays since there were always extra administrative tasks to be done. There were the letters to be opened, the weekend phone messages to be called, and the bank deposits to be made from the Sunday collections.

At 9 o'clock, Christine thought it unusual that Father Tom was not down from his bedroom. Perhaps he had overslept, and so she yelled up to him. After no response, she went upstairs. She knocked on his bedroom door and slowly looked into his room. She then saw him propped up in his in bed with his eyes closed. She also saw the empty vial of prescription pills and the tipped over liquor bottle.

She quickly ran to him. He was passed out in bed. She felt his wrist. His pulse was hardly discernible. She called the emergency number 911 for immediate help.

Before the EMT crew arrived, Christine had picked up the room a bit. This included Father Tom's letter to the Archbishop. Christine read the letter. Her heart sank as she felt such compassion for the young, handsome curate. Some of the typed words on Father

Tom's letter were smudged from his own teardrop stains. Christine quickly reacted. She felt that there was no need for everyone to know about the young curate's personal troubles. As she heard the emergency crew climbing the staircase, she slipped the letter down the front of her dress.

The emergency technicians kept Father Tom Donovan alive. They desperately wanted to save this poor young priest. Whatever his troubles were they did not merit taking his life. If they could save him now, he would eventually recover and be able to resume the rest of his life.

The rest of his life, however, would not take place at the village of Quissett. For the next twenty years Tom would live at the Home for Lost Angels sanitarium. This was a well-respected rehabilitation hospital for troubled priests and nuns, located in the state of Vermont.

CHAPTER ELEVEN

Friends — Imaginary and Real

Jared Thomas Westcott enjoyed the long, sunny, summer days at Chapoquoit Beach. For a five-year-old boy, the beach is the biggest playground in the world. This particular soft, sandy, beach skirts the northwestern coast of Quissett. It is most popular because of its tidal pools for youngsters. It has clean, clear salt water warmed by the Gulf Stream coming into Buzzards Bay. Jared loved to play with the other children in the sand, and by the edge of the salty water.

Jared's mother, Sonny, often asked that Mac take him to the beach. Jared would insist on staying all day at the shore and that was too long for his mother. She was very active in community organizations and conservation committees around Falmouth and the village of Quissett. Mac would make sure that all of the toys would be packed along with the beach umbrella and an ice cooler filled with lunch, cold drinks and snacks.

Mac had become Jared's nanny ever since his birth on that cold November evening in 1978. She was the only person who was with Sonny during her son's birth, since Jim had been away on business. Sonny went into labor earlier than expected. Mac drove her to the hospital and stayed by her side.

Mac was much more than just the Westcott nanny. She was truly the "Gal Friday" for both Sonny and Jim. She was pleasant, energetic, and often served many roles for the family. She was invited to move into the Westcott house a few months before Jared was born. She had remained living there since that time. She was an extended member of the family. She was always included in all of the family functions. She worked hard. She loved the family. She was especially close to her beloved Jared.

As Jared ran long the Chapoquoit shore, or waded in the shallow water, Mac always kept a watchful eye on him. Occasionally, he would run up to her laying on the chaise lounge under the bright colored beach umbrella. He would want to dry off his shivering young body, or get a snack or just talk.

"Mac. Guess what? My friend is helping me to build a big, big sand castle," said Jared as he extended his arms as wide as he could to show the size of the proposed sandcastle.

"Really! That's great, buddy! And who is this friend of yours, Jared? I haven't seen anybody else with you today," Mac replied.

"Oh, you can't see my friend. My friend is invisible."

"Ah....ha. I see. And tell me Jared, what is your invisible friend's name?"

"Hmmmm..... I don't know. I never asked," replied Jared.

"OK," laughed Mac. "Now you and your invisible friend do a great job building that big sand-castle."

"I am serious, Mac. I have an invisible friend." Jared then ran off to the water's edge.

A sunbathing woman on a nearby blanket had overheard the conversation. She lifted up her head and spoke to Mac.

"Aren't these kids something with their imaginations?" "If it isn't their invisible friends, then it's their invisible pets. Mine went through that stage at about the same age as him," she said.

"Yeah.... their imaginations are something, " smiled Mac. "I guess if the kids can't have friends in the flesh, they make them up."

Mac was staring at Jared sitting on the sandy beach just a few yards in from the water. He was such a cute and precocious little boy. It was amusing to watch him chat with his invisible friend while making sand castles.

This new activity, however, was uncharacteristic for Jared, Mac thought. Jared was always such a serious little boy. Everything he did or said came from facts or real experiences that he had encountered. Everything he did had a reason; everything had a purpose. He had never been interested in cartoons or other entertainment programs for kids shown on television. He would much rather enjoy listening to serious stories to be read to him. He enjoyed science and nature. He was obsessed with the US space exploration program since turning the ripe old age of five. Everything had to be precise and truthful. As a young preschooler, he had limited patience or interest for anything else.

Ever since that day on the beach, Jared often referred to his invisible friend with Mac. He also mentioned the friend to his parents. This routine continued for almost a year. He once told Mac that the friend was always with him and that the two of them enjoyed each other very much. The friend was in the house; out in the yard, at the playground, in Jared's bedroom and everywhere else.

Mac went along with Jared's new phase for a while. But she never encouraged this type of behavior. She would listen, perhaps nod her head in agreement, smile, and then let it go. It soon became evident to Jared that he was not convincing Mac, or his mother and father, about his invisible friend. He eventually dropped any reference to his invisible friend as he sensed the disinterest or perhaps disbelief of the adults.

Jared was an unusual young lad compared to his peers. He would spend many hours alone thinking. Jared was a thinker. Often he would then approach Mac, or his parents with a barrage of questions relevant to what he had been thinking about. It was fun for the others to watch him while he was in this deep state of rumination. He also developed a quirky habit while he was in private thought. While he was concentrating about something, he would lightly tug and pull at his left eyebrow with his thumb and index finger.

His mother, Sonny, remembered so well this same habit of years ago. It was her deceased brother, Jared, who had the very same habit. Sonny thought it was uncanny. She never heard or read that physical habits such as this were genetically passed on as hereditary traits.

Mac not only served as Jared's nanny, but she also acted as his playmate when other kids weren't around. She taught him how to catch a ball, fly a kite, hammer a nail, and ride a bike when his father had to be away on his frequent business trips. They were real buddies, as Mac had told him more than once.

One warm, sunny, Indian summer, autumn afternoon, Mac and Jared went to the beach to play kick ball. He had just come home from his first grade class at school and wanted to run off some steam before it got dark outside.

Mac enjoyed outdoor activities with Jared since it gave her an opportunity for some fresh air and physical exercise. Besides, she had such a soft spot for Jared that she would do just about anything he asked her to do. Playing sports with him was right down her alley.

During this particular afternoon, he happened to kick the soccer ball so hard that it flew high over the jetty rocks and curved over to the adjacent sandy beach.

"Go get it! But be careful, Jared," Mac yelled out.

"I will," said Jared as he ran off to retrieve the ball.

When Jared jumped over the rocks to look for the ball, he peered all around. At first he couldn't locate it. He then methodically visualized the path and flight of the ball and tried to determine where it should have landed. When he looked at where it should have gone, he saw a woman, sitting on the sand with her back against the sea wall. Jared's ball was in her hands resting on her skirt. Apparently it had rolled and bounced directly towards her.

Jared slowly walked in the sand and cautiously approached the woman. He stared at her face. She was very beautiful in the young boy's eyes. She had long auburn hair. She wore a pretty skirt that matched the colors of the scarf around her neck. She had not seen Jared approaching since she had a fixed gaze out at the quiet, calm Buzzards Bay.

"Hello. My name is Jared," he said as he bent down to look at her.

When the pretty woman looked up at him, Jared saw that she had been crying earlier. Her eyes were watery and there were some tears still drying on her face.

"Well, hello there, Jared. My name is Paula." She forced a brief, fleeting smile.

"Are you sick or something? It looks like you were crying."

"No..no, I am not sick. Thank you." She managed a grin for the young visitor.

"Well did you lose your dog or something?"

"No, no I don't have a dog. I just got some sad news today. And now I have to go home to tell my husband this sad news. But I will be all right."

"Oh, I am sorry to hear that. Nobody likes sad news."

"I will be all right. You need not worry. How old are you Jared?"

"Six years old. I am in the first grade."

"Well, you a very bright boy for such a young age."

"Do you and your husband have any children of your own?"

"No, ...no I am afraid not." She replied, staring out at the bright, white lighthouse in Buzzards Bay known as Cleveland Ledge.

"There aren't many kids around this section of town. That's my nanny, Mac, over there," he said, pointing out over the jetty rocks.

"Ah, yes, I see her," replied Paula shading her eyes from the setting sun.

"She plays with me a lot since there are no little kids in my neighborhood."

"Well, that's unfortunate that there are no other children your age near your home. Children are such a gift. "

"A gift?" Jared had a puzzled look.

"Yes, a gift of life. Your parents must be very happy that you came into their lives."

"I don't know. I mean they love me and all that so.... I guess they are happy."

"Yes...I am sure they are," replied Paula.

"Paula or ah...ma'am, why don't you have any gifts? I mean kids?"

"Well that is a very long story."

"Would you like to have kids?"

"Why yes, I certainly would Jared." She looked up at him.

"Do you know where you can go and get a baby? I do."

""Where is that Jared?"

"Just go up to the hospital. That's where they keep them. Everyone that I know who has a baby went to the hospital to get one."

"Oh...really? Is that so?" She smiled warmly at him.

"Yup. Ummm. Now. Can I ask you just one more question?"

"Sure, Jared but just one more."

"Can I have my soccer ball back please?"

"Of course." Jared took the ball from Mrs. Parker.

"Well, I got to go now. Mac is waiting for me."

"It was nice meeting you Jared."

"Yeah, maybe we'll meet again."

"I hope so," responded the pretty woman.

Jared would meet this pretty woman again several years later but neither he nor she would recall their first encounter at Chapoquoit beach. Five years later, Jared would be sitting in a front row desk of Mrs. Parker's sixth grade classroom.

* * *

Even though Jared thought that his sixth grade teacher, Mrs. Parker, was beautiful, he had a more serious heart-felt crush on one of his classmates. This girl looked nothing like his teacher. This girl had something that Jared couldn't quite define. There was a special pre-adolescent electricity and chemistry that they had between them.

Melinda Abandando was a slightly chubby twelve-year-old. Her dark toned skin accented her black silky hair. She always had a big smile. She wore thick, dark rimmed eyeglasses and each day her hair was done up in bouncing twin ponytails. Often she had bows in her hair that matched her dress.

Melinda and Jared were the brightest kids in the sixth grade class. Either of them would alternately win the school spelling bees and other scholastic contests. They excelled in every assignment that Mrs. Parker gave to them. Paula Parker had conferred with the Westcott and Abandando parents on separate occasions about their abilities. She had asked their approval to give them advance independent courses at the seventh and eighth grade level.

Soon after, they began taking the advanced mathematics programmed modules and did well. They both began speaking Spanish fluently midway through the school year.

As the academic year went on, Mrs. Parker had a difficult time keeping these two students interested and challenged in the daily subjects. She knew, as a teacher, it was not unusual to have one student in a class of twenty-five who excels academically. But having two students with this intellectual caliber in the same class was considered extraordinary.

In addition, both of them were always willing to help their classmates get ahead. They would tutor the others whenever they had free time. They freely shared with the other children who were academically less gifted.

Mrs. Parker had never seen two students quite like Melinda and Jared. When she talked about them among the other school faculty, she referred to them as her "junior teaching assistants". They each had an air of maturity that was unusual for children of that age. They both showed poise and a natural presence when in the company of adults.

Jared also showed tremendous patience with the other, slower classmates. He was especially good with one boy who had a noticeable learning disability. Jared would read to him, or patiently teach him simple math. Mrs. Parker noticed that the student improved, not just in these subjects, but more importantly, in his own self esteem.

Mrs. Parker had taught hundreds of students, and she would teach hundreds more, but the likes of Melinda Abandando and Jared Westcott would never fade from her memory.

It was also quite evident that Melinda had a romantic crush on Jared. As the year went on, Melinda could be found staring at Jared for long periods of time. He felt the same way about her but always tried to remain as reserved as a twelve-year old boy could. They were special children. The two of them were not anxious with each other and seemed to get along well with each other. Mrs. Parker could sense the youthful, puppy love developing between them. She enjoyed coming to class each day to see how the 'student romance' was progressing.

Mrs. Parker knew however, that Melinda and Jared's future as academic companions was not going to last long. Mrs. Sonny Westcott had told Paula on several occasions that her son, Jared, would not continue in the public school system beyond that year. Sonny was sure that Jared would do much better in a private prep school. After all, he was definitely Ivy League material, just like her brother and namesake uncle, Jared Brooks.

When Melinda and Jared graduated from the sixth grade, they didn't know it at that time, but it would be almost ten years before they would see each other again. It would be through Mrs. Paula Parker that they would again meet. The circumstances, however, would not be nearly as pleasant.

CHAPTER TWELVE

Reunion

The long lines of people were outside of the funeral home waiting to walk by Sam Parker's casket and pay condolences to his popular and lovely wife, and now widow, Paula. It was no surprise that many people had come from the scientific community of Woods Hole, Boston, New York and other parts of New England. There were also many friends, neighbors, and Falmouth townspeople who had worked with Sam on various community committees. They all had come to offer their respect and condolences.

There were hundreds of former students, who had admired and loved their sixth-grade teacher, and her husband. They all remembered Dr. Parker, the man with the wide smile who came to class to speak with them about nature's wonders of the sea. He was the man who took them on those wonderful field trips. They all walked by his casket feeling a sincere loss and heartfelt sorrow for Paula. Most of the former students had to reintroduce themselves to Paula since the years had physically changed their youthful, bright, twelve-year-old faces. It was helpful for Paula to feel all of the love that came through these young people. One particular tall good-looking young man approached her in front of all the baskets of flowers.

"Mrs. Parker. It's me, Jared. Jared Westcott. " He extended his hand. "I am awfully sorry for your loss. He was such a great man."

She hugged him tightly and nervously grasped his hand.

As she stared into the young man' eyes, she had flashbacks of Jared in her classroom several years ago.

"Oh, Jared. Of course I recognize you! Thank you so much for coming."

She then recalled vivid images of Jared in her classroom so many years ago. He was one student whom she could never forget. She had lost track of him and always wanted to know what had happened to him. As she mentally recollected those days with him in school, she also remembered his puppy love romance with another of his sixth grade classmates. She put her arm around Jared and slowly walked away from the casket and towards the group of people sitting respectfully in the funeral parlor.

"Jared, have you met some of your former classmates here tonight?"

"To be honest Mrs. Parker, a lot of us have changed. I really don't recognize any."

"Well, there is one sitting over there who I want you to meet." Paula took Jared's hand and led him to the seats.

"Hello Jared," said the woman, before Paula could make the introduction. She stood up and gave him a light hug. I can see from your expression that you don't remember me. I am Melinda. Melinda Abandando."

Jared couldn't believe his eyes. This beautiful woman who was standing in front of him couldn't possible be the same Melinda whom he knew in the sixth grade. There were no pigtails bobbing up and down. There were no thick, dark rimmed glasses taking up most of her face. The freckles were gone. She was no longer chubby. He felt his face turning warm and he knew that his Adam's apple was moving as he involuntarily took in a gulp of air.

" Ahh...Melinda, yes, yes, how are you?"

As she stood before him, her long black hair cascaded down to her shoulders. She had deep brown eyes and a gorgeous white toothy smile that contrasted against her dark toned skin. She was absolutely beautiful.

They stepped out of the parlor to talk in the hallway. Paula went back to sit in the chair near Sam's casket.

It took Jared the longest time to comprehend that his sixth grade sweetheart had transformed into this gorgeous and attractive adult woman. Staring at her, he was still awestruck at her beauty. After a few minutes of nervous chatting, they both began to feel some familiar ground with each other after all of these years. They returned to the funeral parlor room and spoke briefly with Mrs. Parker. They again gave her their condolences and left the funeral home.

They drove through downtown Falmouth to Betsy's Diner for coffee. It was easy for the two of them to begin telling the stories and experiences that had consumed each of their lives for the past ten years. It seemed incredible that the two of them, now twenty-two years old, had parted after the sixth grade and never crossed paths. They had a lot of ground to cover.

They began telling each other of their most recent activities. Melinda had just graduated from the University of Massachusetts at Amherst, and Jared, was fresh out of Yale in New Haven, Connecticut. They each had followed different directions after their childhood. The years at Exeter prep school and Yale were well planned out by Jared's mother, Sonny. Melinda was grateful to get a substantial scholarship to attend UMASS after graduating from Quissett High School.

After coffee, they left the diner and sat inside of Jared's Volvo station wagon to continue talking. The romantic chemistry that had begun in the sixth grade was quickly reconstituting itself. Although their reunion was created by a sad event, this night had brought to the two of them a new joy and happiness. They both could feel it. Before driving home, they made plans to attend Sam Parker's funeral Mass, scheduled for the following morning, together.

The next morning, as Jared pulled his car up to the Abandando home to pick up Mel, he felt good that he was paying his respects this day *for* someone he had sincerely cared about —*with* someone he had sincerely cared about.

It was a hot, bright May morning. The funeral Mass was well attended by hundreds of people and the eulogies were brief but eloquent. Jared and Melinda walked slowly away from the church reminiscing about their days in Mrs. Parker's class and the fun that they had with her as their teacher.

After leaving the church grounds, and driving back to the Abandando house, Melinda asked Jared if he would like to join her for a day at the beach.

"That would be great, Mel. We could use some relaxation at this point."

"Tell you what Jared. I will pick you up about one-thirty, OK?"

"Great! See you then!"

While Jared was driving his car toward the center of town, he could not restrain the slow, wide smile that was spreading across his face. She looked at him without saying a word and smiled as well.

***

Cape Cod had not yet become crowded. Since the children were still in school this time of year, the family tourists wouldn't arrive for several weeks. The traffic was still manageable, and the beaches were practically vacant. The ferries out of Falmouth and Woods Hole to Martha's Vineyard and to Nantucket carried few passengers during this time of year.

Melinda had arranged to pick up Jared at his family's home. She drove up in her bright, red, new Volkswagen Jetta convertible. The car was a college graduation gift from her proud parents. She was the first Abandando to ever graduate from college. Her Massachusetts license plate was GRAD-00, indicating that she graduated in the year 2000. She had the convertible top turned down. She wanted to show off a little.

They decided to go to Menahuant Beach, which directly faces Vineyard Sound and island of Martha's Vineyard. They had the entire beach to themselves that day. The intense heat of the spring day was slightly cooled by the onshore breezes coming in from the ocean.

It was a pleasant afternoon for the two of them. They spread out a beach blanket and lay down side by side, facing the early afternoon sun. They now experienced a relaxed lightness that balanced off the grief and heavy sadness that they had witnessed for the past twenty-four hours. They talked non-stop. There was never a lull in their conversation. It was almost as though the two of them were twelve-year-old students again in Mrs. Parker's class. Jared looked over at his friend.

"You know, Mel, I feel so good about seeing you after all of these years," beamed Jared with a wide, happy, and boyish smile.

"Me too. You know, Jared, in many ways, you and I haven't changed since our days in elementary school."

"Oh...I don't know about that. You have certainly changed." He stared into Melinda's dark brown eyes.

She stared back at him. She smiled. She got the message. She liked the message.

After the intense sun and heat of the day had warmed their bodies, they decided that it was time to run into the ocean. They knew that the water would be shocking cold this early in the season, but a quick dip would be refreshing.

Melinda unhooked her belt buckle and slowly slid her blue denim shorts down over her long, slim legs. She then reached up and took off her cream-colored tank top. Jared could not believe how beautiful her figure was as she turned towards him revealing her two-piece bathing suit.

She was stunning. At five feet seven inches in height, she stood tall and statuesque. Her figure was full with a tiny waist and there were no soft areas on her taut body. Her naturally dark-toned skin looked as though it was already well tanned. It contrasted with the light, sky-blue color of her bathing suit. Her shiny black hair gave her deep chestnut-brown eyes a sincere, welcoming softness. She looked down at Jared on the blanket and smiled. Her bright toothy smile softened her angular high cheekbones. Her lips were full and inviting.

Jared had taken off his polo shirt and khaki shorts. He held up his hand to Mel for some mock assistance in him getting up off of the blanket. Melinda smiled back at him and pulled him up towards her.

She still remembered his wavy sandy-colored hair from the days together in the sixth grade. But now Jared was more muscular and fit from the rigors of his former collegiate swimming meets. He stood over six feet tall. His back and shoulders were well defined and his biceps were proportioned nicely with the rest of his build.

He maintained his fitness with a disciplined regime of running nearly five miles each day. He was more handsome now than Melinda had remembered him being at twelve years old. He had a strength and beauty about him that not only showed on the outside, but her personal perception could still see through into the warm, inner being of Jared Westcott that was still there.

They both ran into the water giggling when the cold water enveloped their warm flesh. They bravely took a couple of surf dives and then quickly ran back up to the sandy beach shivering. After toweling themselves dry, they laid back down on the blanket to get warm. They finally relaxed quietly without having to say anything. They let the sun warm and dry their bodies. The dip in the ocean was invigorating and it was the ending to a very pleasant afternoon. Later, they folded their blankets and towels and started walking towards Melinda's convertible.

"I promised to help my Mom and Dad out with their fish market business for a few mornings. But next week, I am returning to the Quissett Country Club as a bartender for 5 nights a week."

"Oh, I didn't know that you worked there. I play golf there at times, but I have never spent any evenings there."

"It's a great job. The tips helped me through my college years. In fact, after I start my teaching job at Barnstable High School this year, I think I will still keep it for summertime income."

"I envy you, I am still not certain what I am going to do."

"You had mentioned the possibility of Law School, Jared."

"Oh, I thought a bit about that...But I am still not sure what I want to do."

"Enjoy your summer then and give it some time."

"Well, I do have a summer job, like you, that I really like. I have played guitar in a small band called, 'The Nantucket Sound' for the past few years."

"Cool. I've heard about that band. It plays locally, right?"

"Yeah. Mostly in some Woods Hole taverns and some of the Pocasset clubs."

Melinda smiled. "It looks like you and I have the same working hours for the summer. I don't get out until almost one o'clock in the morning. How about you?"

"Same time, about midnight or twelve-thirty we close down. And then we pack up." Jared smiled at Melinda. She returned his smile with a cute, but seductive, grin.

Melinda drove Jared back to his home. They parked outside of his home and chatted for a while longer.

"Mel, would you like to go out with me for dinner this evening?" asked Jared.

Melinda smiled. "Yes, yes of course. But I have to ask you something first."

"Sure. What is it? Are you a strict vegetarian or something like that?" joked, Jared.

"No, nothing to do with dinner. But I have to ask you something. Are you ashamed to be seen with me driving around in my convertible?"

"Of course not!" replied Jared. He was surprised with the question. "Why ask that?"

"Well, as soon as you got into my car at your house and as we drove all the way to Menahuant, you slouched way down in the front seat. Only the tip of your head barely touched the seat's headrest. Then, on the way back from the beach, as soon as you got into my car, you assumed the same position."

"Oh...I am sorry. I have to tell you something. It is some stupid phobia that I have always had about riding in convertibles. I have been doing this all of my life. Whenever I had to sit in an opened vehicle, I always slouch down. I know its weird but its true." He laughed.

"Really?"

"Yep. See. You are already finding about my most personal flaws."

"Its not a big thing," replied Melinda.

"It has nothing to do with you or being seen with you. I am happy to be with you. Really happy." He reached over and lightly touched her arm.

"Thanks." Mel broke out with a wide smile. "I can be ready by eight o'clock."

CHAPTER THIRTEEN

Bonding Again

Jared took Mel to the 'Nimrod' restaurant in Falmouth that evening. This dining facility was well known for its excellent food. It also had some interesting history to it since part of the building had sustained a canon ball shot from the War of 1812. The history of the house was described in an old newspaper clipping that hung on the wall. It made for interesting reading while customers awaited a table.

As they ate, they enjoyed reliving their childhood days in Quissett and filled each other in on what some of their mutual acquaintances were doing. At ten o'clock they realized that the restaurant staff was waiting for them to leave so that they could clean up and go home. After finishing off their coffees, Jared looked over at Mel without saying a word. Her face looked so beautiful. Her high cheekbones reflected the dim light from the flickering candle on the dining table. He reached across and lightly touched her hand and put it inside of his.

"Mel, would you like to go to he Knob with me tonight?"

"I don't know, Jared, aren't we a little late to see the sunset?" she joked. "That's why people walk out there—for the pretty sky, the sunset and the view." She smiled somewhat coyly.

"Well, those are the reasons that most people go out there."

"Yeah...So why....??"

"Come on," he said as he grabbed her hand and they quickly left the Nimrod.

Jared drove out of the restaurant parking lot and headed back towards Quissett Harbor, which was about three miles away. As he drove his Volvo station wagon along he was excited and animated when telling Melinda about his prior experiences on the Knob.

"I am serious Mel. Most people see the Knob only during the day or at sunset. But to see the evening sky from the Knob is even more exciting! You got to understand that there are no distracting lights from the roads and houses. The stars are so close you think that you can almost touch them...I don't know...to me the sparkling stars and horizon of the sky are just so much more beautiful during the late evening. It's the part of nature that most people miss during their lives since they are asleep."

"Oh really! You sound like you are a frequent visitor out there at night."

"Well I haven't personally been out there in a while. I used to go out there a lot as a teenager. I always brought my fishing rod to catch striped bass, but didn't really care about catching any. The awe of that place was just so pleasing to me." Jared explained to Melinda.

"You went out there by yourself late at night? Come on.... there must have been some other girlfriend who you took with you." Melinda chuckled, but not too strongly.

"No, not at all. I never went out there with anybody else. I had always preferred to go out there by myself then. The peace and quiet was what I wanted. I used to count the number of shooting stars that I could discover in the sky. I was fascinated by them."

"Oh really? And what was your highest record of shooting stars that you saw?"

"Well, you know me. I had to do it somewhat methodically. I would set my stopwatch that I use for running. I would set the stopwatch alarm to go off after one hour. In the meantime I would count the shooting stars."

"And, what, pray tell, is the "Jared Westcott record " for the number of shooting stars sighted in one hour?" Melinda laughed as she looked over at Jared.

"I knew you would ask!" He smiled. "If I remember correctly, eighteen is the record number in one hour."

"Hmmmm. Very impressive."

"But Mel, any night that you want .....We can try to break that record."

Melinda grabbed his wrist playfully and looked at it.

"Thank God! He doesn't have his stop-watch on tonight," she said aloud to a non-existent third party.

There is only one way to get out to the Knob. You must park your car at Quissett Harbor, and follow the one mile walk through the dense woods and trails that have been cut away. It was a bit scary to do this during the late hour. It was pitch dark with only some lights seen from boaters or house lights along the shoreline. Melinda held Jared's hand tightly as he led the way. He would carefully pull back any low lying branches so that she could walk by without getting scratched. The sweet smell of wild honeysuckle filled the warm spring evening. They could not see the abundant flowers in the dark of the night but the fragrance was around them as the walked the trail.

At the beginning of the peninsula section of the one-mile trip, the path opens up. There are no trees and the trail is lined with small bushes. The first thing that you hear is the ocean waves reaching the shores around you. The wide opening which faces the wind enables you to taste the salty air.

As they took the steep steps up to the pinnacle of the Knob, Melinda was feeling more relaxed to be out of the darkened woods. As they reached the top, they had a panoramic view of the adjacent bays and the entrance to the Woods Hole passageway cutting through the Elizabeth Islands. It was truly an awesome sight.

"Jared, it is so beautiful! I haven't been here since a field trip in junior high school. But that was during the day and with thirty other kids. I just don't remember it being like this!"

"There's a bench over there, let's sit for a while."

"I see what you mean about the stars. I feel that I can reach out and touch them. They seem to be hanging only a few feet away from us."

Jared smiled. "I would come out here and sit for hours at night during my late teens. It was sort of my...Oh....I don't know.... like my own private meditation place. Nobody ever comes out here beyond nine at night. I would sometimes stay until the wee hours of the morning."

"Weren't you afraid of being out here all by yourself at that hour?"

"Afraid? No. Not at all. Why would I?"

"Oh, I don't know. If you needed some help, there is nobody around here for miles."

"Yeah, but please don't think what I am going to say is weird. I always felt a sort of spiritual protection each time I was here. It's a little difficult to describe. But it was nice. It was peaceful. You know, kind of serene. It feels good for me to be back here."

Jared paused. He looked into Mel's eyes. "Especially with you by my side."

She too, looked into his eyes. There was a peaceful quiet except for the soft sound of waves meeting the shore beneath them. The time and place were perfect. They were alone except for the stars.

The kiss was soft. It was gentle. They felt each other's warm and honest affection through the tenderness of their lips. It was a loving exchange. Jared put his arm around Melinda and they both sat quietly and took in the view of the peaceful Buzzard's Bay meeting the western sky with the bright stars winking down at them. After a while, Melinda began to feel that there was indeed, some spiritual presence to this special place. She also felt protected.

They kissed again. This time the kiss was longer. They felt the warmth and closeness of each other's bodies. They stayed in each other's arms.

Then slowly, Jared separated himself from their embrace. Almost abruptly, he stood straight up while Melinda remained seated. Jared turned away from Mel and faced the open ocean. He then began to walk slowly away. Melinda was confused.

"What is it Jared, do you see something? Is there something wrong?"

"No, no, I don't see anything."

"Then, where are you going?"

"I....I am not sure, Mel, it's kind of strange. Something is happening. But I can't explain it."

"Are you feeling all right?" Melinda asked anxiously.

"Yeah. I feel just fine. I just don't have control. This is strange."

"What do you mean? Jesus! Jared, what are you doing? You're walking down the side of the hill towards those boulders. Where the hell are you going?"

Melinda stood up and walked over to the edge. Jared was slowly sidestepping down the sandy and rocky slope towards the enormous boulders and ocean. Without looking back up at Mel, he yelled up to her.

"Mel, you're not going to believe this, but I am not walking under my own power! Something is literally moving me down this hill. I can't believe it!"

"OK, come on Jared, the joke is over. You could get hurt down there. You could fall into the ocean. C'mon. Get your butt back up here! Come up here! You're scaring me. This is crazy!"

Jared was laughing, almost giggling. "Mel, I swear to God, I don't know what the hell is happening! It is as though some power or invisible force is bringing me down this hill."

As he walked down the slope to within a few yards of the ocean water, he then sat down at the edge of the water on a large flat boulder. It was about the size of a kitchen table.

"Hey, it just stopped! Mel. It just plopped me down on this huge rock. I can't feel the invisible force any more. Wow, that was strange. I mean weird! But right now I can't feel the force any longer. Its like it wanted me to stop right here!"

"Good! Now that it stopped, why not turn around and get your butt back up here, Jared? It's dangerous down there. I can hardly see you."

"OK.... No argument from me! I'm coming. Wait. There is

something underneath that rock."

"What is it Jared?" asked Mel, very nervously.

"Oh...it's just an empty wine bottle. The label is a little shiny and it caught my eye."

Jared carefully walked back up the rocky and treacherous hill. When he reached the crest Mel noticed that he had carried the empty wine bottle in his hand. He caught his breath, turned and looked back down the steep slope. He shook his head in disbelief.

"I can't explain it Mel, I had no control over my body. Somebody or some thing was literally moving me down to those rocks"

"Jared, are you trying to scare me on our first date?" If so, you've doing a helluva job."

"No, no, not at all. Let's go. I wouldn't expect anyone to believe me. That was much, much too weird. Even for someone like me."

"Well, maybe it was the Environmental Protection Gods getting you to walk down and pick up the wine bottle. It is litter you know," laughed Melinda.

"Come on! Let's get the hell out of here." Jared wrapped his arm around Mel and they slowly walked back through the wooded trail.

As they approached his Volvo station wagon, Jared looked for a trash barrel to dispose of the wine bottle, but there was none around. He brought the empty bottle into his car. As he started the engine, he turned on the car's interior light and studied the bottle. As he concentrated on reading the wine label, he lightly pulled at his left eyebrow with the fingers of his left hand. Melinda vaguely remembered him doing this in the sixth grade when he was deeply focused on something.

"Well. Is it an interesting vintage?" asked Melinda.

"I have never heard of it, but it is beautiful label. What gets me is that it comes from New Zealand. That is unusual for these parts. I don't know much about wines from that country. The vintner is named "Yearling Winery". See the picture of a young deer running over some green hills?" He pointed to show her the deer.

"It was a Chardonnay. Well, I hope they enjoyed it. I'll trash the bottle later."

During the ride home Melinda was very quiet. Jared became worried. He thought that he must have blown his first date with her because of his behavior at the Knob. He hoped that he had not made a fool of himself.

"You're quiet Mel. I hope that you're not pissed with me because of what happened tonight. I mean, it really did happen!"

"No. But I hope that you don't do that again or I will really be pissed."

"Yes my lady. I shall never do it again." Jared was mimicking the voice of an English butler.

"You know something, Jared. I was just thinking about the Knob. Do you really believe that there are American Indians buried underneath that hill? "

"Who can know for sure? It would have been hundreds of years ago if there were any burials there. I have heard that is was a special Indian meditation area, but it could very well have been a burial ground as well."

"Yeah, but you know how folklore is. You get part of the real history mixed in with a lot of anecdotal bullshit passed on down."

"Does it matter to you if there are Indian bodies buried beneath the Knob? I mean ...Do you think that it is sacrilegious that we were there?"

She looked over at him driving the car. "No. Not at all. And, I am not "creeped-out" by it either. In fact, if there are Indians buried beneath that hill, I am happy that we had our first kiss there."

Jared looked at her and smiled. "It only took me ten years to get up the courage."

They both laughed. Jared and Melinda were quiet on the drive to her house. Jared was trying to understand what had happened to him this night. He could not figure it out and that frustrated him. He was more concerned that tonight's events may have screwed up his budding relationship with Melinda.

Melinda was still privately skeptical about what happened on this evening. She didn't know the new Jared well enough perhaps.

Was he now a practical joker that he never displayed when he was younger? She personally doubted it. She also didn't think that Jared could joke about supernatural forces. She would have to think about it a little more and then she would let it go. It was still a very good evening for the two of them. She enjoyed the night. She was very fond of Jared. Just like back in the sixth grade.

CHAPTER FOURTEEN

Integrating Love

As the early days of the summer of 2000 went by, Melinda Abandando was becoming more and more happy with her life. The ironic reunion with Jared at Sam Parker's funeral had changed her life. She knew that it had changed Jared's as well. She was elated with the way this new relationship was developing with her childhood sweetheart and friend.

They began to spend as much time with each other as they could. They each felt that the two of them were always on the same wavelength. They had more in common at the age of twenty-two than they did at the age of twelve. Although they both liked to talk with one another, they also communicated clearly with one another while they were silent. At times they needed to only look into each other's eyes to transfer thoughts and ideas.

He wasn't like any of the others whom Melinda had dated. Jared was so sensitive, caring and in some strange way had another dimension to him that was very much like hers. They both thought differently than most people. Neither of them placed material things at a high priority in their lives. They enveloped themselves only in positive energy. They discarded or ignored any negative energy. Judging other people was as foreign to them as living on another planet. Their conversations were rarely about other people. They talked about feelings or life in general, with all of its attributes, philosophies, and possibilities. They genuinely both felt blessed with all that they had. They sincerely wanted to share and to be of help to others. If there are truly only "Givers" and "Takers" in this earthly world, Jared and Melinda were both "Givers".

Mel loved Jared's non-assuming, unpretentious ways. Jared's mother had wanted him to be someone else, but he stuck to his personal commitments and convictions. While he was in his junior year at Exeter, Sonny Brooks wanted to buy her son a brand new car so that he could come back to Quissett whenever he wanted. She told him that he could have any car he wanted; a jaguar, corvette, BMW in any color or his choice. She was proud of his academic work at the prestigious prep school. He was one of the school's best students. He was also one of the most notable free-styled swimmers on the swim team.

Jared took up his mother's offer and selected the car that he wanted. He did not want a sexy, sports car. He chose a Volvo station wagon. This was not the car that Sonny had in mind for her young, handsome son, Jared. It was not the vehicle that you would expect a young man to select. But Jared loved it. He kept his skis on the rack on top. In summertime, he kept his scuba gear in the back, along with other sporting equipment, a knapsack, hiking boots, fishing gear, tools and all of those things that were of most use to him. Even though he could have the best and most expensive car, he chose only that which he needed.

Melinda truly understood Jared. He was one of the wealthiest young men on Cape Cod but it didn't mean anything to him. He lived within his own principles. He always had an open heart. She loved him.

As the summer romance developed, Jared found in Melinda many of the positive traits that she had discovered in him. Above all, he loved her selflessness. She always thought of herself last. She practiced the theory in life that:

If you think of yourself first, you will *never* be happy.
If you think of yourself last, you will *always* be happy.
Melinda was a very, happy, young woman. In addition to her

internal grace, she was also a beautiful, young, goddess in Jared's eyes. He found it difficult not stare at her. It was no secret that he was falling quickly in love with Melinda. The romantic spark that had started between them in the sixth grade was being re-ignited some ten years later.

Jared also loved and respected Melinda's family. He got along well with her father, Francesco Abandando. He owned and ran Frank's fish market in West Falmouth for over twenty years. His wife, Ann, got along great with Jared also. She appreciated his honesty and integrity. She also knew that he was a responsible young man with her only daughter. She knew that he had true affection for Melinda. It also helped that he was so handsome.

The one member of the Abandando family, who got along with Jared the best, was Mel's younger brother, Michael, or as he was usually called, "Micky". Micky, at the age of sixteen was going through all of the trials and pressures of a young teenager during the new millennium. He really needed a 'big brother' role model to follow and to escape from the constant negativity of his friends. Jared came into the picture of Micky's life at just the right time. Often Jared would ask Melinda for her younger brother, Mickey, to join them on hikes, sailing, or spending days at the beach. Micky enjoyed being treated as a young adult by Jared and by his sister.

By mid June, the summer crowds were beginning to arrive onto Cape Cod at their typical exponential rate. The local radio and TV media would provide people with an estimated delay time to cross the bridges over the Cape Cod Canal. Most people headed to the beaches on hot days. The forecast was for the temperature to reach the high nineties for the third day in a row. The traffic was frustrating and in order to get a good location at the beach, people must arrive early in the morning.

Mel, Jared, and Micky prepared sandwiches at the Abandando kitchen counter. They planned to stop on their way to the beach to buy cold drinks for the cooler and some additional "munchies". Before turning onto Chapaquoit Road towards the beach, Jared pulled in front of the West Falmouth liquor-store. After taking cold drink orders, Jared went into the store while Mel and Micky stayed in the air-conditioned car.

"Morning," Jared said to the proprietor as he approached the counter with his items.

"Good morning! Going to be another hot one! You're lucky! I wish I were you going to the beach today."

"Yeah...we're looking forward to it. I'll just have these sodas, iced-tea and chips."

As the owner was ringing up the sale, something caught Jared's eye. Off to his left, sitting on the floor was a cardboard box. Inside was a case of wine. It was the picture on the outside of the box that intrigued him. It was a beautiful picture of a young deer running over a green hillside. Jared slowly walked over and peered inside the carton. There were eleven bottles of Yearling Chardonnay wine inside. It was not quite a full case.

"Would you like that wine?" Asked the proprietor. I can give you a good deal since it is a broken case."

"Ah...I don't know. I am not familiar with Yearling. How is it?"

"You know, I'll be honest with you. I really don't know. I ordered it by the case every couple of months for just one customer. He would only drink this wine from New Zealand. I ordered it especially for him and his wife for the past seven or eight years."

"Then why do you want to sell it to me and not to him?"

"Oh....ah.... well, he won't be drinking it any longer."

"Really? Why is that?" inquired Jared.

"Unfortunately, he is dead. He drowned in the bay last month."

"You mean Sam...Sam Parker drank this wine?"

"Yep..and he was the only person who ever bought it. He and his wife drank it for years. This was the only place he could get it."

Melinda watched Jared as he came out of the liquor store. She saw him carrying a case of wine in addition to the cold drinks and chips. He opened the back of the Volvo station wagon, put the sodas and tea into the cooler, and then slid in the box of wine.

"Well, Micky, the three of us are going to have some wild picnic at Chappy today," Mel laughed.

"You won't believe what I just learned, Mel."

"What's that Jared?....That if you buy a case of wine before 9AM you get it cheaper?" she joked.

Jared explained about the Yearling wine. Sam and Paula Parker were the only ones who drank it around here according to the liquor-store owner. He then told her that, the West Falmouth liquor store was the only place around that carried that wine. Melinda suddenly became quiet. She had a puzzled look on her face. Micky was totally confused and stayed out of this conversation. Jared then became pensive also. He tugged at his left eyebrow as he drove. Melinda smiled at him without him knowing it.

The three of them enjoyed their day at the beach. Jared, Micky and Melinda brought baseball gloves and played a game of "catch" on the sand. They also brought a Frisbee that kept the three of them entertained and running around laughing. They jumped into the ocean every so often to cool down. By early afternoon, they were exhausted with the hot sun and the activities. Jared and Mel had to leave the beach to return to their homes to catch a brief nap, shower, and then go to their evening jobs.

As they were packing up to leave the beach, Mickey had already run ahead to the car with the keys. Jared occasionally let Micky drive the car home. This was a big deal for the sixteen-year-old, who still did not have his driver's license.

Mel was kneeling down on the blanket folding up the towels. She could feel Jared's eyes looking down upon her. She was also aware that her one-piece, black, bathing suit had a deep scooped neckline. From where Jared was standing, he could catch a good glimpse of her firm breasts as she folded. She purposely bent over a little more and stretched to pick up her purse. This would enable him to see just a bit more to arouse his interest.

Jared's eyes, however, were not staring at her breasts. His attention was fixed directly at the top of Melinda's head. He was looking down and not seeing the beautiful woman whom she had become. The only vision that he saw through the top of her head was a little twelve-year-old chubby girl, with black rimmed glasses, a

sweet smile, and pigtails. He loved that little girl when he was twelve
years old. He now loved her still—ten years later. Jared had a big,
wide smile on his face.

Melinda looked up and saw his smile. She thought she knew
what he had been gawking at. She smiled backed at him coyly.

"And what are you looking at and thinking about, Mr.
Westcott?"

"If I told you, Mel, you would never believe me."

She stood up and smiled and gave him a brief kiss. She put
her arms around his shoulders and let her body fall against his. She
whispered into his ear.

"Just try me, Hon. Just try me."

CHAPTER FIFTEEN

The Knob

It was a busy summer night at the Popponesset Pub. This tavern catered to the summer crowds with light seafood dishes, a well-stocked bar and good music. This evening's entertainment was the local band "The Nantucket Sound". They played music and sang for all ages. Their repertoire included the oldies of the sixty's and seventy's, a lot of "R and B" tunes up through the current pop music. They would also perform reggae and even some "hip-hop" if requested.

During his ten-minute break with the band, Jared picked up the phone and called the Quissett Country Club. He asked the hostess to speak with the bartender, Melinda Abandando.Mel picked up at the bar phone.

"Hi Mel. How's it going over there?"

"The usual. These old guys are really nice but comical.

They have lots of money and lots of stories. I think that they just want someone to listen to them and to stroke their 'senior male egos' a bit."

"I give you credit for your patience. I don't think that I could do that."

"Oh. It's OK. The more they drink and talk, the more my tip bowl fills up. In a strange way, I feel sorry for them. How's it going for you?"

"I'm on my break right now and wanted to call you. How about you and I meeting after work and going back out to the Knob?"

"Sure. If you promise that you won't climb or...... *be led down* to the rocks like the last time."

"I swear. It's such a beautiful night and I really want to be there tonight. There was a brief pause. "With you."

"And I want to be with you. I will meet you there about one-fifteen, right after work. Do you think there will be a crowd out there at that time?" she laughed. "See you at the parking lot.... One-fifteen."

When Melinda pulled her Jetta into the darkened parking lot, her headlights shined onto Jared's station wagon. He got out of his car with a blanket draped over his arm. They kissed and held each other closely. Melinda quickly forgot the night of mixing dry martinis, gin and tonics, and pouring all of those glasses of beer. It was so nice to be held in her lover's arms after a long night of work. She was glad that Jared wanted to be with her tonight. She needed to be with him also. It felt good to be holding his hand, walking through the dark, narrow trail leading out to the mystical peninsula by the sea.

This early summer evening was beautiful and peaceful. There was a very slight breeze coming off of the water. The silence out on the Knob at nighttime was inspiring. The only noise that could be heard was the soft sound of the waves lightly lapping against the shore. There were no other noises. No seagulls, no boats, no fishing lines, nor families running on the beach. The cool, salty air is most acrid at night. It is a beautiful time to breathe in nature. You can smell and taste its life.

This particular night there was a bright moon slowly spinning down to meet the horizon line for the morning. They both thought that it was so nice for the two of them to be able to "unwind" together after working the late hours. Like many people who work the second shift, it was difficult for Melinda and Jared to just leave work, return to their homes and go directly to bed. Sleep never comes quickly for those who work the night shift.

"I thought we would try this Yearling wine that I bought the other day, " said Jared as he opened the cooler.

"Well, I hope that it is good. After all, you bought the whole damned case!" Mel laughed.

"Not quite a case, Mel. Remember, that one bottle had been missing."

They sat on the bench. Jared carefully opened the chilled bottle and poured the wine into two glasses that he had brought. They sipped their Chardonnay and enjoyed each other's company and light conversation. Mel told Jared some of the cute jokes and stories that she had heard at the bar that evening. And then they would giggle. Jared was staring at Mel as she told her latest stories. It was good to see her relax after tending a busy bar all evening. He loved listening to her. He loved the sound of her voice. He couldn't keep his eyes off of her.

They kissed gently at first and then more passionately. They held each other for a very long time. Their hands felt and kneaded parts of each other's bodies as they physically communicated their feelings of love and desire. As they did so, the cool evening breeze enveloped their passionately heated bodies. Their hearts were both pounding with anticipation.

Melinda made the first move. She got up very slowly from the bench. She placed her glass of wine down on the ground beside her. Jared could only stare at her in silence. She picked up the thick wool blanket and spread it out on the ground. She then kicked off her shoes. She continued looking straight at Jared. She watched his eyes without saying a word. She reached up under her skirt with both hands and slowly wiggled out of her panty hose. She pulled them down to her ankles and kicked them off from her. She unbuttoned the top two buttons of her blouse and stood on the blanket staring at Jared. Their eyes met and neither of them moved. They stared into each other's eyes for what seemed a very long time.

Jared got up from the bench and began walking towards his sweetheart, his lover. He kept his eyes focused on Melinda's eyes. Her eyes were speaking an invitation to him. He came within a foot of her and then stopped. He put out his hands to her.

Suddenly something strange happened. Melinda abruptly pivoted around like a marching soldier so that her back was now facing Jared. She was looking out toward the sea. Jared was confused. He started to move toward her but she began walking away. She stepped close to the edge of Knob's steep cliff.

"Mel! Hey Mel! Where are you going?"

" I don't know Jared. I don't know," she answered as she continued walking towards the dangerous Knob's edge.

"Jesus! Be careful, Mel. You know how steep that hill is down there."

Melinda did not turn back to face her anxious and confused boyfriend. She kept moving in short, almost robot-like, steps.

"Jared. You may not believe me, but I am being led down this hill, just as you were a few weeks ago." She kept walking down the steep grade without looking back.

"OK, Mel. Look, the joke is over. Very nicely done."

Jared watched as Mel continued walking down towards the ocean rocks. "Watch it! This joke shouldn't end up being a freakin' accident," he yelled.

"It's not a joke! I swear, Jared. Look at me. Look! It's as if I am being pulled."

Melinda was holding her hand in front of her as though some invisible person was taking it and guiding her to some known destination. It guided her well down the side of the steep, rocky hill. She smiled as though she was with an invisible escort. Just as she looked up at Jared, her hand dropped abruptly and she sat down on a large boulder.

"Jared, Jared! It happened to me too. Look!" she screamed.

"OK, Mel. Great acting! You win the Academy Award! But listen, if you find another empty bottle of wine, I would prefer a Merlot or perhaps a Pinot Noir. Now, come on and get up here, you are making me nervous down there."

"Wait...I do see something, but it's not a wine bottle. It's shining. It looks like a piece of jewelry."

"Well, pick it up and come on back up here!"

"Jared, I swear to God, that I was not joking," she said as he helped pull her up at the crest of the Knob.

"Really? What did it feel like?"

"Like I had no control of where I was going. There was some invisible force leading me down the hill."

"Hmmmm." Jared wanted to believe her. It had happened to him. Why not happen to her as well?

"Jared. Look at this gold medal and chain that I found while I was sitting on that rock."

Jared held the religious medal in his hand. With the bright moonlight he quickly realized that the item had been recently lost, since it was not weathered by the rocks or salt water. It was still shiny and quite smooth. It appeared to be a twenty-four carat gold Saint Christopher's medal.

"Look Jared, there's an inscription on the back."

"Yeah, I can see it." He angled the piece towards the moonlight.

"It reads...To S. P. All my love, P.L. 1977"

"Wow...S.P. You don't think that S.P. is for Sam Parker, do you? I mean first his wine and now this medal."

"It is bizarre," responded Jared.

"I wonder what Mrs. Parker's maiden name was? We know that her first name is Paula. 'P' for Paula."

"I can find out easily by asking my mother, or just looking into her high school yearbook in our study. I remember several years ago the two of them talking about their days at Quissett High. They were both in the same graduating class."

The two of them sat down on the blanket. The passion and romance of the evening was lost for now. Jared was more eager to learn about Melinda's experience with the invisible spirit that guided her down the steep, treacherous hill. He wanted to compare it with his own experience. He wanted to share more of it with her, now that she was a believer. They discussed what had happened to each of them. They understood that their experiences were identical. They believed each other. They had to believe each other. Nobody else would.

"Mel, does this place make you feel uncomfortable, now?" asked Jared.

"No, not at all. In fact, there was an overwhelming feeling of peace when this spirit guided me. I was very tranquil at all times. I feel closer to this spot, the Knob, now. And in a way, I feel protected by whoever else is here with us."

"Who do you suppose it is? This spirit, I mean?"

"I was just thinking about that. When I came here with my class back in junior high, the teacher told us about some old folklore connected to the Knob. It was supposed to be considered a spiritual place. The stories were that some of the younger Quissett Indians came here for answers to difficult questions." Melinda then just shrugged her shoulders. "Who knows?"

"I heard those stories as well. I had understood that this was a special place for the Indians, in addition to perhaps being a burial ground, " said Jared.

"Jared, you told me how you used to come out here at night as a young boy and it made you feel good." She put her arms around his neck and pulled him closer to her. "Let's make this our own special night place, too."

"Of course." They hugged each other very tightly.

They lay down on the blanket. Now they could only hold each other's hands and look up at the sky. They breathed slowly and deeply. They quietly stared at the dark, blue-black sky with its bright shining stars. No words were spoken. They both knew that something was happening to them on the Knob. This was a special place to others who had lived so many years before them. It was now a special place for the two of them.

***

The next day, Jared invited Melinda over to his house for lunch. His former, live-in nanny, and now the Brooks' family housekeeper,

Mac, wanted to meet Mel, since he talked so much about her. His parent's were in Boston and couldn't join them. They had previously met Mel. They too liked Melinda, and were happy to see Jared so much in love. Sonny and Jim Westcott enjoyed Melinda's company very much. They liked talking with her. They respected her honesty and candor. She was very much like their son, Jared. They had made it clear to her that she was always welcomed into their home.

After introducing her to Mac and some cordial small talk, Jared grabbed her arm and escorted her from the kitchen down through the central hallway of the house.

"Oh, Mr. Westcott," she kidded in a silly, childish tone. "Where, oh where, are you taking me?"

"I know what we have to do," Jared said to Melinda.

" Me too. But, let's try it this time without any interruptions!"

"We need to do some research," said Jared.

"Research?"

Jared pulled Melinda by her hand into the Westcott study. Jared walked along the wall's built-in bookcase looking for a specific volume. When he spotted <u>Quissett High 1970</u>, he pulled the book out and they both sat down on the soft, leather sofa. Jared thumbed through his mother's high school yearbook. He quickly went to the students with last names beginning with the letter "L".

"Yup. Here it is. Paula Larson. Her initials were...PL."

"So the medal must have belonged to her husband, Sam."

"Either that or a very strange coincidence."

"First, we find his emptied wine bottle. Now his religious medal. What the hell is going on?"

"Very, very strange."

"Wow, Jared this is amazing! Really amazing."

Jared looked again at the yearbook photo.

"Hey! You know something? This Paula Larson used to be very pretty."

"What do you mean 'used to be'? She still is attractive, Jared."

They spent a little more time thumbing through the yearbook. Mel giggled as she looked at the girl's long, straight, hairstyles. Most of the boys tried to emulate the look of the "Beatles" and other rock stars with their hair grown down to their shoulders. It was amusing to the two of them as they looked through the book. The rebellious attitude of the times came through all of the photos and students expressions. It seemed more like a radical publication of the war in Viet Nam, the racial rioting, the feminine movement, police brutality, and illegal drugs. They quickly read through the yearbook noticing the expressions of anger and dissidence in the student thumbnail profiles. It didn't seem like a high school yearbook. It appeared almost like a social documentary of the times.

They read out loud many of the quotes and expressions that students had penned into Sonny Brook's yearbook.

"Hey Jared, your mom must have had a thing for some guy named Tom. Most of the kids wrote "Good Luck with Tom or Tommy, when they signed her book."

"Yeah, I had read those many years ago. It turns out, that her high school boyfriend became a priest out of college. He is now Father Tom Donovan. In fact, I just heard that he is returning to St. Ann's Church this summer to help out. He's been away from Quissett, living in Vermont for most his life."

Mac called Jared and Melinda to come into the kitchen for some lunch. She had prepared a fresh lobster salad with a side dish of sliced fresh tomato, olive oil, fresh basil, and mozzarella cheese. There was a large pitcher of raspberry iced tea with fresh mint leaves.

Mac could not restrain from smiling. She realized how deeply these two young people had fallen in love. She enjoyed listening to the two of them chatting endlessly. She was extremely glad to see "her Jared" so happy. She could sense the positive energy that sparked between these two young lovers.

"My God, Jared, I have never known you to talk so much. This young woman brings out a hidden personality in you that has never been seen," chided Mac.

"I know what you mean." laughed Jared. "We just never shut up."

"You mean to tell me that he was a quiet boy when he was growing up, Mac?" asked Melinda.

"I'll say. Always thinking, always serious. Very little talk at all."

"What about friends? Did you have a lot of friends growing up, Jared?" asked Melinda.

"No, not really. I mean... I got along with everyone all right, but I just preferred to be alone. Besides, there were never any kids my age in this neighborhood. "

"Oh, Melinda, Jared didn't need *real* friends," interjected Mac. "He invented friends whenever he needed them. You know, about the time he was five or six years old, he told me about his invisible friend whom I could never meet. That friend went everywhere that Jared went. It was really something! Did you ever have an imaginary friend Melinda?"

"No, afraid not, Mac. Nobody that special. Just the ordinary types. School mates and neighbors."

Jared motioned with his hand held in the air that he wanted to make a point. He had just finished swallowing a bite of lobster. He washed it down with some iced tea.

"You know Mac, that friend never left me." Jared used his napkin to wipe his lips. "I just stopped telling you and my parents about my friend because I knew that nobody ever believed me."

"Oh really! And does this friend still stay with you today as it did at the playground and at the beach, helping to build sand castles?" asked Mac with a broad smile on her face.

Jared then sat back and told Mac and Melinda his story about how his invisible friend has been with him for as long as he can remember. Jared was serious. Melinda put her fork down and focused on her lover. She was most interested in what he was going to say. Both Melinda and Mac both knew him well enough. They were certain that he was not joking.

He then told them that his invisible friend had helped him get out of some serious jams and had often guided him throughout his life. He had always sensed another being nearby during his entire life. It was always the same invisible being. He frequently felt this spiritual person near him— especially in times of trouble or challenge. He said that his friend would come to him whenever he called for help.

"I will give you a good example."

"Please," said Mac, sitting down and joining them at the kitchen table.

"You don't know this Mac, nor does anyone else, but when I was sixteen years old, and a pretty good swimmer, I decided that I wanted to challenge myself with a swim from Falmouth Heights beach over to West Chop on Martha's Vineyard. It was a distance of about five miles. At that time of my life, I was confident when it came to swimming distances. And I just wanted to do it. I kept my plan a secret. I didn't want to tell anyone until after I did it. For several weeks, I mentally prepared myself for this swim," continued Jared.

"One early Saturday morning, I dove into water and started my swim. The waves were small; only about two feet. I was stroking real well going with the outgoing current. I was doing very well, for abut the first hour. But I had forgot to check one important thing."

"What was that?" asked Melinda.

"The weather forecast. I had reached the half way point across Vineyard Sound when the sea and sky darkened from the west. Soon, there were black and gray thunderclouds overhead. It was a nasty, windy thunderstorm that had kicked up with hail and lightning. It scared me so much, but I had to keep going. Suddenly the waves became too much for me and I started going under with every other wave. I thought that Saturday was going to be the day that I would die. I would never give up, but it looked real bad. I was being tossed around in six-foot waves. At the same time I was taking in mouthfuls of the sea. The wind and waves sucked out every ounce of energy I had in my sixteen-year-old body. I was praying to God. "

There was a heavy silence that filled the kitchen. Mel and Mac were waiting for Jared to continue with his story.

"And then it happened," said Jared.

"What? What happened, Jared?"

"My friend came and spoke to me and told me not to be afraid.

It was much too early for me to die and there were lots of things that I had to do before I left this earth."

"You could hear this....? You mean your invisible friend was actually talking to you?"

"No..not talking to me in the conventional sense but still communicating with me as my friend always did. It is sort of like a telepathic form of communication where ideas and thoughts are shared without using our mouths or ears."

"So what happened? Did the storm subside?'

"No, not at all, it was a nasty storm. But, somehow, my body lifted high into the air and above the rough sea. I had no idea what was going on. At first I thought I was caught up in a waterspout, which often occur in storms like those. But then I realized that my friend was with still with me and told me that I was going to be set down safely at Tashmoo Bay. I don't know how I traveled. It happened all so quickly. The next thing I knew I was lying safely on that sandy beach between some large sand dunes. I stayed there through the afternoon until the storm blew over. I then took the evening ferry back to Falmouth. I never told anyone else about this until today. Until now."

Melinda and Mac sat paralyzed in their chairs listening to Jared tell his story. They knew that it was true. Jared would never joke or exaggerate about anything like that.

"Wow...Jared, what a story! That's incredible. It's almost as though you had a 'near death experience' on that day. Why didn't you ever tell anybody?"

"Oh, I'm not sure. I guess that I really didn't think it that important to tell anyone else. Besides, who would have believed me? You two are the only people whom I have ever told of that experience. Since Mac brought up the subject of my invisible friend who had been with me since my childhood, I wanted to be open and share that incredible experience with you. There were many more times that my friend was with me, but none as dramatic as during that storm. My friend has always been there for me through high school and college."

"Did you ever think that your friend might be your guardian angel?" asked Mel.

"I just don't know, but I have been blessed with my friend being with me by my side during my entire life. Whenever I was troubled, or in trouble, my friend appeared."

"Jared, my lad," asked Mac in her fading Scottish brogue, "Have you a name for your invisible friend? I mean ...didn't you ever ask it for its name?"

"I did several times especially when I was much younger."

"Did you ever get an answer?"

"It was never clear to me. I couldn't make it out. So I stopped asking it."

"What do you mean not clear? What name did you pick up? Telepathically speaking? " asked Mac.

"Oh... I seem to remember that the name sounded like it began with Je, Ja, or Juh...like in Jesse, or Jerry, or Justin or something like that...I just could never get it."

Now Mac was the one who suddenly became quiet and a little pensive. She still however, wanted to continue her probing about the invisible spirit.

"And Jared, what gender was your friend? Do you feel that it was a male or female?"

He laughed. "That is an interesting question. When I was little, I never thought about the gender of my friend, or angel, as you call it. But as I grew older, I seemed to feel a strong feminine presence when my friend was there. I can't explain it, but it is there. I would bet for sure that my spiritual friend is a 'she'."

"Oh great!" smiled Melinda. "I have competition from some chick, but none of us can see her. What are my odds on this one?"

They all laughed.

"Jared, did you think that the name of your angel could be — — Jessica?" asked Mac.

"Jessica.... Jessica. Yeah that has a very strong possibility. Hmmmm..it definitely could be Jessica."

"Well, now at least I know her name," smiled Mel.

Mac stood up and walked over to the window. She leaned her hips against the kitchen sink and gazed outside the window. There was something on her mind. It was evident to Jared and Melinda that she wanted to say something.

"What's up Mac? Did my story make you feel creepy?"

Mac looked at Melinda first. She was in deep thought. Then she turned towards Jared.

"Look, son. I need to tell you a story of my own. I don't think that you would mind Melinda hearing it with you as well. But I need for both of you to promise to never tell anyone else what I am about to tell you."

"Of course, Mac. What is it? Please sit down and tell us."

"Well, let's see now. Where do I begin? You know Jared, that I was with your mother during the night that you were born?"

"Yes. Mother had told me that you were so helpful and supportive during the night that I was born."

The room became very quiet. Both Melinda and Jared anticipated that they were going to hear something very confidential. They were going to learn something that was very important.

"It was a very, cold, November evening with snow squalls. Your father was away in Europe. He was planning to return home in time for your birth, since the due date was much later. However, Sonny, your mom, went into labor that wintry, November night and I drove her to the hospital at 8pm. We were both nervous wrecks. Your due date was still weeks away. She was in labor much too early. But then at ten o'clock that night you came out and we were relieved and so happy. You were such a beautiful and healthy baby boy!"

A warm smile graced Mac's face. Her blue-green eyes twinkled with love.

"C'mon... Mac... this isn't a story. You're just trying to embarrass me in front of Melinda." Jared grinned.

"Jared, what I am about to tell you is something that I promised your mother that I would never divulge. But now I think I must. I must. So please... "

Again a quiet, nervous expectation filled the room. Jared and

Melinda focused on Mac's face and what she had to say.

"What is it Mac? What is it that you want to tell us?""

"Soon after you were delivered, there was another baby yet to come. Jared, you had a twin sister. And a cutie she was! Unfortunately, she had been born with the umbilical cord tight around her neck. She was born very distressed. She breathed for only a short time and then the poor little one could breathe no longer. She died minutes after her delivery."

Mac took her tissue and wiped her tearful eyes. She was reliving the pain and hurt from that evening so many years ago.

Jared looked shocked. He didn't say anything, but he looked as though he was going to cry. Melinda held his hand tightly. Jared then looked over at her. She had tears rolling down her pretty face.

Mac went on. "Sonny, ah... your mother, was in a very deep state of depression. She asked me to stay with her in the hospital that night, which I did. She told me that the baby girl would be named Jessica. I informed the hospital staff of the name. Then she surprised me with instructions. First of all, she wanted to have a private burial at Cedar Grove Cemetery. She wanted the burial the very next day. She was specific about this. Baby Jessica was not to be buried at Oceanside Cemetery, where the family plot is located. Secondly, she didn't want anybody, I mean anybody, to know about your twin sister, Jessica."

There was a brief pause. Mac had to recompose herself. She took in a deep breath. Her eyes were filled with tears again, as she recalled those days over twenty years ago.

"She didn't even want for Jim, your father, to know about the birth and death of your twin sister. And to this day, he never found out. He still does not know. Jared, you and Melinda are the only other people to know about this. Sonny never told your father, Jared. She never wanted him to know about Jessica. That was something that I could never, never understand. So please, please...don't tell a soul."

Jared was understandably quiet. He now knew why Mac told him this story that had been kept secret all of those years. He understood the link to that story and his guardian angel. His spiritual friend all of those years growing up had been his twin sister, Jessica. He smiled. So many things made sense to him now as he reflected on his twenty-two years of life. His guardian angel was his twin sister. She knew him better than anyone else. It all fit together. The name, the female presence, and the fact that she seemed to know him so well.

"Let's go for a ride, Mel."

Jared stood up and walked over to Mac leaning against the kitchen counter. He hugged her tightly and kissed her on her cheek.

"I love you, Mac."

Mac waved through the screen door as the two lovers pulled away from the front curb in Jared's car. She didn't want them to see the tears of happiness and relief rolling down her face. She knew that she would never regret telling that story. She trusted them. That vital piece of family history was too important. It had to be shared. Jessica had never left her twin brother, Jared.

Mel knew exactly where Jared was going. He didn't say anything as he drove along the back roads of West Falmouth. He didn't need to talk. It was no surprise when he turned into the long flower-lined driveway of Cedar Grove Cemetery. After running into the office to get a plot location, he jumped back into the car.

"It's over there." Jared pointed. "Come with me."

They held hands as they slowly, almost timidly, walked between the gravestones. Then they saw it. The little polished granite marker facing up from the ground had only the words "Baby Jessica" November 8, 1978. That was Jessica's birth and death date. It was Jared's birth date. They both said silent prayers. After a few minutes, Mel walked away; leaving Jared to be by himself. She left him to be alone with the spirit of his deceased twin sister.

Later, as Jared walked back towards the car, Melinda met him and grasped both of his hands. She held his hands tight within hers. She looked at his eyes. Jared looked back at Mel. He had a warm glowing smile that illuminated his face.

"Are you all right, Jared?"

"Sure, Mel. I am fine. I had to stay a little longer because she came to me. She was talking to me. She told me that she was glad that I found out who she was. She told me never to worry about anything and to enjoy life. But sadly, in a way, she told me that she was leaving me. She wouldn't be around me anymore because she had an opportunity coming up. She needed to prepare for that opportunity, whatever that meant."

"Did she say anything else?"

"Yeah."

Jared looked down into Melinda's hands holding his hands. He smiled at her.

"What.....what did she say to you?"

"She said that I won't be needing her any longer, because I was in good hands now."

CHAPTER SIXTEEN

Family and New Friends

Melinda's parents, Francesco and Ann Abandando, hosted an old-fashioned, Cape Cod clambake each year during the last weekend of June. It was a summer celebration for their many relatives and close friends. It was held at Teaticket beach, on the east side of town. This was an ideal location for a clambake since it offered swimming, boating, and ample space for games, cooking, and eating. This area had both the sunny, sandy, beach and many cool, shady, spots provided by the pine trees and tall cedars further inland.

The clambake cooking fire was started in a huge pit dug deep into the sandy beach. Layers of dried wood, stones, and seaweed were placed into this pit. The long burning fire would enable the rocks and cinders to get extremely hot, so that by noontime the lobsters and clams would be put on top of the seaweed to quickly steam and boil. The sweet fragrance of heated seaweed, shellfish, and embers permeated the air for miles around. There was always an abundance of food and drink for the nearly 100 guests to enjoy. The children ran around playing or swimming with their friends and cousins. The Abandando clambake was a success each year. The family all made it so by working together. Everybody had a job or chore to do so that it all came together.

Jared and Melinda's assignment for this year's feast was to pick up the cases of soda and ice. They would deliver them to the beach by late morning.

"Jared, I think I want to stop by Mrs. Parker's house before we pick up the soda. If the St. Christopher's medal did belong to her deceased husband, I think that it should be returned to her. I feel a little guilty holding on to it."

"What if it wasn't Sam's medal?"

"Then I will just tell her that I was mistaken, and we will be off. No big problem."

"OK, Mel, but are you going to tell her *exactly* where you found it?"

"Hmm....I think that I'll side-step that one if I can."

They found Paula Parker on this Saturday morning, working in her backyard. She was watering her herb garden and doing some weeding. The ground displayed an extensive area of green plants of basil, rosemary, oregano, chives, dill, and thyme. She and Sam had always loved to cook together and routinely used fresh herbs in their recipes.

She was happy to see her former students. They chatted for a short time. Paula was delighted to learn that Jared and Mel had been dating. She knew that she had to re-introduce the two of them at Sam's wake. It would have been a shame if they missed seeing one another. She still mentally reflected back on their "puppy love" days at the elementary school. Today she was looking into the faces of two young lovers.

"Well, kids, I was just going to take a break. Please come inside and join me for a cold drink."

"Actually we were just stopping by to see how you're doing, Mrs. Parker," said Melinda.

"Paula. Please call me Paula."

" ....and to see if we may have found something that might belong to you."

"Oh?" said Paula with an uplifted eyebrow. She led them into her house through the back doorway. "Oh really? What is it that you found, Melinda?" asked Paula as she took off her garden gloves and turned towards the couple.

"It's this gold medal here. I found it wedged under a rock. The inscription in the back is what made Jared and me think that it may have been your husband's medal."

As Paula took the medal, she immediately flipped it over to the backside. Jared and Mel watched her, as she seemed to study it for sometime. Perhaps she was reminiscing. She seemed to be trying to feel something through the tips of her fingers as they nervously touched the medal.

Paula then responded, "Yes. Why yes, this was Sam's medal."

There was a long silent pause. A wrinkled frown briefly crossed Paula's forehead.

"I had given it to him as a small gift for our wedding engagement. I always worried when he went out to sea on his research explorations. I don't know why. I guess that I just wanted to be with him at all times. I told him that as long as he wore this St. Christopher medal, he would be protected. And when he felt it around his neck, he would think of me. Since that day, he had worn it every day of his life."

Paula's eyes began to well up with tears. Her voice was a little shaken. Jared and Mel became uncomfortable. Now they regretted that they had re-opened a sensitive area and personal part of her life. Now, they wanted to leave as quickly as they came.

"Well! I am glad that we returned it to its rightful place," said Mel still a little apprehensively.

Paula held the medal tightly in her hand and then dropped it into the pocket of her gardening smock.

"Yes, yes. Thank you so much for bringing it by. I am glad that it is back with me." Paula looked directly into Melinda's eyes. "It must have washed ashore onto the beach."

"Ah....right. That's probably what happened," replied Melinda.

"Can you folks stay to have a cup of coffee or glass of lemonade with me for a while?"

"Well....we....."

Suddenly, there was a light rapping noise coming from the front door.

"Hello! Hello! Anybody home?" a man's voice yelled out from

the front side of the house.

"Excuse me." Paula went to the front door.

Jared and Mel could hear the conversation that echoed in the front foyer.

"Oh! Jack, come in, come in. What a surprise!"

"Hello, Paula, I just wanted to stop by and see how you were doing. Here, these are for you."

Jack Ogren was more than a little uncomfortable as he handed Paula a bouquet of wild flowers. He appeared more handsome out of his police uniform. He was dressed in a dark polo shirt and light colored tan slacks.

He was wearing leather moccasins with no socks. His face was well tanned. There was a strong fragrance of after-shave lotion with a sharp, clean scent.

"Jack, come in. Please. I'd like you to meet two of my friends, and former students, Jared and Melinda. Jared is Sonny Brook's son. And Melinda is Francesco's daughter."

"How do you do," said Jack as he extended his opened hand to each of them.

"Jack and I went to high school with Sonny," she explained to Melinda.

"Oh. I see, " replied Mel.

Melinda hadn't known, however, that Jack was also a high school classmate. She mentally recollected some of the yearbook photos to see if she could recall what this man would look like with shoulder length hair.

"Nice to meet both of you," Jack said politely.

"These two were the best students that I ever had in all of my years of teaching, but I won't embarrass them with that bit of nostalgia."

"Look, Mrs. Parker....ah ....Paula. We have to get going. We have important errands to run. But we did want to return that item to you."

"OK. But promise me one thing? Please come by again. I'd love to talk with you two. It would cheer me up. Will you promise me that?"

"Of course we will. You can bet on it."

"Nice meeting you, Mr. Ogren, " said Jared and Melinda as they quickly exited out the front door.

***

Saturdays on Cape Cod during the summertime is known as "Change Day." That is the day of the week when cottages, rental homes, motels and hotels "change" their guests who had stayed for a week or two. It is the day the new allotment of guests and tourists arrive. These visitors had to be checked out of their rooms or cottage by eleven in the morning. Immediately after they leave, armies of housekeepers and chambermaids would infiltrate and begin to clean, wash, dust, vacuum and to change the bedding. The rooms would have to be prepared for the next wave of guests before three o'clock in the afternoon.

What "Change Day" meant to residents and tourists alike is that all of the roads on the Cape get clogged with tourists' cars loaded with toys, food, luggage, baby carriages, and the ubiquitous bicycles strapped on to the vehicle in some very inventive fashions. There would always be at least one car with a radiator heating over in the hot, summer, and slow traffic. Veteran travelers to the Cape know better. They purposely try to come during some day other than "Change Day".

After Jared and Mel picked up the sodas and ice for the clambake, they encountered some of the snarled traffic.

"Oh, shit! Look at this mess! I forgot that it was Saturday. The ice that I just put into the coolers will melt before we get to the picnic," said Jared.

"Jared, lets take Woods Hole Road out to the shore and go that way. It's longer in distance, but there won't be many cars there now."

"Yeah.... That's a good idea!"

As Jared did a U-turn, Melinda and he engaged in one of their favorite activities. Philosophical Debate. Today's topic for the two of them was the merits of organized religions all over the world. Neither one of them could ever figure out how they got into these discussions, but they loved talking about topics that they felt strongly about. They actually learned more from one another during these talks and it exercised their minds a bit. It didn't matter to them who would be considered the "winner" of these debates. They were each satisfied just from learning something new from one another and about one another.

They love to debate, to discuss, and to share ideas on just about any topic. They both knew that they were different from most other twenty-two-year olds. It didn't bother them at all. They were opened minded about everything. They had so many things in common. They never judged people or their actions. They never expected anything from anyone. They knew that the word "expect" was not a word of love, but rather a word of negativity, with no love attached to it. They were both very slow to anger because they knew that anger was a waste of perfectly good energy. They always kept a balance centered within themselves—emotionally, physically, and spiritually.

As they drove along, they were digressing into the religious beliefs of Daoists from the Far East. This was a topic that Melinda had studied in a college philosophy class.

As they made the turn towards the shoreline, they spotted a very pregnant woman on the side of the road. She was looking down at a flat tire on her older model car. Without saying a word or digressing from their thought-provoking debate, Jared pulled up and parked in front of the woman's disabled car. Melinda and he were still discussing the true essence of a devout Daoist, as they stepped out of Jared's car and walked over to the woman. They had stopped driving to help this woman without mentioning a word about it to one another.

"Hi! I'm Melinda and this is Jared," she said with a big smile.

"Hi! I'm Susan and right now I am completely helpless," she smiled back. Beads of perspiration were dripping down her face.

"That's why we are here. To help," said Jared.

"That's my four year old, Kayla Ann, sitting in the back seat."

"Well..... Why don't we get you and Kayla Ann into Jared's car with the air conditioner. We have some ice-cold soda in the back that will cool you down a bit while we change your flat tire."

Jared was already pulling out the spare tire as Melinda escorted Susan and her daughter into the station wagon.

"It looks like you don't have too much longer to go, Susan," said Melinda.

"That's right. Actually, my due date is next Wednesday," answered Susan a little nervously. "These are anxious times. And today with the heat and a flat tire......somewhat stressful." Susan managed a smile.

Melinda handed each of them a cold soda. "Here, cool down a bit. Well, a new life. That is so exciting! Do you know the sex your new bundle of joy?"

"Yup, it's going to be a boy." Susan smiled wide. "Kayla is going to have a little brother."

Susan looked down at her little girl. She was gulping down the cold drink. Her daughter swallowed loudly and returned a smile that lit up her little face. She hugged her mother's arm tightly.

"You must be excited. Do you have names picked out?"

"Well, you might not believe this, but I haven't one yet! I just can't feel comfortable with the few names that my husband and I have picked out. My hubby's been great, though. This has been a tough pregnancy. He said that I can pick out the name and he will go along with whatever I pick. But, I just have had a mental block with boy's names. I just don't want just any name. It has to be something special."

"Well, I'm sure you'll come up with something that will fit him just right," smiled Melinda.

"Melinda? Is that your sweetie who is changing my tire?" asked Susan.

"Yep. He's a great guy. A real special guy!"

"I can see it in your eyes. And in his eyes too!"

"Yah.... We're very happy!" grinned Melinda.

"I want to thank you for stopping and helping me out. I didn't know how long we were going to be stranded out here. I really have to get a cell phone one of these days. I really appreciate your help."

"That's what we are all here for Susan. To help one another out. Even if it is just changing a tire and giving cold sodas to make cute little girls a little bit happier!"

Mel reached over and lightly pinched Kayla's cheek making her smile.

"Well you know, us Cape Verdeans, or any people of color, that is. We love to meet with people like you and Jared. It warms our hearts and our souls."

"Well today it's 93 degrees out here! Don't get too warm!"

They both laughed. "Let me go and help Jared. You two, aahh...., three, cool down in the car a little bit. We'll be done in a few minutes."

As Melinda slowly let the jack down, Jared tightened all of the lug nuts on Susan's car.

"I don't know about Taoism, Mr. Westcott. I really think a lot of it is bullshit! It has no substance. It offers nothing that I can sink my teeth into. You know what I mean? Which, speaking of sinking teeth into something, I'm getting hungry. Let's get Susan on her way and get to my folks' picnic."

Jared put the flat tire and tire jack back into the trunk of Susan's car. "All set Susan!" yelled Jared.

They each opened a door so that Kayla Ann and her expecting mother could get back into their own car. As they watched her car pull away from the side of the road she shouted through the opened window of her car.

"Thanks guys! Thanks again. You two were angels! *I* thank you. *Kayla* thanks you. And," as she patted her large pregnant stomach, " and *little baby Jared* here." Susan then patted her enormous pregnant stomach again. "He thanks you!"

They waved good bye. The Volvo station wagon then pulled out onto the road. Jared sped off toward the ocean on their way to the Abandando picnic.

"Wow, what are the odds for that Mel? Her baby is going to be named Jared! I didn't think a name like mine was in vogue these days. Her husband must be a little old fashioned."

Melinda smiled. That's a story she would tell him on some other day. She wanted to save it. She reached over and ran her fingers through his hair and on the back of his neck as he drove along. She thought about Susan. Then she thought how she would like to be having a baby some day. Not necessarily named Jared. But fathered by Jared.

***

The Abandando picnic was getting underway as they arrived with the soda and ice. Melinda introduced Jared to so many relatives that he couldn't possible remember all of their names. He enjoyed playing all kinds of games with the kids, running in and out of the salt water to cool down. He was ecstatic. They played water volleyball, and later some basketball and horseshoes. Jared got acquainted with many of the relatives, while Melinda spent time with some of her cousins and family friends.

After they enjoyed the steamed lobster, clam chowder, barbecued chicken, hamburgers, and everything else, Melinda suggested that she and Jared go for a long walk to be alone for a little while.

They found some shaded trails in the thickly, wooded area adjacent to the sunny beach. It felt good to be in the coolness of the shade. They held hands and walked leisurely through the wooded, pine tree area. The late afternoon sunrays were beaming through the tall trees. The shadows created a natural work of abstract art on the sandy trails.

"I met some nice relatives of yours today, Mel."

"Well, it was only a matter of time when the skeletons fell out of the closet. Did you meet any interesting characters?"

"I had a nice long chat with your father's cousin, Jesse Souza."

"Yeah, he is a nice guy. Quite a bit younger than my father though. I think Jesse is only in his mid-thirties."

"Yeah. It was interesting to listen to his professional experiences both at Fall River and now here. He's seen a lot already even though it is early into his career. I guess that goes with the territory when you choose to become a police detective. He invited me to come to his office anytime if I wanted to learn more about the investigative process. He actually told me more about a certain case than I should probably know about."

"Really?...Like what?"

"Well, he started telling me about the Sam Parker drowning."

Melinda stopped abruptly in her steps. She now thought that this drowning incident seemed to be following the two of them wherever they go. It seemed to never leave them alone. She was about to say something but decided to continue walking and hear what Jesse had told Jared.

"That was his most recent case. Jesse informed me about something that never made it to the newspapers. He told me that Sam had died *before* he was drowned. It's recorded in the Medical Examiners report. Sam actually died from an overdose of some flavored morphine, which supposedly he had ingested. Jesse speculates that it could have been administered to Sam orally or he may have ingested it on his own. Then he drowned. Or as Jesse put it, Sam either jumped or was pushed by another person into the bay."

"Pushed? I can't believe...."

"Yeah, I know. But as Jesse said, all angles have to be considered in a case like this one."

"Morphine...wow...Jared, this is weird. I mean it is getting really weird."

"Well, Jesse is still really pissed at the way the Sam Parker case was handled. He said that normally when there is no exact determination of the cause of death, the case must remain open. Sometimes these cases will stay open for several years."

"Really?"

"Yeah, but what I find more interesting is that he and the chief argued over this. The chief wanted this case closed almost immediately. In fact, he closed the case as "accidental" just a couple of days after the drowning."

"Hmmm. That is interesting. So, the chief got his own way and Jesse never got a chance to find out any more."

"That's about it. Jesse was getting pretty fired up over this, but I figured he just might have had too many beers today out in the hot sun. By the way, do you know who the Chief of Police is?"

"No..... I guess I don't."

"It's that fellow we met this morning bringing the bouquet of flowers to Paula Parker. It's Jack Ogren."

"Holy shit!" said a puzzled Melinda.

"My reactions exactly."

Melinda slowed her pace and stared at Jared as they ambled along the wooded trail. They both knew that their thoughts were running a little too fast. Jack Ogren, Falmouth's Chief of Police, was bringing a bouquet of flowers to the widow, Paula, soon after the "accidental" death. It showed that he was uncomfortable this morning when he found Jared and Melinda already in Paula's house. What was going on? Was there anything between Paula and Jack? If so, it was none of their business. They kept thinking as they continued their walk.

As they walked along, Jared stopped abruptly and pulled his left leg up.

"Ooh. Ouch! Wait! I just got a sharp pebble inside my shoe," said Jared. "Let's stop a minute."

Jared stopped to take off his dock-sider shoe and take out the sharp rock. Melinda watched as he sat down on a large rock and he rubbed the bottom of his foot. Then she couldn't believe what she saw. She stared more closely. Then she started laughing out loud.

"What is so funny?"

"Your foot!" She knelt down and looked closely at his foot that he was rubbing.

"What about it?"

"My God! The last few toes of your foot are webbed."

"I thought you knew that. If you think that's so freakin' funny, look at my other foot." Jared took off his other shoe.

"Oh my God! The same thing!" Melinda laughed and quickly brought her hand up to cover her opened mouth. "The last three toes are webbed. Like a duck. You have webbed feet!"

"Of course! How the hell do you think I was a gold medal swimmer at Exeter and at Yale," grinned Jared.

"I don't believe this!" Melinda screamed.

"These were my secret weapons."

They got up still chuckling and started walking back towards the picnic.

"Well, Jared," as she put her arm over his shoulder, "I feel that it is my personal duty to call the athletic department of the Ivy League. I feel obligated to tell the officials that you have held an unfair physical advantage and that all of your trophies and medals should be taken down."

"No, no, no ...you got it all wrong. I actually went forward to the athletic board of directors before anyone discovered the webbed toes and I disclosed my condition. It was perfectly acceptable and all above board. I wouldn't have competed if it wasn't."

"I believe you Jared. I believe you," she laughed. "Only you would do something like that."

They both laughed and kissed as they walked back toward the picnic area holding hands.

The next morning, Jared was up early. Almost every day, since he was a teenager, Jared had the same morning routine. He would wake up at dawn to prepare for his morning run for five miles or more. He would run around the narrow streets of Quissett, Woods Hole, and Penzance Point. Each day before he ran, he would first do some stretching exercises.

As he went through this warm-up routine he had a habit of singing the same song in his head. He couldn't get this song out of his head if he tried. It had been a daily habit of his to hum or to sing this song. Now, after all these years, it would be impossible to drop.

It was a song that he had learned as a young child in Sunday school. The first line of the song went "This is the Day the Lord has Made, Let Us Rejoice and be Glad." He smiled everyday at this routine because he was unable to escape the habit of humming it to himself. After stretching, he would then say the first line out loud and begin his run. It became his Morning Prayer. It was his own personal mantra.

Just as his run had a ritual at the beginning, its ending was always the same as well. No matter how many miles he ran, or which routes that he may have followed, he always ended up in the little meditation garden of St. Joseph's Bell Tower in Woods Hole.

This hidden treasure within the world-renowned research village had existed for a very long time. It is very quaint part of Eel Pond. It had been donated and designed by a young scientific scholar in the 1920's. According to the young benefactor, he wanted this tower and the meditation garden to be created to remind people that there is a much higher and powerful force than us. It is a place for people to visit, reflect upon what is really important in their lives, and renew any personal commitments. The beautiful bronze doors of the bell tower were designed by an Italian artist and modeled from the sculpted art on the doors of the famous Baptistery in Florence, Italy.

The little garden surrounds a few sitting benches that are there for anyone to rest, to relax, and to meditate. It's one of the lesser-known areas within the academic enclave of Woods Hole. Jared would always use this area for his "cool down" period after his morning run. He would slow down, meditate, and get refreshed while his endorphins kicked into his system. It was always a pleasant experience.

When the fog comes into Quissett, it is always very thick. It is almost as though you are in the clouds. This particular morning was one of those days and one could hardly make out objects within ten feet. Jared decided to cut his run a little short since car and truck drivers couldn't see him that clearly on the road. He finished running down the hill and jogged into the Bell Tower garden.

Jared leaned on the wooden fence that circled the meditation garden and the northern side of Eel Pond. He was inhaling and exhaling heavily, trying to catch his breath from his last sprint down the hill. Suddenly, he was startled by a male's voice that came from behind him.

"Hello," the voice said.

Jared turned quickly but could see nothing in the thick, misty, gray fog.

"Hello," the voice said again. "Over here."

"Oh...hi there!" Jared could barely see the faces of two people sitting on the bench. He walked over towards them.

They were both wearing light, gray-colored sweatshirts with hoods and matching sweatpants. With these outfits, they blended in with the thick fog. They were sitting very close together and Jared noticed that they were holding hands.

"Hi...my name is Jared. Jared Westcott."

"Hello there! My name is Riccardo and this is my friend Robert." Jared shook the two men's hands.

Riccardo was a bit shorter and thinner than Robert was in stature. He had a short, close-cropped haircut so that his receding hairline was not so pronounced. His complexion was a light brown. He wore a shiny, round, gold earring in his right ear. He had a distinctive Latino look to him.

Robert was taller with a fair, almost alabaster white complexion. He had dark brown hair that he wore long. It had been neatly tied back into a ponytail. Jared looked at him and sensed that his clear, hazel eyes spoke of a special warmth and understanding.

"We know that its not the greatest day to be here, but it is Robert's last day of vacation before he returns home. We wanted some peaceful time before his plane takes off from Hyannis."

"Oh really! Where are you from Robert?"

"I come from Halifax, Nova Scotia. Have you been there, Jared?"

"No, but it is one place that I would love to visit!"

"He soon will be from Falmouth, Massachusetts," interjected Ricardo. "Robert is going back home to tell his parents about him and me becoming a couple. After that, he is returning in two weeks to live with me."

"Sounds like you've made some pretty heavy decisions."

"Oh yes. We are both so happy."

"Well. I wish you both the best of luck!"

"Thanks."

"That is a very interesting door on the Bell tower," said Robert, as he walked over to it leaving Riccardo still sitting on the bench.

Jared was drawn over to where Robert was standing. Robert was admiring the sculpted bronze door. Jared told him the history of how an artist from Italy was commissioned to create the door during the early part of the last century. Jared also spoke about the background history of the meditation garden, the flowers and herbs grown there, and the bell tower, since he seemed interested. Robert lightly passed his fingers over the sculpted doors as Jared spoke. But he did not look at the doors. It was almost as though he already knew the history. He looked only at Jared. Jared sensed that there was a strange aura about Robert. Not frightening, just strange.

As Jared spoke, Robert was peering into Jared's eyes, as if to get his attention. As Jared continued talking about the door, Robert was staring intensely into his eyes, without winking an eyelid. Jared looked back at Robert. Robert was communicating with Jared in a way such that Riccardo could not be part of the communication. It was telepathic. Jared was getting a telepathic message from Robert. The message was very clear. The telepathy was working. It was a very mysterious message.

"Come on Robert. We must be going. We'll come back here some other day when the visibility is better," said Riccardo.

With that, the two of them left the meditation garden.

CHAPTER SEVENTEEN

Busy Days, Busy Nights

While taking his shower after his morning run, Jared had many disconnected thoughts running through his brain. Besides the unexplainable incident with Robert that he had experienced at the meditation garden, he was thinking back to Saturday's picnic and the open invitation from Detective Jesse Souza.

There was something about this Parker case that intrigued him. It lured him in. This was very unusual for Jared. He wasn't particularly interested in the facts or details of the case itself. But there were much bigger questions that he kept asking himself. Was he supposed to be doing something about this case? Was there even a criminal case at all? Maybe it was merely a suicide. Maybe Sam had known about Paula and Jack Ogren. But, why was the Yearling wine bottle on the Knob? And why did the St. Christopher medal end up there? It could never have drifted there from Chapoquoit beach.

As he washed his hair, Jared continued thinking. Why were there events occurring that were linking he and Melinda with clues to the drowning? Was he supposed to follow up on those discoveries at the Knob? What mystical force led he and Mel to those discoveries? It was odd that finding the wine bottle, and then Sam's medal, happened in such a bizarre way for the two of them. Even the impromptu stopping by an unfamiliar liquor store on the way to the beach was uncanny. That is when he learned about Sam's favorite

Yearling wine in the first place. These events were then followed by the revelation that there may have been foul play. This came to him at the picnic with an unplanned meeting with Detective Souza.

As he was toweling himself dry, he decided that he would pay a quick visit to Detective Souza's office. Perhaps he could pick up a few tidbits on police investigation. He did have some limited interest in that line of work from a purely intellectual perspective. Jared could never see himself in the role of a policeman. The work of an officer or detective would certainly involve helping people, but not in the way that he wanted to do as a career for the rest of his life.

***

"Sure, Jared, why not come down about one-thirty? " Jesse said. "The boss is out for the afternoon and he won't get in our way."

It was not difficult to get Jesse talking. It was obvious that the young detective had an emotional hook into this Parker case. It all stemmed from Chief Ogren closing the case down prematurely. Jesse was also anxious to impress upon this younger student his many, keen investigative skills. Jesse enjoyed the role as mentor. It showed.

Jared asked if he could follow the detailed process in the Sam Parker case since it was so recent. Jesse agreed. He went over to the gray-colored steel filing cabinets. After rifling through a dozen or so folders, he turned to Jared.

"The folder should be in the file drawer here but it isn't. That is strange."

"Could someone else be looking at them?" asked Jared.

"I doubt it. Only Jack and I were working on it. Let's go into Jack's office to see if he was reading it."

"No problem, Jesse. As long as we don't get arrested for breaking and entering." They both chuckled.

Jesse could see that Jack's desktop was cleared and no folders were on it. He then walked around the back of Jack's chair and noticed that the front desk drawer had not been locked. This was not unusual. Jesse pulled on the drawer handle and the Parker file was on top of other paper pens and pencils.

"Here it is, Jared." Jesse pulled the manila folder out of the drawer.

"Oh great!" replied Jared.

"Hmmm .... What the hell is this?" asked Jesse out loud.

He was now pulling a few photographs out of Jack's drawer. Jared walked behind Jesse to get a glimpse.

"Looks like some old photos, but I don't think that they were connected to the case."

They both could easily pick out who was in the photos. One was a faded high school class picture of Paula Larson Parker. Jared recognized the picture immediately. It was the same pose that was in the Quissett High Yearbook. Across the photo she had written.

"To the cutest boy in our class.

You're the one who got away.

Love and Best of Luck—Paula, June 1970."

There were two other photos of a younger Paula and Jack apparently at a teenage house party. Paula is sitting on Jack's lap with an arm around his shoulder with a silly facial expression. One of the photos appeared to be taken during a friendly kiss between the two of them. One of their friends must have snapped it. They were typical high school party photos.

"Well, Jared. These are personal items of Jack's and not part of the case."

"Of course," replied Jared.

He was a little embarrassed, but at the same time he felt a little more intrigued about the relationship between Jack and Paula. They both were quiet as they walked back into Jesse's office to look through the Parker case file folder. Jared sensed that Jesse was doing some thinking about these two old high school friends as well.

Jared read the interviews with all of the co-workers. He saw the hard copy of the electronic mail from Sam to Ted Burford early on that last morning when he was alive. He carefully read it. He read every line of the interview notes with Rita and Roger Anderson, those beach-combing friends of Sam, who knew him so well these past few years. Then he studied the photographs of Sam's body after it had washed up on the shore. He spent considerable time staring at the Polaroid shots of the victim. There was the wide smile on his face. This expression surprised Jared. He stared at the face. With the smile and eyes wide opened, it looked as though Sam had just been introduced to you and was happy to meet you.

He looked carefully at the clothing, the vest, the canvas sacks, and rubber wading boots. As he studied them, he was becoming uncomfortable. Something was not fitting right to Jared as he studied the photos of Sam's body. But he wasn't sure what it was.

Then it hit him. Something was inconsistent. He went back to re-read the Anderson remarks. He read every descriptive line of their interview very slowly. He then picked up the photos once again to verify something that he saw with Sam. It may not be anything. But then again, it might be something more to this mysterious drowning.

He decided not to mention his discovery with Jesse. If he were right, it might embarrass Jesse. If he were wrong, it would embarrass Jared.

"Hey, Jesse, thanks for this opportunity today. I really learned quite a bit. I had no idea the details you guys have to dig through."

"You're more than welcomed, Jared. Anytime you want, just give me a call. It's better when the ol' man isn't around. He would be pissed off if he knew that it was the Parker case that you went through."

"Oh really, why is that Jesse?"

"Well for one thing he was too damned close to this case. He should have let me handle the whole thing and kept out of it. Also, on the q.t.? He has this thing for Paula. I think he's had a secret crush on her for a long time. Some folks say that they liked each other since their high school days. You saw the photos. I guess his feelings for her never went away. I have no idea how she felt, ...or feels about him."

"Do you think that his relationship with Paula could have been a factor in this case?"

"Well, that's something that my instinct says to stay away from for now. Just for now."

"I see". "Jack is really a great guy. But I have to tell ya, he has been a real bastard about this case. It's been a drag. On the one hand there are a lot of unanswered questions, on the other, my boss, the chief, wanted this case shut closed as soon as possible."

Jared had another mental flashback of Jack Ogren handing the bouquet of wild flowers to Paula last weekend. He looked nervous, like he was out of place or perhaps just out of practice. One thing was certain. It was obvious from the way he looked at her that day, that Jack Ogren still had affectionate feelings for Paula Larson Parker.

After work that evening, Jared and Melinda met at the Quissett Harbor parking lot and walked up to the Knob. This had become a steady routine with them almost every night that they worked. It was their place to be alone. Sometimes they would stay until two or three o'clock in the morning. They joked that they were "second-shift" lovers.

Jared wanted to tell Melinda about his encounter with Riccardo and Robert at the St. Joseph Bell Tower garden. He told her how they all met during the foggy morning.

"What do you mean that this Robert communicated with you through his eyes?

"It's bizarre, I know, but I definitely, definitely, felt his words in my head. "

"Was he coming on to you, Jared? You said he gave this message instead of saying it out loud so that Riccardo could not hear, correct?"

"Yes. But that's not it. The message that I felt was something else that he was saying to me. He was trying to give me a warning of some sort."

"A warning! Oh Christ, Jared! Are you in some kind of danger?"

"No, no that's not what I meant. He was giving me a message. He seemed to be saying that 'I am not coming back here. I will not be back. I will no longer be here'. He was telling me something along those lines."

"What do you think he meant by that?"

"I don't know...I mean why would he tell me that or.... I mean... telepathically transmit that particular message?"

"Do you think that he is dying of AIDS and he couldn't tell Riccardo? Maybe that's what he meant by his not returning."

"No. I didn't get that sense at all, Mel."

"Do you think that he just wanted to dump Riccardo? But then, no, no. Why would he feel that he had to tell you that?" questioned Melinda.

"I think that he wants me to look after Riccardo, you know, maybe check in on him at times or something like that. I just don't know why. Maybe I just misunderstood the whole thing."

It had started to sprinkle rain lightly. The two of them would have to jog quickly off of the Knob to reach the car. Inside of the car, Jared told Melinda of his initiation into police work and Jesse allowing him to look at the Parker case files. He had to tell her about the inconsistency that he had discovered at the police station earlier that day.

"Mel, the Anderson's interview clearly stated that Sam always had two canvas bags over his shoulders each day. The white bag was for treasures and the black bag was for litter or trash. The report specifically said that the *white one was always on his left shoulder* and *the black strap always hung over his right shoulder.*"

"So?"

"Mel. That wasn't what the photo showed. The canvas bags were reversed. The white strap was over his right shoulder and the black one was over his left shoulder. They were reversed. "

"Do you think that he changed his habit just for this one day?"

"No. Not at all. The Andersons were adamant about this in the interview notes and said he never changed any of his daily routines. He was an obsessed creature of habit. "

"What do you think Jared?

"I am thinking that someone may have made it look like he was on his normal walking routine and had an accidental fall into the bay from the jetty. Somebody dressed him up like he was on his routine walk. But, they messed up with the canvas bags being on the wrong shoulders."

"They?" asked Melinda.

"Or whoever," replied Jared.

"Jared, this is getting more serious. I really think that you might be on to something. Now, I, am not convinced that Sam accidentally fell off of the jetty after his daily walk, and drowned."

"I think he was murdered, too. He had died before he was drowned according to the Medical Examiner's report. I hate to even think like this."

"I do too."

"Jesus! What the hell should we do Jared? I feel so bad for Paula. She doesn't need this news. It won't bring her Sam back to her anyway."

"I know but Jesse told me something else today that I found interesting."

"Yeah...like what?"

"He said that Jack Ogren had a long time crush on Paula Parker. It goes back to their high school days together. We accidentally came across some old photos that Jack had stashed in his desk. They were pictures of Jack and Paula together some years ago. Why would he keep some thirty-year old photos of his teenage sweetheart in his desk drawer?"

"Jared. Now I am getting uneasy with all of this crap. If Jack Ogren is somehow involved, and he's the Chief of Police, then who the hell do we go to?"

* * *

The next evening Sonny Westcott came up to the Quissett Country Club bar to say hello to Melinda. She had her arm draped through the arm of a very handsome man about her age.

"Mel, I want you to meet a very dear and old friend of mine. This is Father Tom Donovan."

She looked at this tall, striking handsome man and introduced herself to him. Donovan was dressed in a dark blue striped shirt with white slacks. He wore sandals on his feet. He was well built and appeared to keep himself in shape. Sonny was very gracious as she described Melinda and Jared's relationship to her former friend, and now a visiting curate to St. Ann's church.

Sonny continued to smile and gaze at Father Tom with a very different look. She hung on to his arm as she paraded him around the club's restaurant introducing him to the other members. She and Tom were having dinner there. Later that evening, after a few too many martinis in her, Sonny ambled up to the bar and wanted to speak with Melinda privately.

"Listen Mel," she whispered. "Father Tom is going to be around here just for the summer and I want him to enjoy himself as much as possible. He likes to come here because it is private and he doesn't have to worry about who sees him at this club. So, if he orders drinks or meals when I am not here, just put it all on my account."

"Sure, Mrs. Westcott. No problem. Consider it done."

Later, Melinda looked over at the two of them at their table as she wiped down the bar. She thought that they actually made a very good-looking couple. They looked very comfortable with each other. She reflected back to the pictures and signed autographs in the Quissett High School yearbook. Mel could visualize Sonny and Tom as a very "hot" romantic high school duo in 1970. This image quickly faded when she looked up at the clock on the wall. Her own sweetheart, Jared, would be on his ten-minute break soon and she looked forward to his telephone call.

"Hello Mel! How are you doing?"

"Not bad, kind of slow tonight, how about you?"

"Oh it's a long story. The band is having some difficulty. Our drummer may be quitting. He's being a real shit-head lately. It's been a bit stressful."

"Well then, you need to go to the Knob again with me tonight and unwind. It's going to be a beautiful night. And I know someone who can relieve you of your stress."

"Oh, and who might that be?"

"Me. And only me."

There was a long pause and Melinda knew that Jared was smiling. She truly loved Jared. And he was deeply in love with her. It was the happiest times of their lives.

They planned to meet at the usual time, at one-fifteen, in the Quissett Harbor parking lot. They both felt something special about this evening. They had come to know each other very well. They both knew that the love that each of them had for one another was sincere and unconditional. Their love was special. It was the kind of love that was not fleeting. It endured. Their love was not temporal, nor superficial. It was not vulnerable to petty distractions. Tonight they would be together to celebrate their love for one another.

After meeting in the parking lot, they briefly kissed and embraced. They held hands in the darkness of the night going up the to their special hill. There was no moon this night. It was especially dark without the light coming from the sky. The only light that could be seen came from the tiny spots of village streetlights off in the distance.

Jared had spread out his blanket onto the ground. They lay down next to one another and began to relax after their long day. As they spoke, they faced towards the star filled sky. Occasionally they turned toward each other—to hold each other close and to share warm and loving words and kisses. There was no mundane chatting this evening. Melinda would tell Jared some other time about Sonny and Father Tom. Jared could wait to tell Mel about the problems of his rock band. This was their time. This was their night.

As they lay in each other's arms on the blanket, they closed their eyes and kissed softly and affectionately. All other events, surroundings and people in their earthly lives quickly vanished from their minds. Every noise and every movement of the night seemed to leave on queue so that this couple could be completely alone. There was Jared and Melinda and infinite space.

They were lying in each other's arms kissing warmly. Then more passionately. They embraced so that each other's bodies could yield to the power of love. Their searching hands and fingertips felt the warmth, the softness and the hardness of each other. They were in their own world.

Suddenly, as their passion was escalating into a hot, physical crescendo, it was abruptly interrupted. Then there was a tremendous shaking and vibrating to their bodies. At first, they both thought that an earthquake was occurring at their 'special place'. But it was not the earth vibrating. The earth was still. They both opened their eyes and stared at each other. The vibrations were coming from within each of them. They could feel themselves vibrating uncontrollably at a high rate of frequency. It was something that they did not quite understand. At first, they were frightened. These shaking vibrations became more and more intense such that they could not speak or see clearly. Soon they could no longer feel their physical bodies. It was as if someone was shaking them out of their bodies! They couldn't feel anything. They could no longer see anything!

Then they each heard a voice. The voice seemed to come through the vibrations. It said very clearly but very softly, almost as a whisper.

"Let go. Let go. Just let go." It whispered again. "Let go. Leave it to me."

Melinda thought that it was Jared's voice speaking to him. Jared thought that he was hearing Melinda's words. They each obeyed the command that they thought was coming from one another. They would let go.

They purposely let go of everything. They didn't care. They felt faith. They were not afraid of anything. It was the first time in each of their lives that they had no fear. They lost all control and tension over their earthly bodies. Soon they thought that they were letting God take control.

The vibrations then came faster and at a much higher frequency. They both shook internally with a vibrating frequency that is incomprehensible to earthly experiences. They lost all sense of feeling, as we know of it. There was no sense of time such as past or future. They were now on a different plane. A different space. A new dimension. There was no pain, no anguish, and no anxiety. There was a tranquil blanket of love and peace that enveloped Melinda and

Jared.

They were floating up into a space that they never before knew about. They were still in each other's embrace. They were entwined together and spiraling up to a higher level. They soon realized that they were not connected to their earthly bodies. They could now look down below them and see the Knob. They could see their earthly bodies still lying still on the light blanket. It was amazing. They were still on earth and they were floating above it. They realized that they had now become what was considered—bi-locational!

Jared and Melinda looked at each other in this new dimension. They still loved each other as they always did. They embraced. The only emotion was the presence of love. There was no room for other feelings. Only love. Jared saw his Melinda in a much different light. She was as beautiful as ever. He could see her eyes and hair and body as never before. But there was something much more sensuous. He could see her soul. He entered inside of her, not merely with his male sexual organ but with his entire spirit.

He could feel his way into her thoughts, her feelings, her hopes, and her fears. He now understood everything about his beloved Melinda. He learned and experienced where she had been, and who she had been in the journey of her life. He felt the pains that she had experienced. He felt the joys that she had felt. He knew her as he never thought possible.

He experienced feeling himself enter her. He felt his own climactic ecstasy. But at the same time he also felt the orgasmic climax that Melinda experienced. He now could feel the energy of her female sexuality. He experienced his own orgasm and hers simultaneously. It was rapture never before felt. It lasted for a very long time. It was different because this act of love was so different. It was total. It was ecstatic beyond earthly comprehension. There was a harmonious integration of souls that they had never known possible.

He then saw Melinda in the various past lives she had endured in her journey. She had been an Egyptian slave, a Scottish shepherd, a Chinese leper, and a Carmelite nun. While her physical characteristics changed with each role— only her eyes remained always the same. The eyes never changed. They served as her soul's icon of recognition.

Melinda could also feel Jared enter her body, but also enter into her spirit. As he entered into her, so she entered into him. It was beautiful. She felt his soul. His spirit told her all about Jared. She felt his pain and his sufferings for all of his earthly lives. She now could understand him totally. Nothing was hidden. Nothing. She experienced his joys, and his happiness, his fears and anxieties. She now knew who Jared was. She understood him not only in his current carnation, but also in his past spiritual lives as well.

She saw his many past lives as a London prostitute, a Venetian carpenter, a respected African high school teacher in the Caribbean, and recently, an aviator and hero who was killed by sniper fire in the Viet Nam war. As his physical appearances changed, his eyes remained the same in each segment of his journey. His eyes were his identity. They were always the same.

Melinda now knew everything about Jared. She felt and experienced his sexual orgasm as if she were he. She now knew what it was like for him. At the same time she climaxed sexually and shared that feeling with him so that he could understand and know how and what she felt. Waves of ecstasy moved through every molecule of her being. These waves of rapture were then melded and shared totally by each of them.

She now understood that every cell of her being was a life in and of itself. Each cell had abilities and properties never known before to her. She felt that she now knew all of the answers to every question in the universe. The rapture lasted for a very long time. It was beautiful. It was love. There was no difference between them. They were both equal. They could be whatever they wanted to be. The choice was theirs.

They chose to be themselves. Melinda and Jared. They continued floating together, inseparable, entwined in an upward spiraling fashion before returning to their physical bodies.

The loud sounds of children's voices surprised Jared. He couldn't figure out where they were coming from. Was he dreaming? Where was he? Whose voices where out there?

He opened his eyes and looked up directly at the brilliant yellow-white sun. The sharp brightness hurt momentarily. He turned and found Melinda still beside him sleeping on top of the blanket. He adored watching her in her deep peaceful sleep. But the kids' voices continued.

Below them, about fifty yards to the west, was a troop of young, uniformed, Cub Scouts marching up towards the Knob. Jared reacted quickly.

"Mel, Mel, wake up, wake up. We fell asleep."

"Oh shit! Oh no! What happened? Oh my God, what happened?" She squinted up toward the bright daylight.

"I don't know, but, let's get going. We are about to be invaded by a small troop of miniature soldiers down there."

"Huh?....Jared, what time is it?" asked Melinda as she folded up the blanket.

"Let's see. My watch says that it is....hmm 2:21AM. My watch's battery must have died. What time do you have?"

"Let's see". She shaded her eyes from the glare of the sun with her hand. She stared down at face of her wrist watch. "Oh my God! My watch stopped also. It has 2:21AM." She looked up at Jared. "It stopped at the same time as yours. "

Melinda stared at Jared, and he looked lovingly back at Melinda in the bright sunlight. They kissed each other and were quickly on their way to avoid the line of marching troops decked out in the traditional blue and gold uniforms.

CHAPTER EIGHTEEN
Old Friends, New Friends

During the summer months, the Quissett Country Club gets very busy, as do all Cape Cod establishments. This prestigious golf and tennis club is very private. It still has a very old-line legacy of rigid selection criteria for new members. The club is perched on the forested bluffs overlooking Woods Hole. This site affords a panoramic view of Quissett Harbor, Naushon Island, Martha's Vineyard, and Buzzard's Bay. The club's golf course is always in impeccable condition. The fairways are always cut short. The putting greens are smooth and forgiving. It was purposely designed to be an easy course to play for its members and guests. The average age of Quissett Country Club members is 57 years old. It is a very old club. It is very old money.

Father Tom Donovan became very much at ease talking with Melinda at the club's bar during those summer nights. He liked Melinda. She was always upbeat, personable, and was a good conversationalist. It didn't hurt either that she mixed substantially strong drinks. Tom never spoke about his work as a catholic priest, or any religious topics. He'd rather talk about sports or his days growing up in the village of Quissett. He cherished the beautiful life he had back then. He never talked about the work he did in Vermont. He did mention that most of those years were spent at the Home for Lost Angels and left it at that. This was a facility for priests and nuns to get help and rehabilitation from drug and alcohol abuse as well as emotional breakdowns. Club members privately speculated that he had been either a patient or a counselor. The consensus was that he had been both.

Tom was never pretentious or presumptuous. Melinda liked that in him. He did have a gift for the gab, especially after a few gin and tonics. The other club members enjoyed talking with Father Donovan. They also liked his golf game. He was a good player with only a six handicap. He always wanted to play a match with the best golfers. Rumor had it that there were significant sums bet on each hole when Father Donovan played a round of golf. He was well liked by the members.

Usually, during one or two nights each week, Sonny would join Tom for dinner at the club. She glowed when she was in his company. She was a different woman when she was with him. There seemed to be more life and vitality to her when she was in his company. She laughed more openly, drank a little more freely and seemed to let her hair down. This behavior was in contrast to her usual quiet and reserved disposition.

Sonny had lived a quiet and relatively subdued life with her husband, Jim. There seemed that there was little that the two of them had in common. She learned his plastic resin business, not from the desire to know, but as if she owed that to him— to repay him for something that he had done for her in the past. She respected her husband. He was always a good father to Jared. Sonny got more involved with community projects. She was especially active in supporting local and Cape environmental protection and conservation projects.

Melinda got to know Tom Donovan better as the summer went on. He became a regular at the Quissett Country Club bar each week. He always dressed neatly in a summer polo shirt and light colored slacks. Most times he wore sandals on his feet.

There was something about this man, however, that bothered her. It had to do with his smile, his mannerisms, and his physical traits. She felt as though she had already known this man, but she didn't know why. She was familiar with his physical movements, and sometimes she could actually anticipate what he was going to say. She saw many similarities with him and her boyfriend, Jared. He had the same stoic stare. Their smiles were similar when he told a joke. His vocal tone and inflections were familiar to her. If she closed her eyes behind the bar and listened, it could have been Jared's voice she was hearing and not that of Father Tom Donovan's.

Late on a hot July night, Tom was sitting at the bar watching a Boston Red Sox baseball game on television. It was quieting down after a busy evening with the dinner crowd. Melinda was keeping up with washing the glasses clean and restocking the beer and liquor bottles.

"So, Mel, you're going to be teaching at Barnstable High School in September. Are you nervous about that?"

"Not nervous, Father, but excited. I love working with kids, especially teenagers. My brother, Micky, is only sixteen years old, so I pick up a lot of pointers from him too."

"That's good. It is nice to be close to your younger brother."

"Yeah. Jared is good with Micky too. They have a great relationship. They have bonded like brothers. At times, I think that Jared would rather be with Micky doing things than being with me," she said with a grin.

"You know, I am finally going to get to meet Jared."

"Oh really? Is that so?"

"Yeah. In fact he and I have a golf tee time at eleven-thirty tomorrow morning. Sonny felt that it was time I got to meet Jared. She knows how much I love golf and I understand that Jared is a pretty good player."

"Yeah, I heard that he used to be a four handicap. But he's not on his game right now. He hasn't played at all this summer."

"I understand that. I heard some gossip around the club here that a certain young woman has caught his fancy and he just ain't the guy he used to be." Tom had a wide smile.

"Could be, Father," said Melinda with a slight blush. "Could be."

A tall man dressed in a light gray business suit was staring over at the bar. He seemed to recognize Father Donovan, and began walking towards him. Melinda had never seen him in the club before.

"Hey Tom! Is that you? Tom Donovan?"

Tom swiveled his barstool around to see who was speaking.

"Why yes it is.... Billy? Billy Jenkins? How are you?"

"My God, I haven't seen you since graduation from high school! By God, Tom, you're looking great!"

"Melinda, this is Bill Jenkins, one of my best friends from Quissett High. The two of us were inseparable growing up. I think we played every sport known to man. If it wasn't football, it was baseball, soccer, and hockey. You name it Melinda, and we played it."

"Yeah..." Bill laughed. "But that all came to a halt when a certain Miss Sonny Brooks consumed all of your time and we never saw you again."

Both Melinda and Tom looked away and put their faces down a bit, trying to ignore Billy Jenkin's comment and avoid looking at each other. Melinda used her drying cloth a bit more forceful as she wiped the bar. It was the first time that either of them felt uncomfortable with each other. Tom quickly changed the subject.

"And so Billy, what are you doing these days, now that you're all grown up." Tom laughed and firmly grabbed Billy's shoulder.

"I am in sales, Tom. For over thirty years now. Say, Melinda, can I have a Jameson and soda?"

"Coming up," replied Melinda.

"And you Tom, what line are you into."

"Well, I am a priest, Billy. I became a Catholic priest."

There was a long pause in their dialogue. Bill Jenkins looked stunned.

"Wow! No kidding? Say, Melinda, better make that a double. A double Jameson's," Bill retorted. They all laughed out loud.

"Coming up, Billy!" smiled Mel.

Billy and Tom moved away from the bar and sat at a table where they could talk privately and not bore Melinda with their faded memories on the athletic fields. They had a few more drinks together to heighten their conversation down memory lane. Around ten-thirty they both got up and walked over to the bar to give Melinda her tips and to say good night.

"Well, Melinda, it was nice to meet you and of course it was a joy to see you again, Tom. You know Melinda, I told you how ol' Tom here was a good athlete in high school? He played every sport so well that he always made the starting teams. But do you know that he still holds swimming competition records at Quissett High that have never been broken?"

"No, I didn't realize," said Melinda as she was stacking the cleaned glasses behind the bar.

"Yep.... This man here was great in the water, but I will let you in on a long-held boyhood secret." Bill leaned over towards Melinda as if he was going to whisper. "Tom, here, had a secret weapon!

"Oh? And what would that be?"

"Tom here has two webbed feet! The last few toes on each foot are webbed. No wonder he always swam so fast!" Tom and Billy began laughing.

Upon hearing this, Melinda face turned pale. Her arms got weak and she dropped the tray of whiskey glasses. The noisy crash on the floor surprised everyone still at the club. Her mind was racing. She felt herself becoming dizzy and perspiring on her forehead. Tom Donovan. Sonny Brooks. Webbed feet. Jared.

"Mel, are you all right?" asked Father Donovan.

"Sure, sure." She tried to get some words out. Here mouth was dry. She couldn't look at him. She avoided looking at his face.

"I am fine...after all, I haven't broken a glass all year. These are the first of the season."

After the two men left, Mel couldn't stop shaking. She was feeling a little sick to her stomach. She couldn't focus. Her heart was racing. She felt like vomiting.

She telephoned Jared and told him that she wasn't feeling quite right. She told him that she may have she caught a virus. She was going straight home that evening after work.

****

The next morning, Jared woke up early feeling strong and refreshed. It was a beautiful New England morning when the air is just a little cool and so clean. It was a little misty outside. He would run a little longer today and breathe the saltwater-scented mist into his lungs. He enjoyed his morning run. As he ended it, he noticed that the sun was just burning through. It was shining on the Bell Tower in the meditation garden. The purple petunias, red and white begonias and blue morning glories were perked up They added some nice color to the little garden area that was opened for all to enjoy.

Jared did some serious thinking as he leaned over the wooden fence to rest and to cool down. He knew that he wanted to marry Melinda. He wanted to marry her soon. He had been planning to have a diamond engagement ring designed especially for her. He would make a trip into Providence, Rhode Island. There were some close friends of the Westcott family who were jewelers in that city. They would be patient with him as he designed his diamond ring for Melinda.

Her birthday was during the first week in September. It would be his birthday gift to her. This way they would remember their engagement date and celebrate their love for each other on that special day each year. He felt good about his decision and his plan. His thoughts were suddenly interrupted when he heard the muffled crying and sobbing coming from the other side of the bell tower.

Jared turned to look. He recognized Riccardo whom he had met last week in the meditation garden. He appeared very different now. He did not display that glowing smile of love on his face. He did not have that aura of joy and peace that he had when he sat on that very same bench with his friend, Robert. Jared walked slowly over to him so as not to startle him.

"Riccardo, Riccardo, hello, its me.... Jared."

"Oh....oh hello, Jared. How are you?" Ricardo said weakly while raising a handkerchief to his face.

"Well, I am fine. But I see that you're not doing so well. Is there something that I can do Riccardo?"

"No, not really, unless you can bring Robert and me back together."

"I don't understand."

"You know, for the first time in my life of thirty years, I met someone who was good for me. He was the first person to really understand me. He loved me...he loved me, for me, and nothing else." He sounded distraught and helpless.

"I am so sorry, Ricardo."

"Robert was like a gift from God. He listened to me. He understood me. He felt my pain— not only did he feel my pain but he also took it away from me. He absorbed it away from me so that I no longer felt my pain. He did the same thing with all of my anger. He took all of that anger that I had built up over the years. He showed me how my own anger was my worst enemy."

Riccardo sobbed again and then took in a deep breath followed by a sigh. He regained his composure.

"He taught me how to open my heart. He told me how easy it is for all of us to open our mouths, our minds, in the name of love. But he taught me that true love can only happen when we open our hearts."

"Look, Riccardo." Jared tried to interrupt.

"He understood my confusion and my challenge with being a homosexual. He understood the anger that I felt towards my parents. He told me how wrong I was in thinking that I disappointed them. He knew about my teenage years and the ridicule that I had to endure because I was different from the others. In a very short time, Robert understood all of that. Then he cleansed me from all that hatred and negativity that I had accumulated."

"He sounds like a beautiful person," Jared commented.

"You know something Jared, I felt a love for him like no other person. But I will share something very personal with you. We never had a sexual relationship. It was almost ...I don't know...like sex was unnecessary. We would just embrace each other. That is when my pains and my anger left me and somehow.... I can't explain it, but my pain and anger were absorbed by Robert and then discarded."

Riccardo then blew his nose.

"It does appear that you found him at the right time in your life."

"I am so afraid. I am afraid that I will never find anyone like him again."

"I am so sorry Riccardo," said Jared. "Is there any chance of you and Robert getting back together?"

Riccardo stared at Jared. There was a long pause.

"On no, my friend. I thought you must have known as I told you my story. Didn't you hear about it? The small commuter plane carrying Robert and ten other passengers went down in the Atlantic Ocean last week as it was approaching Nova Scotia. There were no survivors. He never made it back home. It was in all of the newspapers."

"I'm sorry Riccardo. I had read about that tragedy but didn't know that Robert was on that flight."

Jared then looked away and out over Eel Pond. He reflected back to the scene with Robert last week at the bell tower. It was clearly the message transmitted to Jared through his Robert's eyes—" I will not be here much longer, Jared, I will not be here much longer". Things made much more sense to Jared. Now he knew what he had to do.

Jared reached over, hugged his friend, and held him in his arms so that he could cry on his shoulder and let it go. Jared went on to tell Riccardo that he must continue to live the life of love that Robert had taught him in those few weeks. He then told Riccardo that Robert had wanted Jared to be his friend. He would explain at a later time. Jared also told him that he wanted to introduce him into his own life. He wanted him to meet his family, his fiancée, Melinda, and her family. They were all loving people and Riccardo would feel comfortable getting to know them. As Jared held Riccardo, he told him that that he and his friends would always be there for him.

Riccardo felt better now that Jared had comforted him in the meditation garden. He felt a strange sense of peace fill his body once again.

CHAPTER NINETEEN

Directions

Micky Abandando had always wanted to learn how to sail. He had gained a lot of experience with power boating with his father, Francesco. When he was out on the ocean, Micky had always been intrigued by the beautiful sailboats gliding through the water. They seemed to move so quickly, so smoothly, and so quietly without the drumming noise of motors. Jared had promised to teach Micky all of the sailing techniques that he had picked up during his many years of navigating the Cape's waters. During an August morning, Jared telephoned the Abandando home. Mrs. Abandando answered the call.

"Micky! This call is for you. It's Jared." Ann yelled out towards the deck.

After hearing his mom, Micky ran so fast to get the phone that he tripped over the threshold entering the living room and almost did a complete flip into the couch.

"Hi, Jared," he said trying to catch his breath.

"Hi Mick. I just wanted to know if you'd like to go sailing with me today?"

"Yeah...sure, I'll be ready in 15 minutes," replied Micky.

"Well, give me at least an hour and I will pick you up." Jared laughed.

The summer day was excellent for sailing in the Cape Cod waters. A light breeze of ten to twelve knots swept over Quissett Harbor. This southwesterly wind would move Jared's twenty-eight-foot Cape Dory sloop, "Servire", smoothly through the waters of Buzzard's Bay.

After Jared maneuvered the vessel out to the open water, he gave the helm to Micky. He immediately started training him on the basics of safe and smart sailing. Micky picked up these valuable lessons quickly from his new role model. He had been already familiar with much of the peculiar jargon of sailboats and sailing. He could identify the mainsail, the jib, the Genoa, and the spinnaker sails. He just never had worked them before this voyage. Micky could follow the compass bearings by adjusting the mainsail, the tiller, and playing with the wind direction. Jared taught him how to "come about" and to always think safety with every action, whether as the captain or as a crewmember. It was a good time for Micky and Jared to be together by themselves, without Melinda. They truly appreciated each other's male company. Jared knew that sailing is an excellent way to experience life together.

The day was enjoyable for both seasoned sailor and novice. Jared, the consummate leader and mentor, used every moment to teach nautical techniques and sailing methods to his younger friend. Micky enjoyed the lessons and knew that he wanted to become the best sailor possible.

On the returning tack into Quissett Harbor, Jared explained that the water's currents and tides were as important to sailors as the wind and its directions. He went down below into the cabin and came back up with a brightly yellow-colored book. Its title was the "Eldridge Tide and Pilot Book". This book was updated and printed annually for sailors of all stripes for the past one hundred and twenty-five years. It was considered to be the "Sailor's Bible" for all serious navigators up and down the eastern coast.

Jared taught Micky how to read and interpolate the speed and directions of the local currents using the Eldridge book. The book has hundreds of pages sorted by calendar dates. Each page or date displays the associated times of high and ebb tides mapped to a specific body of water. The direction and speed of the currents for those areas of water are also listed.

Micky understood some of it. But like most things in life, one must use it often to truly understand it. Jared gave it a rest. He knew that the day was getting long for his student.

Jared idly thumbed through the Eldridge tide book as Micky controlled the tiller. For some strange reason, his fingers stopped at one particular date earlier in the season. Jared had remembered this date. It was the date that Sam Parker's body had washed up on Chappy beach. Jared had remembered that calendar date so well. He stared at the numbers and information on that page. He then looked up from the tide book. Something didn't make sense to him as he read the currents and tides data again. He began tugging at his left eyebrow with the fingers of his left hand. After a while, he folded over the corner of that particular page. Rather than return the book to the cabin area, he put the book into his gym bag to go home with him.

He took the helm from Micky. Jared would skipper the vessel into the narrow Quissett Harbor.

Before leaving for work that evening Jared thought that he would surprise Melinda with a chilled bottle of champagne to celebrate their third month anniversary. They could enjoy it that night after work on the Knob. He pulled in front of the West Falmouth liquor store. As he entered the store he did not see the same owner working as he did during his last visit. There was a middle-aged woman sitting behind the counter reading a magazine. Jared looked carefully for the just the right bottle of champagne for that evening.

As he approached the counter he told the woman that he had purchased the remainder of the case of the Yearling wine a few weeks ago. .

"That's good. How did you like it?"

"Great! It is a good chardonnay. My girl and I both enjoyed it."

"If you want more, give me ample time to special order it."

"The owner had told me that you had sold the single bottle of wine from the case that I bought. You don't happen to remember who that was by any chance do you?"

"Actually I do. Even though it was before Sam had drowned. The guy asked specifically about which wine *Paula* Parker liked to drink. It's not unusual for people to ask us about other people's favorites. It usually involves a gift or sometimes a dinner party invitation."

"Yeah that makes sense. Can you tell me who that person was?"

"Well, it really is none of your business. But I am sure you know who this individual is since he is pretty well known around this town."

"Hmm. I bet I can guess!"

"Really!"

"Was it the Chief of Police, Jack Ogren?" he asked with a smile.

"You got it," she smiled back at him.

Jared paid for the champagne and headed quickly out of the store.

Later that evening, during their rendezvous on the Knob, Jared had some significant news he had to tell Melinda. He explained in a very sensitive way what had happened during his reunion with Riccardo at the Bell Tower garden in Woods Hole. Melinda felt badly for Riccardo and the tragedy that took Robert's life.

"What do you make of it Jared? How could Robert know that he was going to die? I have never heard of such a thing. Of course, with all of your paranormal experiences, nothing surprises me!"

"I don't have that answer Melinda. But see it really doesn't matter because someone has come into our lives who needs love. We can open our hearts to Riccardo and share our love and understanding. I think that Robert ....or whoever he was........"

Melinda looked intently over at Jared. There was a very long pause.

"Yes?" interjected Melinda.

"Whoever he was. I think that Robert may have felt that Riccardo may need us and that we should get to know him. We should become his friends. And that is what I want to do. I think the message from Robert was that you and I should make Riccardo Lopez a part of our lives."

"Well I don't understand all of that, but do you know what?"

"What, Mel?"

"I like the way you said 'our lives'." She leaned over and kissed Jared.

He then changed the subject and told her about the enjoyable sailing lesson that he had given to Micky. He felt like a schoolteacher giving a report on Micky's progress as a sailor. Jared listed all of the sailing techniques that Micky had learned that day. Then he briefly described the Eldridge Tide book. He told her how his fingers had stopped on the page that had the date and currents information on the day that Sam Parker had drowned. He explained what he had discovered on that page.

"So what are you saying, Jared, that if Sam did fall off of that jetty he would have been swept in the opposite direction?"

"Exactly. The currents would have taken his body *out* of Buzzard's Bay and towards Woods Hole. Not, —not towards Chapaquoit Beach. There is absolutely no way that his body could have been dragged in the opposite direction of that current."

"God....this whole thing is really getting to me. It just doesn't leave us does it? Jared I think that we have to do something. I am not sure what the hell that is but we just can't keep this information to ourselves. It is as though somebody wants us to do something."

" I know. That's how I feel, too," Jared responded.

"You know it is so strange. I keep thinking about the series of events these past weeks. It started with those 'spiritual forces' or whatever they were, on the Knob leading us to Sam's wine bottle and later the St. Christopher's medal. Then of all the people you could have talked with at my family picnic, you and Detective Souza become friendly. He kept you intrigued with the case. His invitation to look at the Parker files with the morphine information and the photo with Sam's misplaced canvas bags kept you hooked. And now this. You are saying that if Sam did fall from the jetty he would have gone out towards Woods Hole and into the open ocean.

It would have been impossible for him to float up onto Chappy beach."

"It's looking more and more like somebody may have killed him, and then made it look like a drowning accident. There would be little skepticism since so many people knew his morning routine at Chappy walking out to that jetty," Jared continued.

"And....most people don't understand or think about ocean currents and their directions."

"Christ, Jared. We gotta do something." Mel looked straight at him. "We can't ignore all of this. There is something going on here."

"That was my decision too, Mel. There is some force leading us towards all of this information for a reason. We can't turn our back to it."

"Exactly."

"The problem is.... who do we go to? I am not confident that we should approach Jack Ogren, the Chief of Police."

"No, it's not Ogren. I have someone else in mind. We have to meet with Paula Parker."

* * *

The next morning, after his 5-mile run and subsequent rest in the Bell Tower garden, Jared thought more about Riccardo Lopez. He phoned him when he got back to his house. After some congenial talk, Jared asked if he would like to join Melinda and him that day for lunch. They could meet at the Flying Bridge restaurant on Falmouth Harbor. Riccardo sounded happy for the invitation and looked forward to having lunch with his new friends, Jared and Melinda.

The Flying Bridge restaurant is one of the older establishments in Falmouth. It is ideally located at the mid-point on the western bank of Falmouth Harbor. It is one of the most picturesque harbors in Massachusetts with a busy line of boats coming in from ports up and down the eastern seaboard. The local fisherman and sailors value this harbor for its proximity to the Cape Cod Canal, Martha's Vineyard, Nantucket and the Elizabeth Islands.

Riccardo, Melinda and Jared were a comfortable trio of friends from the beginning. Their conversations were non-stop for almost three hours. They freely shared stories and experiences about themselves without reservation or pretense.

They enjoyed their pitcher of beer, with cherrystone clams, shrimp and avocado salad, crab cakes, and fried calamari. They shared their food with each other as easily as they did their animated conversation.

"I will not dwell on my recent loss folks, but I need you to know that this has been one hell of a bad summer for me," said Riccardo.

"How so?" asked Mel washing down her clams with a swig of cold beer.

"Well. As you know I lost my best friend recently. But prior to this loss, another dear professional friend of mine died this past May.

"Really? Who was that Riccardo?"

"I am sure that you heard about it. It was that sad drowning of Sam Parker in the bay."

"Did you know Sam?" asked Jared. He looked over at Melinda. Melinda stopped chewing.

"Oh, of course. I had worked for Sam for the past five years. I was his research assistant. A lackey really. But I loved working for him since he was such a sweet man. He really played the role of my surrogate father for me many times over the past few years."

"Yeah... we knew him too. We actually know his wife. She had been our sixth grade teacher many years ago."

"I had never met her. Paula, isn't that her name?"

"Yes it is."

" Sam was so good to me. I confided in him and he confided in me. I knew about his illness before any of his associates did, including his wife. It was so sad."

"So you knew about his brain cancer early on. How so?"

"Several months ago, he had surmised something was seriously wrong with him. He went into Boston for some clinical tests without anyone knowing. He learned then that he had an inoperable tumor.

The doctors and he could only hope that the mass would increase in size slowly so that he could maintain some quality of life. But it was doubtful even back then."

"So he knew that he was dying some time ago?"

"Yes, but for some reason, he decided to tell only me. I was always his confidante as he was mine. My job at the Marine Biological Laboratories in Woods Hole had been to schedule and arrange all of Dr. Parker's experiments and research trips. He told me that he wanted to cancel all research trips from that day forward. I had to take him off of the master schedule for all upcoming trips aboard our research vessel. I then assigned other associates to take his place."

"Really! So then, he knew several months before his death that he would never again go on a research trip?" asked Jared.

"Oh, yeah. He knew that he could not take the pitching and rolling of the ship now matter how short a trip it was. He would just get sick and be a burden to the crew."

Jared's mind was working fast. He recalled the day spent in Jesse Souza's office. He remembered the paper copy of the electronic mail that was in the file. He could picture it almost word for word in his mind. The e-mail stated that Sam was canceling the research trip at the last minute. It implied that he had always planned on sailing out on that research trip. But according to Riccardo that could not have been the case. There was also mention of going for a walk along the beach in that e-mail from Sam. Jared then wondered if Sam was the person who had sent that e-mail message.

"Riccardo. Did someone else take Sam's place on the trip scheduled on the day he drowned?"

"Of course. I got replacements for all of the trips planned this year," replied Riccardo as he shook the saltshaker over his fried calamari.

Jared ate no more food. He now understood that his meeting Riccardo some weeks ago had dual purposes. He now had picked up another clue that Sam's death was more planned than accidental, based on Riccardo's story. The e-mail was set up as a decoy. Someone had access to a computer and sent that e-mail to make it look like his plans were changed at the last minute. It also set up the time for his walk and subsequent death. Somebody murdered Sam Parker. The murder had been carefully planned out. Except the killer was missing some information that Jared and Melinda now knew.

Jared was mulling over a nagging problem. That email message could have originated from anywhere. It could have come from any computer with access to the Internet and electronic mail. He knew that it could have come from a neighbor, a school, or the public library. It could have come from the Falmouth Police station.

"Riccardo, just one more question about Sam," said Jared.

"Sure. What is it Jared?"

"Did anyone else, besides you, know that Sam's sailing research trips had been canceled for the remainder of the year?"

"Oh, I don't know. We kept it confidential. None of his associates knew about his plans."

Jared decided to drop the topic about Sam Parker and returned to more positive topics. Melinda and Riccardo found that they had similar interests in art and Asian history. Jared learned that Riccardo had been an avid sailor for several years. He had been a competitive racing sailor on the J-24 sailboats. They made plans to meet again on the weekend, and talked about a day-trip to Boston. Their friendship was genuine. They all wanted it to last for a very long time. As they said good-bye, the three of them felt blessed that they had encountered each other.

Melinda felt much better after their lunch. It took away the mental anguish that she had been feeling lately. The relationship between Jared's mother, Sonny, and Father Tom Donovan— both past and present, had been bothering her. She was not sleeping at night. She couldn't get the personal and physical similarities of Jared and Father Tom out of her mind. It made her sick. If her theory was true, then Jared had been living a twisted lie through all of his innocent life. She tried to believe that this couldn't have happened. She loved Jared so much. Jared didn't deserve this. It was sick. Melinda, at times, rationalized that she was making too much of what she was seeing and hearing at the Quissett Country Club. She was now looking forward to her bartending job coming to a quick end.

CHAPTER TWENTY

Memorials and Memories

The rain came down in torrents that hot, humid, Friday night in August. The rain was a welcome site for the Quissett residents. The extraordinarily dry spring and summer had exhausted much of the stored water in the local reservoirs and private wells. This night, however, was uncomfortably sticky with the rain, high humidity and dense, thick fog.

The antiquated air conditioning in the Quissett Country Club could not bring any relief when the humidity reached such high levels. The working staff, and members alike, all felt uncomfortable. There was only a small dinner crowd at the club restaurant on this oppressive evening. Melinda dreaded staying behind the bar until closing on such a slow and dismal night. She asked her boss and club manager, Patrick, if he would let her leave around nine o'clock. Patrick was very understanding. He told her that one of the other waitresses could easily tend the bar. He didn't expect much of a crowd beyond that time on this sticky, August night.

At seven-thirty, Father Tom Donovan came in for his usual relaxing Friday night of drinks and conversation. He settled into his favorite bar stool to watch the Boston Red Sox play the New York Yankees on the bar's large screen TV.

Fifteen minutes later, Sonny Westcott joined him at the bar. She was wearing a very short khaki skirt that accented her well-tanned legs and a new pair of espadrilles on her feet. She had on a soft, periwinkle blue, tank top that revealed enough cleavage to let her feel cool and to tease others with her inviting well-shaped breasts. While most people were suffering through the oppressive humidity, she appeared to be in a very fresh and bubbly mood this evening.

"Good evening Melinda, and....Tom. How is everyone tonight?" as she slipped onto a barstool.

Melinda felt herself tensing up. She just didn't want to be in the company of these two former lovers on this evening. She wasn't sure that she ever wanted to be in their company at all.

Melinda answered. "Hi....Well, to be honest, I feel great now, since Pat has given me the rest of the night off. The club is really slow tonight. I'll be leaving at nine. How are you doing?"

"I am great. Just great!" Sonny had a glow on her face. "I feel so honored. I have to tell you something that has made me so happy. But first, Mel, could you please mix me a tall, cold "T and T" with a twist? And ...oh yes, another one for Tom here."

Melinda turned to make the gin and tonic drinks. She peered out of the corner of her eye to the clock on the wall wishing that it were already near nine o'clock.

"Let me tell the both of you. I have some exciting news! Today, I received an invitation from the VFW to speak at a dedication ceremony in September. There is going to be a beautiful Viet Nam memorial monument erected on the lawn at Quissett High School. It is to remember all of the school's graduates who had lost their lives in Southeast Asia. Because of my brother's heroism over there, they have asked me to participate at the ceremonies. I am thrilled! The VFW wants me to speak about the sacrifices that my brother, Jared, and the other Quissett boys had made during that ugly war."

Tom lit up. "Sonny! That is wonderful. What a great honor to represent Jared and the others. Congratulations!"

Sonny continued to glow. "Melinda, as soon as I get the confirmed date for the ceremony, I want you to put it in your calendar. I would love to have you beside my son, Jared, at that ceremony. I know that my brother would have loved for you to be there!"

"Sonny, that is so nice of you. You can bet on me being there. I wouldn't miss it."

"He was a great guy, Mel. I wish he could have met you."

"I hate to ask, Sonny, but how did your brother die in Viet Nam? Was it during a battle?"

"No dear. I still have that dreadful copy of the report from the Department of Defense. He had just returned to Da Nang Air Base. He had come back from a mission where he flew in and scattered the enemy and saved many of our own GI lives. He was being driven in one of those opened convertible Army jeeps back to the Officers' barracks. Tragically, a hidden Viet Cong sniper took a shot at him and got him in the side of his head." Sonny's eyes welled up.

"Oh! I am so sorry Sonny."

"Yeah. It was a tough time for all of us back then."

Melinda then had a puzzled look on her face. "Did you say he was shot while riding in a convertible? A jeep convertible?"

"Yes. I always felt that if had he been in a truck or armored vehicle he would still be with us today. Those opened convertibles offered no protection."

"And Tom, I have a favor to ask of you." Sonny turned to face Tom. I think that, you, as a priest, and a former Quissett High 'grad', should give the invocation at the ceremony. Please say yes?"

"Oh, Sonny....Oh, I don't know....Viet Nam....you know....."

"Here, lets take our drinks over to that table and we'll have a nice dinner, and I will convince you."

She turned and winked at Melinda as she slid seductively off of the barstool and took Tom's arm.

At eight-fifty-nine, Mel bolted from the club's back door and ran to her car in the rain. She drove her car very slowly out of the parking lot since the rain and fog were so heavy. Mel felt so much better being out of the club restaurant. She wasn't about to experience another night with Sonny teasing Tom with her eyes, her body and those memories of their old high school days and nights. She wished that Jared could get off from work now.

Since she had some extra time, she decided that she would give Riccardo Lopez a phone call as soon as she got home. They needed to discuss plans for their upcoming trip to the Boston Symphony. She needed a pleasant distraction from her evening's experience at the club bar.

Sonny and Tom had several drinks with appetizers and a light dinner.

"You know Sonny, I am really proud of you and this Viet Nam Memorial ceremony. But you know, I have told so many people in town that I dodged the draft to avoid that war. It wouldn't be right for me to be there. It would be much too hypocritical."

"I know. I already had thought about that. It's just that you were so much a part of my brother's life growing up and all of Quissett is so proud of you!"

"Well, with respect to Jared and the others, that war is one that I still cannot condone. We lost too many good, young people in Viet Nam including your brother. I am sorry but its one thing that I cannot do for you."

Sonny looked down into her lap, disappointed, but she knew not to press him on this. "I understand," she replied.

"By the way, do you know if anyone from *our class* of 1970 was lost over there?"

"You know, its funny that you should ask." Sonny grabbed her pocketbook and opened it.

"Did they give you a list of students by graduating class?"

"Yes. Our class had several men and women who served over there. But according to the list of names who had been killed in action, there was only one who had been in our Class of '70." Sonny opened the envelope and began reading the letter.

"Really, who was it?"

"Well, it is strange. I don't remember this person in our class, and I thought I knew everyone. Here it is. The name is Whitestone. David Whitestone. He was killed in Saigon about five months after graduation from Quissett High. Do you know who he was?"

"Hmmmmm .....you know me..... I remember just about

everyone. I believe that he was a transfer student who came in late during our senior year. A quiet guy. Didn't really get to know him. I recall that he was in my gym class."

Sonny's eyes were fixed on Tom's face as he spoke. She had a very longing smile. "You know Tom, I wish I were in your gym class at Quissett High." She giggled. " I need another drink, can you get the waitress?"

"OK, but I am just going to have some iced coffee." Tom replied.

Tom excused himself to go to the restroom. Sonny knew that he would stop by at the bar to check the latest score of the baseball game. While he was gone, Sonny smiled as she thought about the honor to speak at the veterans' ceremony. She felt so good about this. She was happy that she could finally do something for her deceased brother and the other village casualties of the war. As she sipped her cold drink she suddenly had a very vivid flashback to the last time when she was with her older brother. She quickly sat straight up. The reflection rattled her.

It was at Squibnockett beach on the island of Nantucket. It was some thirty years ago. She remembered her discussion that day with her brother, Jared. He had brought her out to the island to tell her that he was leaving her. Did he know more than he had shared with on that day? The shocking news of his enlistment had taken her off guard. She couldn't hide it. As they hugged each other on the sandy beach for what was to be their final time, she told him that she could imagine him serving his country well and becoming a war hero. She remembered how she further told him that she envisioned him being honored later at a special ceremony. Jared had responded that he did not want any ceremony to happen in Quissett unless she was there with him. A sudden chill went down her spine, as she recalled that conversation on the Nantucket beach, over three decades ago. Next month there would be a ceremony to honor him. To honor him in spirit. Sonny would be there with him. He would be there with Sonny.

The waitress brought over a tall glass of iced coffee for Tom and another gin and tonic for Sonny. They were the only two members still in the club by ten-thirty. The waitress was attempting to signal a hint to Tom and Sonny. She asked if they were ready to sign for their club check. Tom caught the subtle hint.

"You know Tom, I look at you today in August of this year 2000 and wonder what our lives would have been like if we had stayed together."

"Ohhhhh, now Sonny, lets not go there. I worked too hard to get over what happened between us and I am content with the life that I have been living."

"I am sure, Tom. But in a special sort of way, you and I were something together. We ignited sparks every time we were together. It was as if you and I were.........I don't know...maybe 'soul mates'".

"Look, Sonny, you have to be happy with your life. It has been comfortable, problem-free and happy. Especially with your son, Jared. You must be so proud of having a son like him. He is such a joy! And look, you're probably going to have a beautiful daughter-in-law soon with Melinda. You'll have not one, but two children then and perhaps grandchildren in the future. I envy you Sonny, more than you'll ever know. Not becoming a parent was the biggest void in my entire life."

"Really?" Sonny asked incredulously.

"Yes of course. You will never know how I envy what you have. Having children of my own was always my ultimate goal. You are so fortunate to have a son. Especially Jared. I think that he is so special."

"Why, Tom. I.... I never knew....we never discussed....."

Sonny looked away into thin air. She began to think about all of the times that she had been in Tom's company. They never really had any in-depth conversations about anything. They always resorted to their instinctual physical lovemaking. Sonny realized that although she was so intimate with this man, she never got to know Tom Donovan, the person. Their relationship was always superficial. That was her fault. She knew this. That's how she was with all of the men in her life. No other man would understand her. No other man could understand her. Except her brother. Jared was the only one who totally understood her. She also knew that she didn't rally care about the inner feelings of the men in her life.

"Yeah, it's not so much the easy living, and the wealth that you have always had during your marriage. I could have survived well enough without that. It's your son, Jared. I would give anything to have had a son like him. You don't know how lucky you are! God really blessed you with a beautiful human being and human spirit in that young man."

"I know, I know...." Sonny replied.

She was feeling awkward with this conversation about Jared. What happened twenty-two years ago had been totally suppressed in her mind during all of these years. She never again thought about the decision that she and her husband, Jim, had made back then. She had rationalized from that day forward that it would be healthier for her to mentally suppress not only the decision, but also how she had mistreated Father Tom. Until now, she had succeeded.

Sonny's emotions were reeling while Tom continued talking to her about Jared. Her head was swimming with many different thoughts all at once. She had to change the subject. She always had avoided any detailed conversations about Jared since Father Tom had returned to Quissett. She had recommended that they meet only on the golf course since the conversations would be light and their focus would be on the game.

She was feeling very sorry for Tom on this night as he opened up about having a child of his own. Her heart was still pounding. She had trouble processing all of this. She needed to get up. She had drunk too many drinks to think logically. She needed some fresh air.

"I really enjoyed playing golf with him the other day. We hit it off extremely well. It seemed strange, Sonny. It was almost as though we already knew each other. We were really comfortable together. I sensed that he was comfortable with me, as well. I really wished that I knew him as a youngster, you know, as he was growing up."

Sonny then became quiet and pensive. Tom looked over at Sonny. He was surprised to see that a tear was falling down her cheek.

He was confused. What did he say that brought this on? Why would she be so emotional about her grown son?

"Sonny is there something wrong?" Tom asked.

"No, no. I just get...."

Sonny excused herself to go to the ladies room. As she ambled away from the table, Tom noticed how unsteady she was walking. She had consumed many drinks this particular evening. Tom thought they should leave the club. He also realized that in her condition it might be best that she not drive herself home.

He signaled, the manager, Patrick, over to his table and told him that he would be driving Mrs. Westcott home. He explained that she had "overindulged" a bit this evening. Patrick need not worry about Sonny driving home. Her Mercedes Benz would be staying in the club's parking lot, locked up, overnight. Patrick was in full agreement.

When Sonny returned to the table they sat for a few minutes longer and then left the club. She had regained some of her composure. She had refreshed her makeup. She looked better. They walked slowly as he escorted her out of the club.

"My God, is it foggy tonight!" said Sonny with a noticeable slur in her words. " I don't mind you taking me home Tom, but I really think that I am all right to drive."

"Oh now, Sonny, it's not a problem. And you never know when a cop might pull you over. Then you'd have an embarrassing situation. Nobody needs that."

"Hmm..I guess that your are right," she said with a sly smile.

Tom opened the passenger door of his car for Sonny. She deliberately turned slowly to get into the car such that her short skirt slid up. This gave him a long look at her legs, her upper thighs and beyond. After all, she thought to herself, he has seen it all before. And he has been there before. Many times.

Tom started his car and immediately turned on the air conditioner for relief. The cold air felt good to the both of them. He then cautiously started driving down Woods Hole Road with its serpentine twists and turns. With the thick fog and wet roads, there wouldn't be any speeding tonight. It would be a long, slow drive to the Westcott house.

"You know something Tom? In a way, we never got to really know each other when we were younger."

"Oh no, Sonny, *au contraire*. I think that we knew each other very well."

"Well..I mean.... what you said back at the club. About children. I never, never really knew that children were so important to you. I never realized that you wanted a child. That was a subject that we never discussed years ago."

"Yes. That is true. We never discussed it. But children were always in the back of my mind. You know I never told you this, but there were times that I had hoped that I got you pregnant so that we would create a new life in this world. I wanted so much for you to have my baby. But, of course, my other agenda was to make you my wife. And as I painfully learned...that was never to happen." There was some disappointment and sarcasm in the tone of his voice.

Tom slowed his speed to get his bearings in the thick, white fog. Sonny became very quiet while she was in deep thought. Her mind was hazily working to recall scenes that took place so many years ago. She looked over at Tom as he struggled to see the road through the windshield wipers and the dense, wet fog. The headlights of the car only made it worse. It seemed like he was navigating through clouds. She then leaned her head on his shoulder. She let her hand drop so that it rested on his leg. With her fingers moving lightly on his thigh, she could feel the warmth of his skin through the linen material of his slacks.

"You know Tom, there is something that I want to tell you now. It is something that you have never known and I think you deserve to know. I have kept something very important from you. I have kept this secret for many years."

"And what that might be, Sonny?" asked Tom squinting through the windshield.

"Tom. I just hope that you will understand."

"Understand what, Sonny?" asked Tom as the car sped up going down a steep hill.

"Tom. Maybe you should pull the car over to the side of the road."

"No. No, it's all right. I have control now. I think the fog is lifting. What is it that you have kept from me all these years?"

Sonny was quiet again. Then she took a deep breath. She had to tell him.

Now was the time.

"It's Jared, Tom. I need to tell you something about my son. Jared is really......he is really....."

The next thing that Tom saw coming through the fog was the rack of antlers. It was a six point buck. The big black eyes had been fixed on the car's headlights. Instinctively, Tom stomped on the brake as hard as he could. It was too late. The deer came hurtling through the windshield, cracking the glass with its hooves. The car went into a wild spin.

Tom's car rolled over several times on the dark, slippery, and unforgiving road. It stopped turning over only after it slammed into a large oak tree. Flames were flaring from the engine through the front hood.

The emergency technicians arrived on the scene quickly. They used their powerful floodlights to look into the crushed vehicle. The light shone on a woman's leg outstretched in a grotesque fashion. Her khaki skirt was bloodied and raised up on her body. Her left buttock was completely exposed. The intense bright emergency light then found a neon green, orange, and blue-colored butterfly tattoo. The butterfly did not seem to be flying as it once did, but rather suspended in flight. Sonny had been killed instantly.

The paramedics quickly used the "Jaws of Life" to extricate Father Donovan from the vehicle. He was critically injured with head and neck wounds. The ambulance whisked him away to the local hospital. He would need to be transferred to one of the other hospitals better prepared for trauma cases such as this one. If they could stabilize his vitals, they would air lift him into one of the Boston Hospitals. His injuries were extensive and he had lost a lot of blood.

CHAPTER TWENTY-ONE

Revelations

Jim Westcott and his son, Jared, had decided to hold a single evening wake for Sonny at the local funeral home. The wake had to be held with the casket closed. The tragic and fatal accident had disfigured Sonny's face and body beyond recognition and repair. Jim had the funeral director place a recent oil painting portrait of Sonny next to the casket. The Provincetown artist had captured the beauty and magnetism of this woman on his canvas. The likeness was incredible.

There was a significant turnout for the wake. Most of the people were the local Quissett citizens. Sonny had been generous with her time and her energy over the years. She had served on many environmental and civic committees for the village. She was well known for her tenacity to maintain the conservation of the land and natural wildlife habitats.

Jim had asked Melinda Abandando to stand in the funeral parlor receiving line. She stood alongside Jared thanking the visitors for their warm support. It would be a solemn evening after such a tragic and untimely death.

Mel was a source of strength for both Jim and Jared during this stressful time. Jared was so proud that she could socially handle the line of visitors so capably. While she spoke to the visitors, Jared reflected on his mother and his childhood years with her.

He thought how she had been a good mother to Jared. She attended to his childhood needs. She motivated him to always do his best. She kept his nanny, 'Mac", on board to supplement in those areas that she had difficulty as a mother. She did this so that Jared wouldn't lose out. Sonny did not have "instinctive" warmth in her love for him or for most people. Jared later learned that people who are distant or cold or negative are those who have never known what real love is during their lives. He often felt that was true for his mom. She never really knew what love was all about. If she never received love, she didn't know what it was, and therefore couldn't give it.

People would mention as they passed by that they would be praying for Sonny's soul and for the recovery of the good Father Donovan. They hoped that he would pull through from his injuries. He was still in critical condition at the intensive care unit at the Boston General Hospital.

Near the end of the evening, it was Paula Parker, who surprised Jared and Melinda. Paula walked nervously into the parlor. She gave each of them warm and sincere hugs. She deeply felt compassion for the two young people having to experience such a tragedy. She told them that after things had settled that she wanted Jared and Melinda over for dinner at her house. It would be supportive for all of them and especially uplifting for Paula. She had tears coming down her cheeks.

Jared stared at Paula Parker crying. Those tears were for him. He focused on those tears slowly rolling down her face. For the first time, he had a clear recollection that brought him back to a time when he was five-years-old. It was an Indian summer day.

On that fall day, Mac had brought him to the beach to play kick ball. He had to retrieve the ball when it had been kicked too far away. He found that it had landed in a pretty woman's lap leaning against a sea wall. He recalled her aura of beauty and grace as seen from the eyes of a little boy. He still could see her auburn hair blowing in the breeze. He remembered that her voice was gentle and her smile was soft and warm. Her beautiful green eyes were sad that day. He focused on the tears rolling down her cheeks much like they were this evening. He now knew that the beautiful but sad woman, who caught his ball that day, was Mrs. Paula Parker. He must tell her that story when the time is right. He was still a little curious to know what the sad news was that she got that day.

The funeral service and motorcade held the next day seemed terribly long for the family and friends. The day was hot and humid with thunderclouds making threatening noises from a distance. After the burial ceremony at the Westcott family plot, everyone was invited back to the Westcott home for refreshments.

Jared kept close to Mel. He needed her support and love to get him through this raw and emotional event in his life. He was very pensive after returning to the house. He was cordial but emotionally distant from the friends and relatives. Mel filled in the empty pauses with social grace and kindness so that there were no awkward moments for anyone.

Later after the guests were gone, and the caterers were finished cleaning up, Mel asked Jared if he wanted her to stay.

"No, no. Thanks Mel, you have done so much for me and for my father already. Please go home to your family and get some rest."

"OK, Jared. I will. You need some time alone with your father. I will call you tomorrow in the morning." She kissed and hugged him.

Mel felt such deep love and compassion for Jared this day. She knew him so well. She knew that his mind was processing so many thoughts. She felt helpless because she wanted to take his emotional pains away from him but that was impossible. She turned quickly and ran out of the Westcott home with her eyes filled with tears. It was the first time that she had lost control and cried since learning of the death of Jared's mother. She didn't want Mac or the others to see her crying. She hurried to her car and sped off. She drove with tears in her eyes. It was unbearable for her to think that Jared was in emotional shock and pain. She didn't want her Jared, her best friend and lover, to feel this way. She felt helpless. She couldn't do anything for him to make the pain go away. He had to live through this by himself. It was part of his journey, she thought.

Jared took off his shirt and tie as walked into the kitchen. He didn't even know why he came into the kitchen. He seemed to be walking around aimlessly. He looked over at the kitchen counter.

Mac was getting herself a glass of iced tea. She looked over toward Jared. Then she silently nodded her head toward the study.

Jared walked over towards the door to the study. He stood at the room's threshold and saw his father sitting on the leather couch staring into space. He had been crying. His eyes were still very red. As Jim turned, he noticed Jared at the doorway and motioned for him to come and join him.

Jim stood up and put his arms around Jared's shoulders and then hugged him. They held their embrace for several minutes patting each other's backs. Jim then walked over to the portable bar cart. He poured a brandy over ice for both of them. After giving Jared the drink, he walked over in front of the picture window and turned and faced Jared. The sun was setting through the window behind Jim. This sunset had an effect of rays emanating from Jim's body as he looked at Jared.

"Jared, I know that this has been rough for you, as it has for me. It will take me some time to get used to the fact that your mother is no longer with us. I can't believe that she won't be walking through that door any moment now."

"I know Dad, but we can help each other through this. We have to."

Jim looked at his son with a long, sober expression. This moment was going to be the most difficult time of his entire life. He prayed silently that he would have strength. He prayed silently that Jared would have understanding.

"Jared, I just received a phone call from the Boston hospital."

There was a brief pause.

"Son, Father Donovan just died about an hour ago. He didn't make it. The physician told me that it was probably for the best since he was severely and permanently injured."

Jared put his head down. "God, that's too bad. Poor Father Donovan. I liked him. We seemed to hit it off so well the one day that I was in his company. He struck me as being a good and honest man."

Jim stared at Jared. He took a long drink from his glass and let it burn his stomach as though that would make his next obligation easier.

"Jared, I have something more to tell you. Something that is very important. But before I speak to you, I am going to ask that you open your heart as you always have since you were a young boy. This is not a time to make judgments."

"What is it Dad, what do you want to tell me?"

"Jared is your heart opened? I mean   really, really opened?"

"Yes, Dad. My heart is open and I am not about to make any judgments. I never have. You know me well."

Jim looked directly into Jared's eyes.

"Jared,......Father,....Father Donovan,......he was not just a father in the church. He was......your father. Tom Donovan was your biological father."

There was a deafening silence in the study. The only sounds were the pounding of the men's hearts in their internal chambers. Jared couldn't speak at first. He looked confused and shocked.

"What? "What are you talking about?" The color of Jared's face was rapidly changing hues. He stood up from the couch and walked towards his father. "What the hell are you talking about?"

"Please, please sit down, Jared."

Jim told Jared that he would explain everything to him. He described the marital crisis that he and Jared's mother experienced in early 1978. He began with the revelation that Sonny and he had discovered Jim's sterility early in their marriage. He described the emotional depression that they both experienced. This had put a critical stress on their relationship. At that time, they were both devastated and disappointed since they loved children and wanted to have them.

He told Jared that there was an "estrangement period" in early 1978. It was during this period that his mother and her former high school boyfriend, now Father Tom Donovan, had unintentionally reunited and conceived Jared during a brief romantic affair.

Shortly after, Sonny discovered her pregnancy. She privately confessed everything to her husband and she anticipated that he would leave her.

Jim now told Jared how it was his idea to hold onto the marriage and bring the child up as though it was conceived by Sonny and him. Father Donovan never knew that he had made Sonny pregnant. He never knew that he had conceived a child. The child was Jared. He and Sonny were confident that Tom had no idea about the pregnancy. Sonny and Jim agreed to never let him know. They had a covenant that they would work on their marriage and bring up this yet unborn child with all of the love and caring possible. They agreed to never let Father Tom know about his child. Tom Donovan had died an hour ago never knowing that he had a son.

"Jared, I am sorry to have to tell you all of this, and at his time, but I thought that it had to be done. Sonny and I had promised each other not to ever, ever, tell you, or Tom. You will never realize how we both wanted you so much. We wanted you and we needed you."

Jared was frozen. Not one muscle of his body was moving. He was in complete shock.

"I...I just don't get it. All my life...I....I..."

"But...Jared,...... Please, please try to....... That was long before we could ever imagine what has happened this past week. I am telling you now only because I love you, Jared. I always have and I always will. I thought that since you just had to properly say good-bye to your mother, you should have the opportunity to now say good-bye to your father. I didn't think it fair to keep it from you any longer, under these circumstances. You should know the person who is your real father."

Jared's brain was racing faster than his heart beating.

"Dad....Dad! *You will always be my father!*" Jared said in a loud and stern voice. "You chose to have me born with your name. And you made the decision to bring me up under your love and care. So, I did not come from your blood. Dad, I will never, never think of you as anyone but my father."

"Yes...but I wasn't perhaps fair with both you and Tom Donovan. Each of you lived your lives not knowing the circumstances. He never knew that he had a child. He had a son. You never knew who your biological father was until, now, today. The day that he died."

Jared was regaining some of his emotional strength. He did not know from where it came, but it came. "Dad. Listen. I will pay my respects to Father Tom Donovan. Not as my father, but as another spirit like all of us who journey on earth to do what we are supposed to do—love one another."

"Yes, yes...son," answered Jim. Then he broke into tears and cried loudly.

"In a way, Dad, he was an innocent victim of these circumstances. And if we all think about it, nobody was truly hurt. He didn't know about my conception, so he was detached and didn't feel the emotional pain. It doesn't matter to me because I had a loving father and mother all of my life. It wouldn't have made much of a difference. Dad, you taught me how to love and to be patient and to forgive. And those are the feelings that I am calling upon now to get me through this and to understand. We will all be OK. I know that we will."

"Jared, I loved your mother so much. I didn't want to lose her *and you* back in 1978. I told her that I thought her pregnancy was a gift from God, even under those circumstances." Jim began to weep. There was a long pause.

"Dad....I understand. Don't worry, I understand. I love you."

"And I love you, son." Jim wept.

Jim walked around the study. The sun had now set and dusk was slowly darkening the room.

"Jared, I felt terrible about the situation even though I was so happy that your Mom and I were going to have a child brought into our lives."

"I know, Dad." Jared began to stand up.

"But Jared, please sit down there is more." They took long sips from their drinks. " I have to tell you everything. You deserve to know everything."

"What is it, Dad?" asked Jared as he sat down on the leather chair.

"After your Mom and I relocated permanently down here at Quissett from Boston, I received a hand written note from a woman by the name of Christine Stanton. She was a secretary at St. Ann's rectory. Her hand-written letter only said— —"I think that you should be aware of this letter. It was never sent out."

"A letter?"

"Attached to her hand written note was a typed letter on St. Ann's letterhead from Father Tom Donovan to the Archbishop. The letter was brief. It informed the bishop that Tom wanted to resign from the priesthood. He wrote the bishop that he had fallen in love with a woman in his own parish. It went on to describe that she was someone whom he had known for a long time and was now seriously contemplating nuptial vows of marriage. He confessed that he had not been faithful with his vows of celibacy and requested release from the priesthood as soon as possible."

Jim paused and looked long at Jared. He had to tell his son this information so that he would not think any less of his biological father.

"You see son, Father Tom Donovan truly loved your Mom, as did I. He had planned on marrying her even without knowing about the pregnancy."

"Do you know why the letter had never been sent to the Archbishop?" Jared asked.

"I met with Miss Stanton to learn that. I called her and arranged a private meeting with her. She told me about Tom attempting suicide with liquor and narcotic pills. The letter was found on his nearly comatose body. She found him in an overdosed condition in his bedroom and immediately called for help. She actually saved his life. He was eventually sent to a sanitarium in Vermont. This Christine Stanton had snatched Tom's letter and did not let anyone else see it."

"Oh my God. He really was hurt. He did love mother."

"Jared, all of this happened the day after your Mom told Tom that it was over between them. She called him and told Tom that she and I had conceived a child prior to our estrangement and before their winter romance. She informed Tom that we were now working hard on reconciling and saving our marriage and bringing a new life into this world. I don't know why, but I never destroyed that letter about his love for your mother. I locked it up in my safe in the Boston office. It belongs to you Jared, if you want it."

There was a brief silence. "Thanks, Dad. I think that I would like to see it some day. He must have really loved Mom. I do feel sorry for him."

"You see, son, Tom *was truly* the innocent victim. He had always loved your mother since he was a teenager. He followed the vocation as a priest to escape and to get through his initial pain of losing Sonny. When your mother was considering the future of our own marriage in a very dim light, the brief affair ensued."

Jim then went on to explain to Jared how he felt guilty about Tom's plight. He never let Sonny know what had happened to her former lover. She never knew about the letter to the Archbishop. She never knew that he had suffered an emotional breakdown. She merely thought that Tom had requested a transfer to another parish up north.

Through his connections, Jim was given updates on Tom's progress from the Home for Lost Angels. Without Sonny or Tom knowing any of this, Jim made sure that Tom had the best clinical care and psychiatrists to help him recover from his emotional illness. Jim had made sure that when additional money was required it was sent to Vermont immediately. The recovery for Father Tom Donovan was long, but effective. Jim had felt some degree of responsibility and insured that the young priest always had the best of care. But his actions were very discreet. Sonny never knew of Jim's guilt, love and ultimate responsibility for Tom's recovery. And Tom never knew that he had an anonymous benefactor in Jim Westcott.

Jared was now pacing slowly around the room. He sipped his drink and began tugging at his left eyebrow. He had something that he now had to tell his father.

"Jared, are you OK, son?"

"Dad, I wish that someone else was here with me right now to help me sort things out."

Jim had a puzzled look.

"Oh.... and who could help you with this, Jared?" asked Jim.

"Jessica, my twin sister, Jessica."

"What...what are talking about, son?"

Jared began telling his father what he had had learned this summer. He carefully told Jim that while his birth came weeks too early, it was accompanied with a twin sister who did not survive. Jim wasn't there to witness the birth. The burial was done quickly without anyone knowing about it.

"So. You see Dad; I had a twin sister. Mom had named her Jessica, just before she died. She didn't want anybody to know. You or me. And for over 22 years it was a well-kept secret. But I found out a few weeks ago. I even went to the cemetery where Jessica is buried on the other side of town. Mom probably didn't want you to know, since it was so painful, especially under the circumstances. You were away, and she quickly had Jessica baptized at the hospital. She was buried across town on the very next day."

"She named her Jessica?" Jim began sobbing.

"Yes, I presumed she name her Jessica after your mother."

Jim, nodded, still weeping, still in shock.

Jared then described to his father the closeness that he had felt with Jessica's spirit during all of his life. She had been with him since his childhood days, but never knew exactly who she was until recently. He told his father how she had communicated with him telepathically throughout his life. At the graveside, she communicated with Jared. She informed him that she was moving on and that he now was in good hands with Melinda. He told his father that it was times like these when he found her support and love for him so helpful.

"I just can't believe it!" said Jim. "And she kept her promise. She named her Jessica after my mother. She kept her promise to me."

"Yes...Jessica."

"Twins. All these years and I never knew that Sonny had given birth to a daughter. She had twins. I never knew it. I just never knew about it!"

There was a brief silence. Jared looked over to Jim. He looked into Jim's eyes.

"Neither did Tom Donovan, Dad. Neither did the father, Tom Donovan."

* * *

That night, Jared could not sleep. He tossed and turned and could not stop his mind from racing. He was perspiring profusely. There were multiple vignettes playing through his mind. He visualized his mother and Tom together as lovers, as his parents. He speculated on those difficult and painful discussions between Sonny and Jim when she discovered her pregnancy. He thought about the tragic scene at the hospital when his twin sister had died. He wondered what Sonny and Tom were discussing before the tragedy occurred on Woods Hole Road. He wondered if Sonny truly loved Tom and not Jim. All of these thoughts cluttered his mind and made him confused. He was never relaxed enough to fall off to sleep. As soon as the sun came up, without any sleep at all, he jumped from his bed and put on his running clothes.

He was anxious to run so that he could mentally and physically exhaust himself. He needed to escape this emotional turmoil. He did not do his stretching exercises on this particular morning. He just started running as fast as he could with no particular course in mind.

Jared ran over fifteen miles. He ran as fast as he could. The sweat poured down his face mixing with his tears. Finally, he became tired. Finally, he was exhausted. He could hardly run. He felt a little light-headed. He began to slow down his pace almost to a walk. He turned the last corner limping and headed towards the St. Joseph's Bell Tower garden. He felt better being in the meditation garden.

As Jared paced around the garden area, his breathing began to slow down. He was gradually recovering some of his strength. He finally sat on the bench and looked out upon Eel Pond. He focused straight ahead at nothing, unaware of the sailors raising their mainsails. He didn't hear any of the powerboats revving up their motors leaving their moorings for the day. He was unaware that tears were still rolling down his cheeks. He didn't know why or what he was feeling. It wasn't self-pity. It wasn't anger. And then he knew. It was the lack of something. Love. Love was missing. There was no love. He needed love. He couldn't stop the tears.

"Jared! Jared! Are you all right?"

Jared turned and saw Riccardo coming through the garden's little wooden gate. He wore his light gray sweatsuit. He had a look of concern across his face.

"Oh...Hi Riccardo. ...Yeah, I guess that I'm OK," he coughed.

He then lost control and started shaking and broke down audibly crying and sobbing. Riccardo was quickly at his side. He opened up his arms and embraced the distraught and shaken Jared. He hugged him firmly and said to him.

"Jared, let it go, let it go, leave it to God. Just leave it to God."

Riccardo held him for a long time repeating those phrases until Jared obeyed him. Jared soon began to feel light, as though a burden was lifting from him. Soon his mind was no longer confused. He was getting messages that helped him to understand. He now knew that there was nothing he could have done to alter the events of the past. It was God's plan that these events had happened for reasons he may never understand.

Jared slowly began to feel different. He felt better. He and Riccardo were still embracing. His tears had dampened Riccardo's sweatshirt. He had let go. He felt as though Riccardo had absorbed all of his confusion and emotional pain and then discarded it. He brought in love as they hugged, so that there was no room for any other feelings. Jared knew that love takes up all the space it needs. Then there can be no room left for pain.

They sat down. Riccardo still had his arm draped over Jared's shoulders. Jared turned to his friend and thanked him. He needed love and Riccardo was there for him. He regained his composure and told Riccardo that he had just gone through the most emotionally heart-breaking time of his life. He wasn't sure that he could still make sense from it.

"Jared, Jared."

He turned to look up the street and saw Melinda running

towards St. Joseph's meditation garden. She turned sharply through the gateway. Jared stood up and quickly ran to meet Melinda. He ran to her and Jared brought her into his waiting arms. They embraced and hugged each other tightly for a long time without any words.

Jared broke the silence.

"Mel, Mel, I have to tell you.......I found out that...."

"Don't worry," she smiled. "Don't say anything. I know, I just know. Are you all right? You're going to be all right, Jared. You will be all right. We are *all* going to be all right."

Melinda, Riccardo, and Jared all embraced in a circle fashion. They loved one another. They had helped one another and came to each other's side during times of need. They took away the pain from one another and displaced it with pure unconditional love for one another.

***

Several catholic priests concelebrated Father Donovan's funeral Mass at St. Ann's Church. The procession was very long. It was well attended by Quissett people and relatives from Prince Edward Island. There were several acquaintances from Vermont's Home for Lost Angels. It was an uplifting ceremony since Tom was now truly at peace. Jim and Jared Westcott carried the casket as the front leading pallbearers. They sadly helped put Father Tom Donovan to rest. They prayed for his soul to be happier in heaven than it was on this earth. They knew that it would be.

CHAPTER TWENTY-TWO

Suspicions

Vincenzo Vendrasco was a very large and intimidating man. He stood over six feet four inches in height and weighed close to 290 pounds. His head of thick, silver hair was pulled back and tied up in short ponytail at the back of his neck. His face had a stubby white beard. He had deep penetrating dark eyes and a wry, snarling smile. He always smelled of stale cigar smoke.

Vendrasco filled the entire entranceway to Paula Parker's house when she responded to the front doorbell. She hesitated at first, but then decided to courteously let him into the house after he introduced himself. She did not ask him to sit down.

Vendrasco told her that he was sympathetic about her husband's passing a few of months ago. He did, however, quickly tell her that he and Sam had some discussions about his taking the Parkers' Quissett Harbor boat mooring when they no longer wanted it. Vincenzo explained that he was the next person on the coveted waiting list for a town mooring in that harbor. Because of the recent tragedy of Sam's death, he asked Paula if he could assume ownership immediately and then file with the harbormaster later.

Paula was taken aback. Sam would have told her if he had conversations with Vendrasco or anybody else about taking over their mooring. Sam had secured the mooring soon after they were married. She never paid much attention to it. It was just something that they always owned. She was aware, however, how valuable the Quissett Harbor mooring was since they were in such demand. They were extremely difficult to get. Some families left them in their wills so that a Quissett Harbor mooring became a legacy for younger generations to have in their name.

Mr. Vendrasco's tone had become more aggressive about his taking the harbor mooring. He told her how it wasn't good for people to waste valuable resources. He had told her that it really wasn't fair to those who had been patiently waiting. When he spoke to her, he came closer to her. She actually backed up a few inches to get away from him and his stale breath. He stared at her eyes as he spoke.

Paula was not comfortable with this impromptu meeting. She politely told him that she would seek the counsel of her attorney on such matters. Her attorney would get back to him later. Nothing would take place now. Vincenzo then countered with a financial offering to Paula to temporarily rent the mooring. He wanted to do this until such time that her attorney completed all of his paperwork.

Paula, stood firm with an emphatic "No"! She then asked that he leave her house immediately. She showed him another side of her that was not particularly polite. Vincenzo shook his head, uttered something in Italian that sounded very profane and then left her house, slamming the screen door.

Paula knew that her attorney was vacationing in Europe with his new wife. There was no sense calling his office about this annoying incident. Yet, she was still upset. She paced the floor and couldn't get Vincenzo Vendrasco out of her mind. He had intimidated her. She didn't trust him or what he might do. Her mind was developing violent fantasies over this foolish mooring. She began feeling more uncomfortable and nervous about this encounter. He was not a gentleman and looked like he was capable of inflicting physical harm if he didn't get his way. She decided to call her friend, Police Chief, Jack Ogren.

"Hello Jack! This is Paula. I know that you're probably getting ready to leave the office after a long day, but I need to run something by you."

"Paula, please. I told you to never hesitate to call me for anything. I am happy to hear your voice. Now, what can I do for you?"

Paula explained her earlier visit from Mr. Vendrasco. She told Jack of the demeanor of the giant fisherman and how adamant he was about taking over the mooring. She confessed to Jack, how she felt intimidated and that she was more than just a little nervous with this Goliath. She needed his advice on how to handle the situation.

"Look, Paula, I know about this Vendrasco character. I never wanted to bring it up to you last May because of the raw, emotional pain that you were experiencing from Sam's drowning. I think now I should spend some time with you and explain a few things, and maybe ask you a few things, before we decide how to handle our friend Vincenzo."

"Like what, Jack? What is there that I should know?"

"Paula, look. I'm just going home to take a shower and then I was going out alone for dinner. Would you please do me a favor and join me? I'd love to have dinner with you and then explain where our 'mooring-monger' fits in. How about it? I will pick you up at seven-thirty. OK?"

"Sure, Jack. I really want to know what I can do about this guy. Do you think that you can help me with that? He's a bit creepy! He scared the hell out of me today."

"Seven-thirty," Jack replied.

Jack told Paula that he wanted to take her to the Daniel Webster Inn located in the town of Sandwich, for dinner. The Inn is an upscale restaurant as far as Cape Cod eateries go. It is a very quiet, romantic place with authentic colonial decor and an excellent menu and wine list. People always dressed up from the typical Cape Cod casual look to a more distinguished style when dining at the Daniel Webster Inn.

This restaurant was located outside of the Falmouth area. They were less likely to meet any acquaintances in the town of Sandwich. Jack did not want to be perceived as someone who might be taking advantage of a recent and vulnerable widow. Everyone in town had known Sam and Paula Parker. Most people knew Chief Jack Ogren. They also knew that he had been divorced and was still single.

When Jack arrived, Paula sensed for the first time, that Jack's interest for her was not strictly related to police business. He was dressed extremely well. His after-shave lotion was especially strong this evening. As they got into his car, Jack told her that he wanted to take the longer shore route. This would give them a chance to chat a little and see the beautiful sunset over the Quissett beaches and coastline.

His timing was perfect. The Cape Cod sunsets are especially beautiful in late summer, as the huge ball of fire slowly drops down behind the ocean's blue horizon. The colors in the sky change quickly from light orange and pink, to fiery, ruby red and finally a variety of purple hues. Jack purposely drove slowly along the shore. Paula watched the entertaining sunset perform for them behind the several couples and lovers walking the beach hand in hand.

Most people go to the Webster Inn restaurant for special occasions. Paula was sure that this was not a place frequented by one divorced policeman, Jack Ogren. She had never given any thought to a different man in her life. She didn't know how she and Jack were going to act since she and Sam had always considered him to be one of their best friends. She was more than a little nervous on this late summer evening.

The hostess led them to a room with darkened pine paneling on the lower walls. There was a wide railing of wainscoting with flowering print wallpaper on the upper half of the walls. It had a warm and cozy feeling to it. Jack requested a private booth that would enable them to talk without being overheard.

As the hostess led them to their table, Jack had a broad smile on his face. This grin spoke volumes of his pride and affection as he held Paula's arm escorting her to their table. He couldn't understand completely what he was feeling. He hadn't felt this way in many years. It was commonly known as feeling happy. Jack hadn't known this emotion for a very long time.

The waitress recited the special meals of the evening. Jack ordered a scotch whiskey on the rocks and Paula requested a Manhattan. Paula now noticed the smile on Jack's face. She decided to quickly get to the topic that brought them there. She asked about what she should do with Vendrasco.

"Paula, I've got to tell you about this guy, Vendrasco, and how we might handle him. But first, a toast, if you don't mind. To the both of us — — may our *future* days be light and filled with good health!"

They clinked their glasses, and then started on the cheddar cheese spread and crackers.

Jack explained to Paula that Vendrasco, had a criminally checkered past. He had been associated with the mob in the cities of Providence and Boston during his younger years. He had been involved with some drug transporting from Columbia and several money-laundering incidents. On two occasions he was investigated for murders that took place in the Boston Harbor. Each victim had been killed with a large steel fisherman's gaffing hook through the neck. The murders were never solved and were commonly known as the "hook" murders. Vendrasco was suspected but never convicted for the murders.

Paula was getting very nervous as Jack spoke about Vendrasco. She was sure that this big ugly man was capable of committing murders and other crimes.

"Actually, my detective, Jesse Souza, investigated this guy. Vincenzo is not someone with whom you want to be associated. I don't want to go into the details about Sam's death, Paula, but there was always the remote possibility that foul play may have been involved. After some legwork, we could only come up with Vendrasco as anyone with a possible motive. It didn't go anywhere. It's wasn't so much the mooring as it was his reputation for dealing with people who crossed him."

Jack looked for a reaction from Paula. She was losing some of the color in her face.

"Jesus, Jack. You're not making me feel any better about this guy. I told you that he scared the crap out of me earlier today. I am afraid that he will not go away."

"I'm sure."

Paula emphatically stated her nervousness about Vendrasco as she sipped her Manhattan cocktail. "Is there anything that I can or should do? I don't want him coming back to my house!"

"The only thing that we can do is to wait to see if he does come back to visit you. You did the correct thing by telling him that your lawyer would be looking into it."

"Can I get a restraining order or something like that? I really don't want that bastard coming back to my home."

"I wouldn't do that now. If he should return just don't let him inside of your house. Talk through the door. Let's see if anything develops. All of the boats have to be pulled from Quissett Harbor in about two months. It isn't worth him pursuing this now. I really don't think that he will cause you any problems."

As they ate dinner, their conversation shifted to more mundane topics. Jack asked about her sister's medical clinic on Martha's Vineyard. He also inquired if Paula had any plans for going back to work.

"I'm really burned out as a teacher, Jack. Even substitute work doesn't appeal to me. About a year ago, I really had thoughts of opening up a small, quaint bookstore in the Woods Hole area. You know something a little different with rare or hard to find titles. Perhaps a little coffee shop included. I just don't have the confidence right now in doing anything like that. Sam was going to help me set it up since he had a better financial and business sense than me."

When the waitress brought the check, Paula excused herself to go to the ladies room. As she walked down the aisle towards the restroom, she heard the waiters and waitresses singing "Happy Birthday" in a booth nearby. She stopped and listened. She could see a small birthday cake with some lit candles being placed in front of the customer. As she focused her eyes, she could now make out that the birthday celebrant was Jim Westcott. As the wait staff scattered after the song and brief applause, she could see that Jared and Melinda were with him. She walked towards their table.

"Well! Happy Birthday Jim." Paula smiled as she approached their booth. It's good to see you out and about."

"This is a pleasant surprise, Paula," replied Jim. "Thank you. Jared and Melinda asked if they could take me here for my birthday. I think they just wanted to get me out of the house. I had forgotten that I even had a birthday!"

"Well, they are sweet, special people." Paula bent over and kissed both Jared and Melinda on their cheeks. I am still waiting to have a dinner with them myself!"

"We haven't forgotten, Paula. We are looking forward to it," replied Jared.

"It's funny," Paula continued, " this is my first night out of the house in long time. I had some police issues today and Jack Ogren wanted to get me out of my house to discuss them. It was so nice of him to bring me here."

Jared's mind went back to the photos of Paula hidden in Jack's desk drawer. He thought that maybe Jack was moving in on Paula quickly. Jesse's thesis may have been right. He had been after Paula for a long time.

"Police issues? I hope that there is nothing wrong Paula," asked Melinda.

"Well, I had someone quite scary unexpectedly stop by my home today. He is pressuring me to give him my Quissett harbor boat mooring, now that Sam is no longer here."

"That doesn't sound too sensitive or compassionate!" said Jim.

"No, and that is why I called the police. This guy was quite overbearing today."

"Do I know him?' asked Jared.

"I doubt it, hon'. He comes from the mob out of Boston and Providence. Not someone you would come across in your travels. That's for sure. Evidently he's had his eye on Sam's mooring for a long time. His name is Vendrasco. He came into my house trying to make all sorts of deals with me to get the mooring."

"Wow, that must have been tough for you to deal with today," said Mel.

"Yes it was," answered Paula.

"Can we be of any help?" asked Jim.

"No. No thanks. Jack has been looking after me quite closely. At least I have the cops on my side," she laughed. "Listen I've got to go. Please, please give me a call, kids. Jim, enjoy your birthday." Paula blew him a kiss.

As Jack and Paula were driving back to Quissett, there was too much silence. It bothered Paula, more than it did Jack. She made small talk, which was unusual for her. Anything to break the silent pauses. As Jack pulled his car up in front of Paula's home he told her that he had an idea that may diffuse the Vendrasco situation.

"What is it Jack?"

"Paula, we know that this ape is interested only in your mooring. He told the harbormaster and you that it was just going to waste since you only tied your skiff up to it. Your boat is hardly ever used. He is pissed off because its just floating there and nobody is using it."

"Yes, I understand that. I know where he was coming from."

"Well, what if Vincenzo saw that it was getting used again? Then he would have no argument that it was going to waste, and he would back off."

"Well, even if it wasn't used, I still don't have to give it up legally."

"I understand that. You understand that. But when you are dealing with the mind-set of Vendrasco, you have to use a different psychology and strategy."

"But, Jack, I only took the boat out a few times. It was mostly when Sam and I had a picnic on the Elizabeth Islands. Vendrasco knows that I don't take the boat out alone."

"Precisely."

There was a pause. Paula wasn't following his logic.

"You see, I will be going out with you. I will take the boat out with you such that Vendrasco will see us together. I know that he will back off then. Especially since I am the Chief of Police. I was thinking about trying that routine on this Sunday. I will even pack the picnic lunch for us. You pick our destination island."

This completely caught Paula by surprise. She couldn't think fast enough. She knew what was happening and she didn't know how to deal with it. Jack was pursuing her. She had to think. She couldn't think.

"Jack....I...ah....let me consider that, all right? I have a lot to think about and my mind can't handle as much as it used to. I really appreciate what you are doing for me. Thanks for dinner this evening. It was good to get out of the house. Thanks, again"

"Sure Paula. I will call you later in the week. You know, just to give you time to think about my plan."

"OK, Jack," she gave him her hand gently. "Good night."

As Jack got back into his car after walking Paula to her door, he noticed a very shapely woman just a few yards away on the other side of the street. She was walking a small silky terrier on a short dog's leash. He could make out that she had short blond hair and was wearing a black, tight, sleeveless, tank top. She also wore dark colored shorts.

He thought it unusual for someone to wear such dark colored clothing on a late summer evening especially on a road with very little street lighting. He started the car. He then made an immediate U-turn to get a better glimpse of this woman walking her dog. Jack saw that the turn and the bright headlights startled the woman. He got a good look at her before she turned away. Anita Vendrasco could not avoid Jack Ogren's headlights. He looked straight into her eyes. She pulled the dog's leash sharply and turned her head away. It was obvious to Jack that she did not want to be seen. She ran quickly down a side street.

CHAPTER TWENTY-THREE

Love, Death, and life

The next day Jared telephoned Paula Parker. He asked if he and Melinda could come to her house for a brief visit. With Mel now teaching at Barnstable High School, her free time during the week was limited. They decided to meet at three o'clock on Saturday afternoon.

Jared did not tell Paula the reason for the visit. She presumed it was a social call. She would convince them to stay for an early dinner.

It was a beautiful, warm Indian Summer day. Melinda picked up Jared in her convertible but with the top up so that Jared wouldn't have to slouch down in the seat as soon as he sat on the front seat. The angle of the late summer sun illuminated the sky with a light, tranquil, blue color. There were pink and orange streaks emanating from the fading sun. As they drove along they chatted about the hint of autumn in the air. It made the two of them think of school, football games, and apple picking. They joked about snuggling together when the darkness of the chilly evenings came.

As Melinda drove, they avoided discussing any strategy or agenda with Paula. Their minds would be relieved after they tell her what they had learned about her beloved husband's death. They each felt as though they had been harboring information that should be disclosed. Their friend, Paula, would be the first to know. Even though their theories were speculative, they must inform Paula that all is not what it seemed to be concerning her husband's death.

Paula greeted them at the door with a quick embrace and kiss. She glowed with happiness that her friends had come to her house for a visit. She had coffee and tea prepared for them with some cookies that she had baked. Paula was in her comfort zone when hosting a tea, a party or a gourmet dinner. She thoroughly enjoyed entertaining at her home. She enjoyed serving others so that they would be happy.

After Paula led them into her living room, they all sat down and became relaxed. After some cordial small talk, Jared looked directly at Paula.

"Paula, Mel and I have come here today not only to visit with you but also to let you know about some information that we have come across related to Sam's death. We have been troubled keeping this information to ourselves over the past weeks. We also thought that the one and only person with whom we wanted to share this information-----was you".

Jared started the conversation, but Melinda chimed in when appropriate. They covered everything that had occurred to them in a chronological way.

They discussed the phenomena that each of them had experienced at the Knob with the 'invisible' spiritual forces. The guide who brought them to the wine bottle and the St. Christopher medal. They described finding the empty Yearling wine bottle and how they coincidentally learned later that the New Zealand wine was a unique and special order for Sam and Paula.

Finding Sam's St. Christopher's medal at the Knob triggered a curiosity for them to reflect more on how Sam had died. It was evident to them that Sam had been at the Knob recently —either alone or with someone else. The spiritual forces at the Knob had been leading Jared and Mel to clues about Sam's recent death. If Sam was at the Knob during the night of his drowning, how did his body get all the way over to Chappy beach— some three miles away?

The irony of meeting Jesse Souza at a picnic kept Jared

intrigued and more interested in the so-called "drowning accident". The Medical Examiner's official cause of death with morphine was perplexing. He was dead before he was in the water.

The photos of Sam's body with the draped canvas bags created additional signals that they could not ignore. Why...... on the day that he died, were the bags on the wrong shoulders? More convincing evidence registered when Jared found the tide and current data on the day that Sam died. After looking at this information, Jared was firmly confident that the tides would have taken his body away from "Chappy" beach and not towards it. He then told her about the e-mail message that was sent by someone who did not know that Sam had never intended to go on that research voyage. He learned this after meeting a new friend who turned out to be a lab assistant and professional confidante to Sam. Jared theorized that the person who sent that e-mail had been involved in his death.

In effect, Jared told Paula, they had uncovered clues that Sam had been murdered. But they had no direction where they might go to find any possible suspects.

Paula listened to the two of them tell their story without interrupting their chronological presentation. They told their story without animation or emotion. It was purely factual. Paula knew that these two were special people were concerned for her as they told their story. As they spoke their words, they showed sensitivity, compassion and a love for other people. They never judged other people.

Paula had a wistful smile on her face as they spoke. She watched the two people intently as they told their story. Although it was not rehearsed, they blended and dovetailed their descriptive parts very well. Paula felt that these two young, attractive people were like two halves of a whole. It seemed that they each knew what the other was thinking without asking.

Paula got up and poured more coffee and tea for all of them. Both Jared and Melinda focused on her facial expression, which appeared very serene. She listened without showing any emotion. There was no change from that slight smile on her face. She sat back down and looked at the two of them.

"Well first of all, you did the right thing coming here. And in a while I will tell you why. But first, I want to tell you something about me and my life," Paula said, as she lifted he cup.

"I will be telling you some things that I have never told others, but I feel that I owe it to the two of you."

"When I was eighteen, a terrible, horrible, thing happened to me. Something for which no young person is prepared. I was drugged and raped at a party during high school graduation week."

Melinda's jaw dropped upon hearing this. For a few seconds she just sat there with her mouth wide open in shock. Jared winced.

"Soon after the rape by someone I hardly knew, I discovered that I was pregnant. Not a great way to start your eighteenth summer is it? " Paula said with some cold, disgusted sarcasm.

"I had to arrange for an abortion, which you know was illegal in those days. Although the fetus was aborted, unbeknown to me, I was rendered infertile from the procedure. The only thing that I wanted in my life after marriage was children but with one slip of the midwife's hand, this was not going to be."

Paula stared through the window at the huge old elm tree that shaded her front lawn. She placed her cup down on the saucer. It was obvious to Jared and Mel that Paula was personally reliving these events as she articulated them. The air in the room was suddenly much heavier. Jared looked over at Mel. He did not know why Paula was telling them this personal and intimate story. They now were uncomfortable that they may have stirred up negative and deeply personal experiences in Paula's life. They felt responsible that they had come to her home and initiated a discussion that forced her to relive some old and distasteful memories.

Paula continued while she walked slowly around the room.

"I went on to college and got my degree in teaching, as well you two know. Soon after, I met Sam in a Woods Hole pub. We fell in love immediately." She smiled briefly. "I think that you two know what that is like."

Melinda looked over at Jared. He was staring directly at Paula.

"My life had turned around. I thanked God each day for bringing Sam to me. He was the love of my life, and still is today," said Paula, her eyes welling up with tears.

She drew in a very deep breath. Jared squirmed. He was feeling uncomfortable. He still didn't know where she was going with all of this personal history.

"We both wanted to raise a family in the worst way. It was not to be. When I discovered that I was to be barren, I walked the beach every day after school to plan how I would tell Sam. It was the worse time of my life."

Jared now distinctly remembered, for a second time, when he met the pretty lady at the beach who had caught his kick-ball. He specifically recalled the tears that had rolled down her beautiful face that day. He remembered how sad he felt for her then. He was beginning to feel the same way again.

"At times, I didn't want to upset Sam about the circumstances of my infertility, but then I knew him too well. He had an unconditional love for me. I found the right time to tell him. He reacted with love and compassion. Sam quickly redirected our energy away from these negative events. We began making plans to interview with adoption agencies. I was becoming happy once again. I was going to become what I wanted to be since I was a young girl. I had only wanted to become a mother."

Paula slowly stood up and walked over to the bookcase that had several framed photos on it. She picked a large photo. In the picture she was wearing a plain sweatshirt and jeans. She was snuggled under Sam's right arm. They were leaning against the drawbridge railing at Woods Hole. It was an older, black and white photo. It was obvious that this photo had been taken on a special day in their lives. It was one, which she had cherished. She held it for a while, smiled as she privately reminisced, then slowly put it back in its place.

"One night, after we had just returned from visiting my sister, Pat, on the Vineyard, Sam received a telephone call. The family doctor had informed him that his mother had just experienced a cerebral hemorrhage resulting in a moderate-grade stroke."

Paula then picked up a smaller photo of her mother-in law. She stared at it warmly as her fingers stroked the gold frame.

"Sam was an only child. His mother was a beautifully warm and caring person. Sam had adored her. She was a good mother to him and he loved her dearly. We had no alternative, but to take her in. She needed a great deal of assistance. Nursing homes were not the answer."

Jared looked away. He was not disinterested. He felt helpless. He had difficulty hearing sadness and wanted to somehow make it go away.

"I had no regrets. I loved her too. She did not want to live with us because she did not want to be a burden. But Sam and I convinced her that this home, our home, was the best place for her."

Paula explained more of this story as she slowly walked towards the enormous picture window decorated with flowers and plants on the sill. She was continuing to re-live these events as she told them to Jared and Melinda.

"We just never picked up the ball on adopting a child as we had planned. Taking care of Sam's mom was more overwhelming than we had anticipated and for fifteen years we did what we had to do," Paula said with a weak and fading voice.

"When did she pass away?" asked Jared.

"Oh...several years ago. But, by that time, Sam and I were much too old for any adoption agency to consider us as appropriate parents. We never talked about it. You know, it's kind of ironic. Because of my horrible experiences, we could never have a child naturally, and because of Sam's commitments, we could never adopt a child."

Jared wanted to ask what this all had to do with Sam's drowning, but since Paula was going through a very personal revelation, he did not want to distract or upset her in any way. He would be sensitive and let her continue talking.

"Sam and I went on with our lives. We both figured that we were supposed to care for his mother in this lifetime. That's what we were here for. There was no need for us to care for and love small children. We rationalized that I had children in my classes that I cared for. Maybe that was enough. And I did care for all of my students."

Paula looked up at Melinda and then to Jared. They all managed a smile.

"We can both attest to that," said Melinda.

"Well, Sam and I accepted it. Just as I accepted my rape, my abortion, my childless marriage and then our caring for his mother. We accepted all of that. But then this past spring God threw another curve ball at us. Sam's migraine headaches that had come on suddenly were diagnosed as an aggressive form of brain cancer."

Paula stood silent for a couple of minutes. She now had a tear coming down her face and her eyes were both water-filled. Jared got up and walked over to her and put his hand on her shoulder. His hand felt good to Paula. She reached up with her right hand and laid it on top of his. Some of the hurtful pain began to leave Paula. She felt some healing coming into her body through Jared's hand. She turned toward him and asked that he sit down again next to Melinda. What she had to tell them was very important.

"We were both devastated with the news. When you are in your fifties you begin to plan the autumn and winter of your lives, as Sam used to say. We had just begun that planning when Sam's disease came in to de-rail all of our intentions. I was told that he had, only at best, one or two months left on this earth. His quality of life was going to degrade each day. There was going to be excruciating physical pain for him. There would be the emotional pain for both of us. The doctors could only recommend counseling and medication. Strong medication."

Paula picked up some tissues to wipe her eyes. She walked over to a large, overstuffed chair at the window that faced the short, cobblestone street below and overlooked Buzzard's Bay. She put her hands on the top of the chair's backside. She caressed it slowly with the tips of her fingers.

"This was Sam's favorite chair. He sat here every day and did his best thinking. One day in early May, I left him here while I went out do some errands. I was getting into the car when I realized that I had left my pocketbook on that table over there." Paula pointed to an end table next to Melinda.

"I came back into the house. Sam did not hear me. I looked over at this chair with him sitting in it. Then I saw the shiny, glint of the gun's barrel reflecting in the sunlight. I was in total shock. I yelled to Sam, ran over to him and grabbed the handgun." Paula took a deep breath.

"He did not want to be a burden to me. He knew what the next few weeks were going to be like for the both of us."

Paula then sat down again across from Melinda and Jared. She put her face down into both of her hands and lowered her head half way down to her lap. She then recomposed herself and went on with her story.

"And now....... my young, super sleuths. I will answer some questions that have been plaguing each of you this past summer." She flashed a quick smile.

Paula then looked up at Mel and Jared with a very serious look on her face.

The room seemed to become very quiet and still. The light wind that had been blowing outside had died down. The sun was preparing to set for the day. The shadows were getting longer in the room where the three of them sat.

"The next morning, I went over to the Vineyard to see my sister, Pat. We met at the outpatient clinic, which she runs. She gave me the bottle of morphine. I had called her earlier and asked her to secure it for me. We didn't say anything. I quickly made the return boat ferry back to Woods Hole at 4:15. The next day I told Sam that I wanted to spend the evening at the Knob. It had been a special place for us before we married and during our younger years."

Jared briefly glanced over at Mel who was staring at Paula with an intense but warm and understanding look. She sensed Jared's looking over at her, but she did not look back at him. She did not move.

"I went out by myself in the afternoon to do some preparation.

When I returned, Sam was already dressed to go to the Knob. He had packed our picnic basket with wineglasses and a chilled bottle of Yearling wine. This was our own specially ordered wine that we had shared together for years. As you two just learned." Paula had a brief smile run across her face.

"We struggled a bit to hike up to the Knob. We sat down on the bench that was there. I opened the bottle of wine and as Sam was staring out to the sea, I mixed in a large dose of the flavored morphine into his glass. Sam had not yet lost his sense of taste yet with the brain cancer. I had the drug masked so that he would not have to taste it. We sat quietly for a while. It was almost twilight time. That was our favorite time, when the color of the sky is such a beautiful blue color, from the last few beams of the fading sun. It would be our last twilight together. Sam turned to me, looked deep into my eyes and said, 'Thank you Paula, thank you'. It was then that I knew that he was clearly aware of what was happening. We drank some more wine. Again, his glass was laced with the lethal morphine." Paula turned and looked away.

Jared was listening intently as Paula described what had occurred that last night of her husband's life at the Knob. As he listened, he was more engrossed in feeling the love and emotion that she had for her husband rather than the mechanics of what she was doing.

"It wasn't long before I knew that the morphine was doing its thing. He was fading quickly. In one alert moment he turned to me. I thought that he was going to say something. Instead he looked over my shoulder and up toward the sky. He managed a broad and wide grin on his face. It was Sam's typical smile showing his beautiful white teeth. He kept staring up over my shoulder to something behind me. Then he said very clearly..... "Mother, mother... Yes, yes I am coming." Paula managed these words with a cracking in her voice.

"He passed, still with that smile frozen on his face. I took the empty bottle of wine and flung it down the hill. My throw didn't quite make it to the water and I didn't care. I dragged Sam's body down the steep slope to the base of the Knob. I left him there and ran to the dock on the other side of the Knob. That is where I had tied up our motor boat in the Quissett Harbor. I had prepared this earlier in the day. I already pre-packed his beach combing clothes, boots and canvas bags in our boat. I motored around to the base of the Knob. I struggled to carry Sam's body inside of the boat. As I did so, I noticed that his St. Christopher's medal was still around his neck. I held the gold medal in my fingers. I thought about the night that I gave it to him so many years ago. I then remembered that salt water fish, and in particular, barracuda, would snap at anything shiny. I took the chain and medal off of his neck and threw it toward the rocks on the Knob. I didn't want any fish bothering his body. I was awash in emotions— hate, anger, love, fear and self-pity. I was feeling them all at once. I didn't even know at that point what I was doing. Then I dressed him in his beach combing clothes, and yes, Jared, I am sure that you were correct. I wasn't thinking about his usual routine when I draped the white and black canvas bags over the wrong shoulders."

There was another long and heavy silence. It filled the room. Paula was deep into her own thoughts. For a brief moment, she thought she was alone and reliving that night in their small motor boat in Buzzard's Bay. It was a night that she would never forget for the rest of her life.

"I motored towards Chapaquoit beach, where he walked each day. I headed for the jetty where Sam finished each daily walk with his morning meditation. I cut the motor. I wasn't aware of the currents, which you discovered in your tide book, Jared, but I knew that we were drifting. The boat was quickly floating back out to sea. I had to start the motor again to stay in the area. I don't know why, but since I knew that Sam was no longer physically with me, I wanted to talk to him in his spirit life. I thought that he must have been going through his own personal earthly life review soon with angels and guides by his side. We had always shared our experiences with one another. I still wanted to be part of him and his new life— even in his spiritual life."

Paula began to weep and shake lightly. Melinda then got more tissues and brought them over to her. There were no words spoken.

"I then began to speak with Sam in his new spiritual plane. I told him to take care of himself. Isn't that something! He is in heaven and I am telling him to be careful!" Paula chuckled.

"Paula, do you want some water?" asked Jared.

"No, no thanks. Isn't that silly? Me.... telling him to take care of himself. I spoke with him as though he was still with me. I looked at his warm, loving smile with his body propped up against the inside of the boat. I told him not to forget me. I told him that when he went through his life review in heaven not to forget the love we shared, the walks in the woods, the time we baked our first blueberry pie together and ate the burnt crust and laughed about it. I told him to remember the fun we had together biking, and fishing and swimming. I told him not to forget the intimacies that we shared, the day we made love on a bright summer's day in that remote, grassy orchard in Maine. I asked that he remember our private walks around the harbor, the whispering in bed at night. I asked that he never forget me, as I would never forget him. I told him that I would meet him in the spiritual world and that he shouldn't worry. I then told him not to be concerned. I would recognize him when I got there by his beautiful, warm smile. And then I said my good bye to Sam with a final kiss."

At this time Paula burst out crying uncontrollably. She ran into the open and waiting arms of Melinda. They embraced closely for a very long time. They all sat for a while without saying anything. Jared went into the kitchen for glasses of water.

Paula smiled for the first time. "You know, you two make good detectives. With or without the help of spiritual guides."

"How is that, Paula?" replied Jared.

Paula drank some water. And then she turned to the two of them.

"The e-mail message. You see. I sent that e-mail myself the very next morning. I sent it from our computer in the den. What I knew was that it would be time-stamped and imply that Sam was still alive that next morning. What I did not know was that he had canceled his sailing research trips. He never told me. But you two found that out. Now, I suspect that he knew the gravity of his disease long before I did. He didn't want me to know until the time was close."

The telephone rang. Paula signaled with her hand to let it ring. The answering machine went on. The caller was her sister, Pat. Paula again signaled quietly with her hand that it was OK for them to listen.

"Hello, its me, Pat. I don't know why, but I had this strange sense right at this moment that you were going through an emotional, time. So I decided to call to make sure that you were OK. Maybe it is just me worrying about you but I had some vibes that you needed someone to talk with this afternoon. Give me a call when you get back home.....Love you."

Paula slowly regained her composure while the three quietly sipped their glasses of water. It was a heart wrenching experience for all of them. Paula fidgeted with her tissues and then she stood up and walked around the room slowly.

"I apologize for laying all of this on the two of you. You are both so sweet. I am glad, however, that I confessed the story to you. Nobody else knows exactly what happened. I know that you have to turn me into the police. It still is against the law to take anyone else's life. Even if it was an act of euthanasia for someone you love. You two just do what you have to do." Paula's voice was fading.

Jared walked over and stood directly in front of Paula. He took both of her hands into his own hands. He squeezed them slightly. He looked deeply into her eyes and smiled.

"Paula, we are not going to turn you in to the police. We don't have to do that. We don't have to do anything in our lives except love one another. You don't need to be incarcerated. You need to be loved, as we all need to be. You loved Sam. We all did. His dying was inevitable. What you did was done out of your pure love for him. We are here for you now and we will be here for you forever. Please never, never forget that."

Paula smiled. A glow seemed to come out from within her and to surround her whole body.

"But what about all of your detective work? And your spiritual sleuth detectives that guided you? Do you want all of that to go for naught? I do believe that those spiritual forces and coincidental events occurred for a reason."

"As do we," interjected Melinda. "All of those things happened to bring us to this very moment in time. Those events had a specific purpose. They all culminated in bringing the three of us very close to one another and to share our love."

"You see Paula, because of those clues and revelations we are here with you now," said Jared. "We would never have become this close with you if these clues didn't lead us to you. We are here today; not to have you arrested, but to go on with our lives together. We all need each other. Especially now. I need you and Melinda does too. I just lost my mother. You just lost the love of your life. We can help each other get through these times and get on with our lives. We have lots to look forward to and lots of love that we can show each other. That's why we were brought together. That's why we are all here today. "

Paula sat down again. She seemed overcome with emotion. She managed a nervous smile with her two new companions. They had lots to talk about. They had lots to share.

Jared knew that Paula was going to become an important person in his life with Melinda after they get married. There will be children for he and Mel to love and to parent. They would need another grandmother to look after them and to spoil and to love them. Jared and Melinda would make sure that Paula was included in their life. She was a loving person. She had been denied before, but this time with the love of one another they would all lead happy and memorable lives in the village of Quissett.

CHAPTER TWENTY-FOUR

Circle of Love

It had been almost a week since Mel and Jared had met with Paula. The session at her house had a tremendous impact on their lives. They were very happy that the drowning incident had been solved. And it had been resolved privately among the three of them. They were also happy that the two of them would always be an important part of this woman's life. They both sensed that Sam was spiritually aware of their encounters with Paula and their new, special relationship with her.

Jared felt very positive now about his own future. He explained to Mel that he had some of his own plans to help reinforce the new bond with Paula Parker. He would work as a partner with her to locate and to set up the quaint old bookstore that she wanted in the village of Quissett. He would be happy helping out Paula with something that she now needed in her life. Perhaps it was also a project that he personally needed. After all, he needed to heal the emotionally torn wounds that he had experienced recently.

The following Saturday Mel picked up Jared in her Jetta convertible. They had scheduled a meeting with their wedding coordinator to go over their reception plans. Since Jared had given her the engagement ring, they both wanted to get married sooner rather than later. A nice, big wedding with friends and relatives would help bring back the positive feeling in all of their lives. Ann and Francesco Abandando were very supportive and happy that they decided to marry soon rather than delay the wedding. Jim Westcott was elated that his son, Jared, would be bringing in another new member to the family. He also loved Melinda very much. He was happy for his son.

While they were driving along for a few miles along the shore, Mel slowed her car down and pulled over to the sandy side of the road. She stopped the car and then pulled the lever to let the convertible top down.

"Hey Mel! What the hell are doing? Do you think it's warm enough today to have the top down?" asked Jared.

"We'll, see," she replied. She locked the vinyl-covered top down in place.

"Huh.....?" Jared quickly began his usual routine of slouching down whenever the convertible top was down.

"Jared, I have to ask you just *one* question," as she pulled the car back out onto the road. " What are you afraid of when the convertible top is down?"

"I am not sure if I am afraid of anything. What are you talking about?"

"Well we went through this discussion earlier in the summer remember? And..... You told me that it was some sort of phobia with you whenever the top was down. You had an impulse to quickly slouch down in the seat. I had thought you were embarrassed to be seen with me. But you were the one that said that you had some weird phobia about convertibles."

"Yeah. So what ? We all have our private weaknesses. Right?"

"Jared. Let me ask you something. Do you think that there is someone out there who is going to fire a gun at you and shoot you in the head?"

"No. Of course not. What the hell are you talking about?"

"Well, if you are really not afraid of anyone taking a shot at you while the top is down then you should sit up like normal people.

"Yeah I know."

"Then why don't you move your ass and sit straight up in the seat like everyone else. After all, as I said, nobody is going to take a shot at you."

Jared's heart suddenly began to palpitate quickly. He frowned and began to freeze in one position holding on tightly to the arm of the car door. He did not respond to Melinda's question. He knew that his forehead was beginning to perspire.

"Jared, nobody is going to shoot at you. It is perfectly safe riding around in a convertible car with the top down. Do you understand? Nobody is going to aim a gun and shoot you while you are riding around in a convertible."

Jared thought about what she had just said. He looked over to Mel behind the wheel. He began to smile. He slowly edged his body up on the seat until he was finally sitting up in a normal position. He began to chuckle. Then he giggled. Then he started laughing out loud.

"You're right! Nobody is ever going to take a shot at me with a gun just because the top is down. Why would anyone ever think that? This is great! I feel so free! I am free!"

"Well, hallelujah! It worked! It worked!" said Mel.

"What worked? What do you mean? What are you talking about, Mel?"

"I will tell you some day. Some day when we are old and gray." She smiled.

She continued smiling at him. He looked puzzled. Jared was confused. But it didn't matter. He was happy. He had just conquered a weird, old phobia.

After they completed their meeting with the wedding coordinator they took a brief ride along the southern side of Vineyard Sound. It was a day to celebrate. They could now have their wedding ceremony and get on with their own lives as a married couple. They felt different this day. It was time for them to be alone together where nobody could see them or find them. Every couple needs one of those days every now and then. Melinda continued driving along the shoreline but then headed toward the south side of town. The beaches were rocky there. It was a place that tourists or residents hardly visited.

Melinda grabbed a soft, navy-blue blanket from the trunk of

her car. They went for a walk along the rocky beach to a section of the beach that has some prehistoric caves hidden in the cliffs. They came across one cave that was private and comfortable. It probably had housed some of the earlier Quissett Indians when they first migrated here from the west.

Mel and Jared were in an especially intimate mood this day. They had just completed what was sure to be the most emotional summer of their lives. They were faced with many unexpected personal events involving mystery, love and death in a matter of a few months. Through it all they felt that they were being guided and guarded by something that they could not fully understand on the earthly plane. And more importantly, through it all, their love not only survived, but it also grew into something that was special. It was now an exciting time for them.

After they had placed the blanket on the floor of the cave, they both knelt down and held each other's hands. They expressed their own personal vows of love for one another while kneeling on the blanket looking into each other's eyes. This was their personal wedding of love. Only the two of them would ever remember this private and personal marriage vow in this Cape Cod cave. It was their marriage of unconditional love.

Jared spoke the words first:

"Melinda. Today I give you my heart, my body and my love. My love for you is special. It is a totally unconditional love. It will never judge you or expect things from you. My love for you will always be there for the rest of our lives."

"Jared. Today I give to you my heart, my body and my love. My heart will always be filled with love for you. There will never be room for anything else in my heart. There will be no jealousy, no anger, no judgment, nor hate. Only love. My unconditional love."

Jared and Melinda embraced and kissed. Today was their day. They made love. They became purely intimate and familiar as they made love. They made love on this late summer day in a secluded coastal cave that was just for them. They knew that they were in love. They knew that they were so compatible together. They knew that they would become a happy married couple. They knew that they would enjoy each other for the rest of their lives. On this day, they thought that they knew everything.

But they didn't know everything. What they didn't know was that this act of love, on this day, would begin the biological process known as conception. What they didn't know was that the egg inside of Melinda, that was to be fertilized, would eventually split into two. They didn't know that out of their love for one another, they had conceived twins during their special intimate wedding day.

They also had thought that they were alone this day in their cave of love. They were not, however, alone in this old, coastal cave.

What they didn't know was that there were two invisible spirits who watched them closely, looking over them, and smiling. These two spirits were anxious to become those twin life forms soon to develop inside of Melinda. They were the new lives that would once again come down to the earthly plane.

One of these spirits had recently lived several decades. She had a troubled adolescence and an unfulfilled adult life. She had never understood love. Since she had never opened her heart to give love, she was never open to receiving love. She had never known love so she didn't know how to give it or share it. Perhaps during this next journey she could experience unconditional love and share it with other people in her life.

The other spirit had her earthly life cut short soon after her birth. She lived for only a few hours. She never got to know and experience her parents or her twin brother. She now understood life and love much more. But now she wanted to experience it so that she could give love, feel love and share love in the physical world. She now would get her chance, her gift of life. She would have an opportunity to live and to love in this special place known as earth.

Their spiritual souls would take earthly form in a region known as Cape Cod—in a very special, quaint and charming, village called Quissett.

ABOUT THE AUTHOR

Gordon Mathieson has spent most of his professional life in Computing and Information Systems. He retired early from the Yale School of Medicine as the Director of Clinical Information Systems. Since then he has done consulting to large and small companies in the field of Information Technology. He has published many non-fictional pieces of work. In the year 2000, along with his wife, he invented and developed a trivia boardgame, called "The Cape Cod & Islands Challenge Game" (website www.challengegame.com) which has been hugely successful. While doing the reading and research for this trivia game, Gordon was inspired to write his first novel, Quissett. It is a small Cape Cod village not far from where he and his wife, Ann, live. They are the parents of two grown daughters.

Additional copies can be ordered on-line at

www.challengegame.com

Or, you may call GMCI Books toll free 877-757-4358
(8am to 5pm EST) to order.

There is an additional $3.00 shipping and handling charge.

Please specify if you want an author autographed copy.

Booksellers may use this same number to call for wholesale
pricing and distribution information.